THE GREAT BOOMSKY

THE GREAT BOOMSKY

The Many Lives of Magic's First Black Superstar

MARGARET B. STEELE

Peekskill, New York

The Great Boomsky: The Many Lives of Magic's First Black Superstar

For information about this title or to order other books and/or electronic media, contact the publisher:

Floating Lady Publishing LLC
www.floatingladypublishing.com
info@floatingladypublishing.com

ISBNs:
979-8-9889560-2-0 (hardcover)
979-8-9889560-0-6 (softcover)
979-8-9889560-1-3 (eBook)

Library of Congress Control Number: 2023950862

Printed in the United States of America

Disclaimer: This is a work of creative nonfiction. All people, places, and dates are real as sourced. Re-creations of historical events may include the use of imagined dialogue, educated speculation, and circumstantial evidence.

Sensitivity: Segregation, Black minstrelsy, racism, racist language

Cover images courtesy of Dale Penn. (1) Cabinet card photo of Milton Hudson Everett, circa 1892, by José Maria Mora (2) One-sheet lithograph portraying Léon Herrmann and Isaac W. Willis, circa 1903, Metropolitan Printing Company, New York.

Edited by Marianne Ward
Cover, interior, and logo by 1106 Design
Logo art by Patrick Conlon

For Phyllis Marsman, Yvonne Glover, and Sheila Ryan,
granddaughters of Isaac Willis, The Great Boomsky, who so
generously shared their stories but did not live to see them told.

~

"I am especially glad of the divine gift of laughter:
it has made the world human and lovable,
despite all its pain and wrong."

~ W. E. B. Du Bois

CONTENTS

☙ INTERLUDE ❧

☙ ACT TWO ❧

BOOMSKY WITH HERRMANN'S SUCCESSORS 183

❧ ᴀᴄᴛ Tʜʀᴇᴇ ❧

❧ ᴀᴄᴛ Fᴏᴜʀ ❧

Contents

FOREWORD

BEHOLD!!! You ARE HOLDING IN YOUR HANDS a story about transformation. I say this not only to describe the journey of the main character(s) in this book, but also to describe the journey of the author.

Margaret Steele is recognized as the leading authority on Adelaide Herrmann, who, among other things, was the wife of Alexander Herrmann, a.k.a. Herrmann the Great. Margaret has done extensive research on Madame Herrmann and published the highly respected book *Adelaide Herrmann, Queen of Magic: Memoirs, Writings, Collected Ephemera*. She has also created and performed magic scenarios that give homage to the groundbreaking magic artist. Generally speaking, magic historians have overlooked/ignored the work of Adelaide Herrmann. Margaret's goal has been, and continues to be, one of illuminating the life and artistry of the "Queen of Magic," as well as other women in the magic arts. Approximately twenty-five years ago, while seeking more information on Madame Herrmann, Margaret discovered yet another overlooked character in magic history: The Great Boomsky. And thus, her transformation began!

As Steele journeyed down the rabbit hole, she discovered that Boomsky was not only Herrmann the Great's onstage assistant and personal valet, but he was also a very significant force in helping Alexander create and execute the magic for his elaborate theatrical productions . . . as well as helping Herrmann maintain the persona of a wonder-worker while in the public eye offstage. As audiences and critics lauded the artistry of Monsieur Herrmann, they had no idea how much his wife, Adelaide, and his assistant, Boomsky, facilitated making Herrmann the Great truly great! Even today, this is generally the case with those of us who enjoy theatrical performances. We tend to overlook the creators, builders, technicians, cast, and crew that help make the magic happen. If the individuals behind the scenes happen to be women or persons of color, it is even more likely that their contributions will be swept under the rug. We are living in a time when blatant omissions, alternative truth, and whitewashing history are becoming more accepted as the norm. In spite of this disturbing fact, it is encouraging to know that there are still writers/artists like Margaret Steele who exhibit unwavering conviction and choose to stay on the path of pure, uncut Truth!

In 1999, just before Margaret discovered The Great Boomsky, the film *The Matrix* premiered in theaters. The basic plot centered around the premise that one could take a blue pill and continue to see the world from one's own comfort zone . . . or take a red pill and see the world without any filters. To write this book, Sister Steele metaphorically took the red pill so that she could clearly see Boomsky beyond what I refer to as "white eyes." She could see him beyond her comfort zone. Margaret immersed herself in a wide variety of print and digital media; viewed artifacts, posters, photos, etcetera from assorted private collectors and museums; and even visited grave sites. She also had many significant conversations and conducted interviews with people that were integral in bringing this masterwork to fruition . . . including relatives of The Great Boomsky, whom she had tracked down.

Margaret Steele's conversations and interviews ranged from relatively casual to very intense. At least one potential publisher said: "A white woman has no business writing about Black history." Conversely, several people of color encouraged her to continue her work, and in one of those conversations (concerning a particular racial slur that was spoken by one of the characters in the book), she was told: "If you're gonna do it, go all the way! Please don't whitewash history. If you do, I will lose some of my respect for you!" One of her most eye-opening exchanges occurred while Steele was interviewing Boomsky's granddaughter, who expressed gratitude for Margaret's work . . . but also gave her a verbal spanking for misinterpreting a bit of information. The elder then followed up the tongue-lashing with an actual slap on Margaret's hand! Sister Steele admitted to me that she was indeed looking at the information through those aforementioned "white eyes."

As a result of Margaret's clear-eyed approach to this book, you are about to experience a work of nonfiction that reads like a novel. A story of genuine transformation . . . filled with glitz, glamour, jealously, intrigue, espionage, triumphs, tragedies, romance, racism, villains, sheroes, and heroes! On a personal note: When I read this book, I experienced joy, sadness, tears, anger, empathy, jaw-dropping shock, and peaceful resolution.

For thirty-seven years, I worked as Artist-in-Residence at a small liberal arts college in Virginia. During approximately twenty-five of those years, I produced a program that featured African American prose and poetry, enhanced with music, movement, and theatrics. Inevitably, every year, someone would ask me if it was OK for white people to attend! I have found this is often the question when there is an art exhibition, arts festival, television show, film, play, or book in which the main characters are "Black." This book is not intended to be experienced exclusively by non-white people. It is not to be pigeon-holed into the category of "Black history," but rather, it should be read and appreciated as a significant story in our American history!

Furthermore, this is not a mere tome of historical data to be read exclusively by magicians and their allied artists . . . or placed on various niche reading lists by educators, researchers, and erudite book clubs . . . or displayed (perhaps pretentiously) on one's coffee table or bookcase to give the impression of being "woke." Instead, this is a masterwork that should be read by anyone who has a genuine interest in Truth and the resilience of the human Spirit!

My Sisters and Brothers, I invite you to take the metaphorical red pill, so that you can clearly view this amazing story of The Great Boomsky . . . a story of transformation, and pure Life Magic!

Hiawatha Johnson Jr.

∾

PREFACE

If a book is a show, the preface is the warm-up act. The author rolls out the red carpet, walks you to your seat, and prepares you for what you are about to see. But a magic show is all about surprises! The less you know in advance, the better. So, grab your hat and valise. We're hitting the road with the world's greatest magician. Just a couple of brief notes, and we're off.

We'll be keeping a brisk pace and meeting lots of people. I have included a Cast of Characters appendix to help you keep track of everyone.

Please note that this story takes place during a time when racism was accepted and normalized in America. Boomsky's descendants have insisted that I not whitewash history. Therefore, quoted material has not been censored. Be warned that you will encounter words and expressions that are jarring and offensive by today's standards.

But take heart. In this real-life fairy tale, magic prevails. By all accounts, seeing Herrmann the Great and his assistant Boomsky onstage together was just about the most fun anybody could have. Their hilarious act left audiences breathless, satisfied, and unburdened of their cares. Now, over a century later, they are together again, ready to perform just for you.

Herrmann's train is leaving, so I must wave you off. Bon voyage!

In 1890s America, mass-produced, full-color art lithographs were new and stunning. For people who had previously seen only lettered broadsides, the posters were as startling and transformative as motion pictures would be two decades later.

PROLOGUE

AMERICUS, GEORGIA, OCTOBER 19, 1891

THE FANCY TRAIN CHUGGING TOWARD AMERICUS that Monday morning was an unusual sight, and the field workers paused briefly to gaze. Thirteen-year-old Milton Hudson Everett took a long look at the train's shiny green private car before turning back to work the cotton row alongside his parents and brothers. Excited chatter rippled through the groups of pickers. Everyone knew who was on the swanky car. Full-color posters all over town blazed the arrival of the devil himself.

At least that was what some folks were saying. The field workers could not read the words, but the fantastical pictures were weird and shocking. The poster was so riveting, it almost seemed to be casting a spell itself. Nobody passed it without stopping to stare. In the lower right stood Satan, dressed head to toe in vivid red, pointing and swirling his cape. On the opposite side stood a robed wizard, his wand held aloft. Between them, a lady's body sat separated from her head, which rested upon a nearby pedestal. Overhead, a skeleton danced, an angel hovered, and a woman flew out of a hat! These images made some older folks tremble with fear. But for adolescent boys, the vivid pictures thrummed a thrilling, overwhelming curiosity. The whole town was talking the world-famous *magician* performing in Americus that night—Herrmann the Great! It was the most excitement since early summer, when a circus hyena had escaped and killed local dogs and chickens.[1]

The magician's arrival that day stirred arguments out in the cotton field. Some warned everyone to keep far away from this wizardry. The field workers could not attend the performance, of course. The opera house admitted whites only. Anyway, tickets cost money, which they did not have. But local teens could make a few pennies, sometimes even a nickel, working backstage for touring theater troupes—pulling curtains, pushing scenery, and hauling trunks. Best of all, they got to watch the show.

Despite the elders' warnings, Milton Hudson Everett ("Hutchin" as everyone called him), his brothers, and all the other boys desperately wanted to be on the crew for this sensational spectacle. Competition would be fierce. Hutchin was young and small for his age, but he already worked as an errand boy at Glover's Opera House. Hutchin had watched, starry-eyed, as actors, singers, musicians, dancers, and stagehands bustled to prepare for their performances. Once, he had even stood on the stage by himself and imagined that *he* was performing for a cheering audience. He and his older brother, Sidney, always did everything together. But that night, it would be every man for himself.

Cotton pickers in Georgia, circa 1890.

That day in the cotton field, as the Everett family worked their way down the row, picking boll after boll, tossing each one into cotton sacks, Hutchin impatiently watched the sun travel oh so slowly across the sky and longed for the quitting-time bell with every fiber of his being.

A crowd of curious townspeople met Herrmann the Great's train in Americus. The railroad was just a few years old, and nobody this famous had ever visited. Practically overnight, sleepy little Americus had turned into a booming cotton distribution hub with new electric street cars—Georgia's first—and a new opera house, little used so far.

The Next Attraction!
The World's Greatest Magician,

HERRMANN,

Prince of Prestidigitateurs

King of Illusionists!
Emperor of Magic!

Aided by

Mme. Herrmann

Direct from his Cozy Palace of Amusement at New York. Assisted by

ABDUL KAHN,

Presenting His Most Brilliant and Bewildering of all Entertainments, Including the Latest Puzzling Sensation,

STROBEIKA AND BLACK ART!

This is his First and Only Appearance in this Section of the Country in Seven Years.

MONDAY, OCT. 19.

The Americus Times-Recorder, *October 18, 1891. In his twenty North American tours, Alexander Herrmann performed in Americus just once.*

Herrmann's crew got off the train first. The stars—Alexander Herrmann and his wife, Adelaide—would emerge from the private coach car later. Herrmann's chief stage mechanic, William E. Robinson, scanned the scene. Normally, the theater sent a horse-drawn wagon and some stagehands to help with their equipment. But nobody was there. Robinson and his crew found their own way to Glover's Opera House, which was locked up tight. The manager let them in and told them the part-time theater had no regular staff. Local hands would arrive before the show. Will Robinson told his men they would have to load in all the equipment and hang the sets and backdrops themselves, in addition to all their regular tasks. With much grumbling, they got to work.[2]

After finishing in the fields, all four Everett brothers dashed straight for the theater. The older two, Sidney and Hutchin, ran ahead of the twins, eleven-year-old Cook and Fort. To their dismay, about two dozen boys were already there. The stage door opened, and a man stuck his head out. The boys—teens and younger—clamored for his attention, shouting over each other. "Stagehand!" "Electrician!" "Property man!" "Fly man!" Hutchin himself was a fly man, but he knew that most of the boys didn't even know what those jobs were. They just wanted to see the show.

Nonetheless, the man flung open the door and all the boys rushed in. The doorman motioned them forward, but Hutchin broke from the group and scurried up a ladder to claim the fly-man position on the catwalk above the stage. Up there in the fly zone, curtains, backdrops, and scenery hung suspended from battens, waiting to be lowered on cue down to the stage. The fly man would help guide them down.

From the catwalk, Hutchin looked down upon a remarkable sight. Sitting in a chair center stage was the most elegant man Hutchin had ever seen. His clothes were from another era—silk knee breeches with hose and polished, pointed shoes, topped with an impeccably tailored white blouse. His wavy black hair was combed back, accentuating his high forehead, strong nose, and magnificent pointed mustache and goatee. He smoked a cigarette, gesturing delicately as he spoke to the wide-eyed Black boys who crowded around him from all sides. He spoke with a strange accent. It was *him*—Herrmann the magician!

The front curtain was closed, but Hutchin could hear the audience filling the theater. The pubescent field hands' pungent sweat sharpened the stagnant backstage air. But Herrmann didn't seem to notice as he pulled out some playing cards and performed a trick. The teens jostled each other for a better look.

As Herrmann lounged with the youths, his crew seemed rushed and stressed as they scurried about preparing the show. Since arriving at the locked-up, unstaffed theater that morning, Will Robinson, who doubled as the stage manager, had faced one problem after another. The stage of the five-hundred-seat Glover's Opera House was cramped and too small for some of Herrmann's illusions. The tiny orchestra pit was completely filled by a piano, with no space for Herrmann's music director/violinist.[3] Now, right before showtime, Robinson learned that his local crew was this gang of ragtag juveniles. Irritated, Robinson checked his watch as the boys gathered around Herrmann. They should have been getting sorted out and to their stations. Suddenly Herrmann asked them, "Who is the best buck and wing dancer among you?"[4] With his French accent it sounded like "boohk and weeng."

Up in the flies, Hutchin's heart sank. He was the best dancer, and everyone knew it. At every holiday celebration, when Hutchin danced, the floor cleared. It had been that way since he was little. But now he was stuck in the rafters instead of down on the stage where he could leap in the air and shout, "Me! Me!" Then Sidney looked upward and pointed at his brother. "That boy up there," he said. "He done wing best."[5] Herrmann tilted his head up and Hutchin smiled his broadest smile. Herrmann gestured him to the stage, and Hutchin practically flew down the ladder to the magician's side. Herrmann looked him up and down. The boy was small, which was good. When asked his name, Milton Hudson Everett pronounced with his thick Georgia accent, "Milton Hutchin Everett."[6]

Herrmann said to Hutchin, "Let us see you dance."

Wearing just a threadbare shirt and a pair of ragged butternut trousers held up by one rope suspender, Hutchin proceeded to "wing" like nobody's business. The boys clapped the rhythm as Hutchin strutted about, shuffling his best fancy footwork. He beamed a radiant smile and flapped his elbows like rubbery chicken wings. Not only the famous magician watched. The entire Herrmann company paused their preshow bustle to see this boy buck and wing his heart out. Just offstage, an odd-looking white boy stood next to a young girl wearing spangles. A closer look revealed that the boy was actually a woman wearing a man's tuxedo and short wig. Madame Herrmann was temporarily back in a role she had retired from years earlier. Now, her filled-out figure strained both the seams of her costume and her character's credibility. The young girl in spangles was also not what she seemed. Angel-faced and tiny, Dot Robinson was a mature woman of twenty-eight.

When Hutchin struck his final pose—onstage, behind the closed curtain—the backstage group of the Herrmann company and the sweaty local boys burst into spontaneous applause. Out in the house, arriving theatergoers exchanged looks, confused by the uproar behind the curtain. On the spot, Herrmann asked Hutchin if he would like to travel with him and be his new assistant. He would leave with the company that night.

Hutchin was stunned. As later recounted by Madame Herrmann, Hutchin exploded in response, "I jes' worship to go with you-all!"

"All right," Herrmann told him. "Bring your father or mother to see me."

"Ain't got none; only got a aunty."[7]

This was a lie. Milton Hudson Everett had both a mother and a father.[8] But he could not risk their saying no.

"Well then, bring your aunty down," Herrmann said.

Hutchin flew off and returned with an "aunty" who signed his contract with an *X*.

"Go get your things," said Herrmann, "and meet us at the station. Our special sleeper leaves at midnight."

That night, Hutchin did not work the flies or see the show. Instead, he hung around the train depot, waiting. He wanted to go home and wake his parents to say goodbye. But he did not dare. Late that night, when the Herrmann company and their equipment finally arrived at the station, Hutchin was there. So were all the other boys, there to send him off. Come dawn, they would be back in the cotton fields. More than a few would likely catch a licking for being out past midnight. Hutchin hugged his little brothers, Cook and Fort, then gave Sidney a fierce final embrace. When Herrmann's manager, Mr. Bloom, asked about his baggage, Milton Hudson Everett said simply, "Got none." With that, Mr. Bloom gestured him aboard. Hutchin climbed the steps and waved to his friends. Then the door closed and the train rolled off into the night.

~

ACT ONE

ONSTAGE
WITH
ALEXANDER HERRMANN

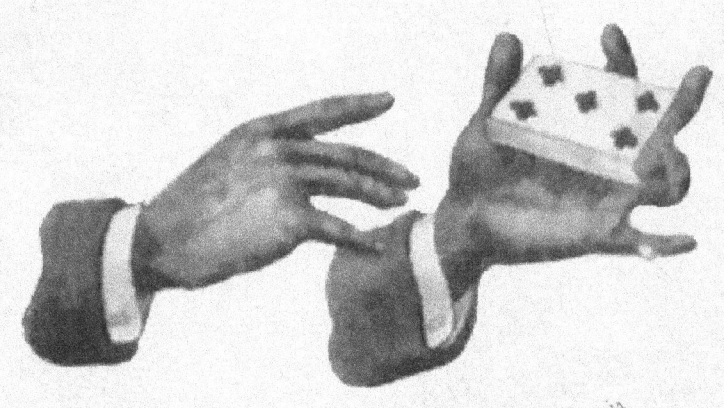

CHAPTER ONE

Monsieur Alexandre, Clever and Stealthy Child

Paris, 1852

Alexander Herrmann was eight years old when his older brother, the magician Carl Herrmann, kidnapped him. Not that Alexander had resisted. For as long as he could remember, he had loved magic more than anything. Alexander practiced his tricks day and night, planning to become a famous magician himself. But his parents firmly said no; their youngest would become a doctor. No matter that their magician son Carl, the oldest of the sixteen Herrmann children, had bought them their ample house in Paris and that Carl and Alexander's father, Samuel, was a legendary magician himself. Born in Germany, Samuel Herrmann had emigrated to Paris after Napoleon granted full French citizenship to Jews. Samuel had retired from touring and worked as a physician to support his wife, Anna, and their huge family.

Europe's top two magicians were already reaping box office gold by featuring children as assistants. Frenchman Jean-Eugène Robert-Houdin and Scotsman John Henry Anderson were blessed with sons, every magician's dream. Both boys floated in the air in ether-induced trances. The two young boys, as well as Anderson's tiny daughters, also exhibited the astonishing gift of Second Sight. Blindfolded and seated onstage, the children were able to accurately describe borrowed objects that their fathers merely touched as they wandered among spectators, barely speaking. Audiences flocked to see the amazing magical children.

Alexander Herrmann as a boy.

Carl Herrmann had been running a distant third when he snatched his youngest sibling. While avoiding the search parties of their furious parents, the Herrmann brothers headed toward St. Petersburg. On the stagecoach trip to Russia, Carl taught Alexander his role. Hour after hour they practiced Second Sight, until the boy was fluent in the secret code by which Carl transmitted information hidden within common spoken phrases. At night, in dark rooms in roadside inns, Carl set up the apparatus for the Aerial Suspension so that the boy could practice floating in the air. As they traveled, both brothers compulsively manipulated cards, coins, rings, and any other small object within reach.

When they arrived in St. Petersburg, the Herrmann brothers received a royal command to perform for Czar Alexander II. Carl told little Alexander that if he performed well, the Czar might give him a watch and chain. Eight-year-old "Monsieur Alexandre" proceeded to baffle the ruler and his guests with tricks with cards and coins. Afterward, the Czar took the boy on his knee, patted him on the head, and said, "That was a very clever bit of magic, my little Alexander. Now you are going to tell me how it was done."

Carl Herrmann's rival magicians, including John Henry Anderson, floated boy assistants in the Aerial Suspension.

The boy replied, "I don't know, Your Majesty, but is it true that you are going to give me a watch and chain?" Mortified, Carl expected a rebuke. But the Czar replied, "Yes, it is true" and presented to the little boy a magnificent gold watch, enameled and set with diamonds, with a chain of heavy, twisted strands of gold.[9]

Carl realized his little brother had a natural gift and a raging passion for magic. The older Herrmann brother quickly gained ground against his competitors. With Alexander working invisibly behind the scenes, Carl's tricks began to look truly magical. Unlike most magicians who cluttered the stage with apparatus, Carl stood alone on a nearly bare stage, well away from any tables or curtains. Cards, scarves, rabbits, and doves would appear in his hands seemingly from nowhere and disappear just as suddenly. Awed reviewers, who coined the term "the no preparation school" to describe Carl Herrmann, never suspected the little boy who took away the produced-from-thin-air parakeet or guinea pig of secretly passing a bunny or a chicken to the magician for his next baffling production.[10]

Though twenty-eight years Carl's junior, little Alexander quickly became a star in his own right. The Herrmann brothers were the toast of Europe. But they fought bitterly, and often. When patrons presented the boy with gifts, Carl confiscated the precious items, infuriating Alexander, who wanted to play with his bejeweled toys. But the brothers' differences went deeper. Desperate for noble patronage, Carl distanced himself from low-class carnival magicians with his impeccable dress, etiquette, and deportment. Carl's magic was elegant and smooth, his presentation formal and proper, like a scientist presenting his experiments. Alexander, on the other hand, was a mischief-maker whose silly side prompted screams of laughter from audiences, noble and common alike. To Carl, slapstick humor was a debasement of the art, yet ticket sales soared. The older brother fumed as Alexander stole the spotlight night after night, season after season.

While the brothers were touring in Spain, fifteen-year-old Alexander stormed off after a particularly bad fight. He made his way to Madrid, where he convinced a wealthy friend of Carl's to bankroll a new magic act of his own. Alexander Herrmann, the teenaged magician, soon performed for Queen Isabella II of Spain then toured throughout Belgium and France. Impressed, Carl enticed his teen brother to rejoin him by offering him a contract to tour America, where they performed for President Abraham Lincoln. The brothers toured together off and on for another ten years until one final explosive argument in San Francisco when Alexander quit for good. The brothers did not speak again for sixteen years.

The Herrmann brothers, Carl and Alexander, at about ages 44 and 16, respectively.

As Alexander sailed from New York to England after the split, he was certain of two things. First, he loved America and would return. Second, if he wanted his tricks to look like real magic, he would have to find an excellent assistant.

∽

A poster promoting Alexander Herrmann at Egyptian Hall, featuring Alexander Osmann.

CHAPTER TWO

Magicians in Training

(1873–1890)

Alexander Osmann: African Mysteries at Egyptian Hall

In 1871, Alexander Herrmann began performing nightly at Egyptian Hall, a small, ornate theater in Piccadilly in London. He was an immediate hit. Soon, Egyptian Hall was the place to be seen. Alexander became quite the dandy about town, spawning fashion trends, especially with his jaunty hats. On any given night, Herrmann's private smoking lounge backstage hosted a stunning array of guests, including the Prince of Wales and his entourage. High society flocked to Herrmann's show, but so did middle-class Londoners. His successful show ran for nearly three years.

At first, Herrmann brought in variety entertainers to fill out the evening. During his first year at Egyptian Hall, Herrmann featured a juggler, a ventriloquist, and a slack-wire walker. But the perfect magic assistant proved to be elusive. The Herrmann family had no available sons, brothers, or nephews to train. The English assistants that Herrmann hired could not grasp the intricacies of the job and had to be let go. Finally, during Christmas week of 1872, Alexander Herrmann introduced his new assistant, Alexander Osmann, who, to everyone's surprise, was Black.

Rumors circulated that Osmann had been Herrmann's manservant whom the magician had trained; however, unlike Herrmann's future Black assistants, Osmann was already performing his own magic show, "African Mysteries," when he joined Herrmann at Egyptian Hall. Osmann had performed at London's Polytechnic the previous spring. Now he expertly supported Herrmann at every performance. The novelty of a Black assistant drew audiences. Osmann also presented "African Mysteries"—on his own, without Herrmann—four afternoons a week.[11] As Herrmann's fame grew, lucrative performance offers followed. Into the spring, while his employer tended to other engagements, Osmann stood in for Herrmann at Egyptian Hall for all but two shows a week, a testament to Herrmann's faith in his assistant.

Alexander Osmann remains mysterious. No images or reviews of Osmann have surfaced. His origins are unknown. Contemporaries described Osmann as being very dark-skinned. Yet he could have been a white man blackening his face and hands with burnt cork, the method used by blackface minstrel performers in the US. This accomplished magician appeared from nowhere and performed for just two seasons in London. A few months after Herrmann ended his run at Egyptian Hall, the African Wizard performed in a London review under the name Alexander Hausmann. Then he vanished from the historical record.

ADELAIDE HERRMANN: THE LADY IN TROUSERS

One night in 1873, a young, auburn-haired woman with intense ice-blue eyes sat near the Egyptian Hall stage. Herrmann noticed an engagement ring on her finger but no escort. He asked her to assist. She replied, "Oui, Monsieur." Herrmann borrowed her engagement ring. It dissolved at his fingertips then reappeared on a ribbon tied around the neck of a snow-white dove. Although she did not expect to see the magician again, something moved her to write to her fiancé, canceling their engagement.

Miss Adelaide Scarsez was a dancer and trick bicyclist. Born in London to Belgian émigrés, she spoke French at home. When her disapproving parents tried to squelch her show-business dreams, Adelaide took ballet classes in secret.

At fifteen she had landed a paid role in a holiday pantomime ballet. A year later she sailed for America with the Kiralfy Hungarian Dance Company. At eighteen she toured Belgium and France with Professor Brown's Lady Velocipede Troupe, the first-ever stage act featuring the newfangled, two-wheeled precursor to the bicycle.

In late March 1874, twenty-year-old Adelaide Scarsez departed England on a New York–bound steamship. Professor Brown's Lady Velocipede Troupe had joined Schumann's Transatlantique Vaudeville Company—a newly formed troupe of European variety artists—for an exciting American tour. When the steamer stopped in Queenstown, Ireland, a tall, distinguished-looking man in a luxurious fur coat walked up the gangplank. "He must be a prince!" someone said. Mrs. Schumann, wife of the tour manager, spoke up. "That is Alexander Herrmann, the famous magician."

Adelaide wondered if Professor Herrmann would remember their brief encounter, more than a year earlier. The answer arrived that night at dinner, when Adelaide was served a glass of champagne and a dish of cracked nuts, "compliments of the gentleman." She looked up and met Alexander's twinkling eyes. By the time they docked in New York two weeks later, the thirty-year-old conjuror and the red-headed bicyclist were engaged. They were married in New York City on the steps of City Hall by Mayor William H. Wickham. Alexander, feigning he had no money to pay the mayor's wedding fee, suddenly produced a wad of bills from the mayor's beard. The Belgian-blooded Londoner and her German-Jewish Parisian felt at home in America, especially in New York.

Adelaide and Alexander Herrmann's 1875 wedding photo.

The two Europeans would become US citizens, crisscrossing America together for most of the next twenty-two years.

Alexander soon had a new boy assistant—his wife. Dressed in a tuxedo and a short blond wig, Adelaide cut a striking figure, taking her husband's boyhood stage name, "Monsieur Alexandre." Already an experienced performer, Adelaide quickly became a skilled magic assistant. Her cross-dressing was cutting-edge and daring. In an era of strictly proscribed gender roles, dressing as the opposite sex was illegal in many countries. But American audiences found the conceit charming. The lady in trousers raised eyebrows and sold tickets.

Newlywed Adelaide Herrmann dressed as a boy to assist her husband.

After playing Monsieur Alexandre for a few seasons, Adelaide became frustrated with playing a boy. Madame Herrmann—a beautiful woman and a trained dancer—was eager to appear as herself. Adelaide was already performing her bicycle act to fill out the show. She zig-zagged through a line of a hundred glass bottles—each topped by a flaming alcohol-soaked rag—never knocking down a bottle, all with a young local girl riding on her shoulders. But the quick specialty act, however impressive, was over in the blink of an eye. And it was not magic. Adelaide envisioned herself as something new, something never-before-seen in magic—a glamorous, bejeweled lady illusionist.

STAGE ILLUSIONS

In the late 1870s, Adelaide Herrmann originated the role of the alluring, athletic female illusionist. Prior to that, large stage illusions had not yet become a big part of magic. In an era when athleticism in women was discouraged, the most-seen illusion, the Aerial Suspension, was usually performed by young boys.

M'LLE ADDIE ASLEEP IN MID AIR

WITH THE GREAT HERRMANN

A.S. SEERS PRINT. N.Y.

Herrmann trade card featuring Adelaide performing the Aerial Suspension.

An illusion partner is essentially a secret gymnast, ideally strong, small, and light for fitting in tight spaces and floating in the air. Adelaide had always been athletic. At five-foot-two, she was not tiny, but she was small enough. In Adelaide's day the audience would not have suspected that the workings of the illusions were all her doing. (This remains true in modern times.) The necessary strength, stamina, flexibility, balance, speed, and perfect timing, as well as a tolerance for getting banged up, were not considered ladylike traits, or even possible for women. These biases provided perfect cover for the secrets, but the work carried dangers. Appearing or disappearing through trap doors could seriously injure an extraneous limb, head, or chin. Levitating or hanging above the stage risked a bone-breaking fall. And those swords being thrust through the basket were real. It was no job for a lady, and no woman had seriously attempted anything like what Madame envisioned.

Adelaide Herrmann's illusions were a smashing success, inspiring a new generation of female illusionists and an entirely new genre of magic, the grand illusion show.

Adelaide called her vision "Spectacular Magic." Nothing like it had ever been done. She and Alexander would perform grand illusions presented as magical fairy tales, with elaborate sets, lavish costumes, and original music. Alexander loved her idea. "The bigger the better" was his motto. And with Adelaide out of the boy assistant role, Alexander could finally add slapstick comedy to the part. It was all well and good for Madame to dress as a boy, but she could not do pratfalls. Everyone knew the boy was really a lady, and the audience would not think a lady falling on her face was funny. An actual boy slipping and falling and messing up *would* be funny. Funnier still, as well as novel and exotic—a little Black page.

EDWARD JOHNSON, THE FUTURE BLACK CARL: NABBED ON THE RUNAROUND

Edward Johnson, of Topeka, Kansas, was around twelve years old when Herrmann hired him as his first African American assistant. In 1881, the *Milwaukee Sentinel* reported, in language common for the day, "As

Prof. Herrmann says, there are ten and a half people in his company, counting the little darkey who helps him as the half."[12] Though young, Edward became a skilled magic assistant. Every night, he disappeared from a box onstage then reappeared in the audience at the back of the house. One night in St. Louis he did not reappear, leaving Herrmann noticeably flummoxed. The magician suspected his young assistant had been "nabbed on the runaround," a known hazard for tricks requiring exiting the theater by one door and entering by another. After the show, the company visited the police station where they found the despondent boy locked in a cell. A police officer had spotted the lad running through the theater's alley and had arrested him. The young assistant was overjoyed to be released and back with his company.

Over two seasons, young Edward traveled with the Herrmann company all through North America. The teen became keenly interested in magic, studying Herrmann's tricks and practicing his own magic moves in his spare time. The tour was a thrilling adventure for Edward Johnson, whose best job options back in Kansas would likely have been cart driver or doorman. In Mexico, before there were railroads, the Herrmann company's equipment and crew were transported by mules, and guarded by fifty Mexican Army troops. In Central America, Madame rescued an injured monkey, little Jimmie, as they navigated by river through rainforests and jungles. They toured from Bogota to Caracas where the Leopolds, a trapeze couple, suddenly left the show, abandoning their cannon act. Every night, the Beautiful Geraldine had been shot from the cannon, flying over the heads of the audience into a net stretched across the stage. The hit act had been heavily advertised, and Alexander fretted that without it they would have to cancel a series of shows. To his shock, Adelaide stepped up and performed the dangerous stunt herself. That night, and for the rest of the season, Madame Herrmann flew headfirst fifty feet from the theater box into the outstretched net, sometimes with her slippers and costume on fire from the gunpowder blast. Although stiff, sore, and bruised from bad landings, Adelaide performed the act for months. Finally, after dislocating both shoulders and almost breaking her nose, she abdicated the role to a male acrobat.

Edward Johnson was about fourteen when the tour ended. But he had seen and learned plenty. He had fallen head over heels in love with magic. Before long he had mounted his own magic act, using the stage name Black Carl. He would go on to become the most celebrated African American magician of his day.[13]

WILLIAM ADAMS: SOUTH AMERICA, EUROPE, AND RUSSIA

In July 1883, an African American teen named William Adams joined the Herrmann company as they set sail for Brazil on the SS *Reliance*. Adelaide's little monkey, Jimmie, dressed in a tiny sailor suit, sat on Madame's shoulder.[14] Over the next sixteen months, they performed throughout Brazil and Argentina, always to standing-room-only crowds. Herrmann's reception in Rio de Janeiro was especially grand. The Emperor, Dom Pedro II, attended sixteen performances and awarded to Herrmann the Cross of Brazil.

A popular and progressive ruler, Dom Pedro was tirelessly battling powerful opponents in his quest to end the last vestige of the African slave trade in the Americas. Millions of African Brazilians were still enslaved and would remain so for another five years, until May 13, 1888, when slavery was finally abolished in Brazil. The African American teen William joined the entire Herrmann company as they lined up onstage to receive Emperor Dom Pedro and his entourage. Madame Herrmann had instructed William to look straight ahead and bow when the Emperor passed by. William did as he was told, glimpsing Dom Pedro's impeccably tailored suit, covered with medals, and his bushy silver beard. Later, at the Emperor's grand reception, William stood like a statue with his back to the wall—his uniform crisp and his posture razor straight—ready to spring into action at Professor Herrmann's signal to assist in whatever the moment called for, from handing out cigars to being handed a flapping goose, magically produced from under a guest's coat.

In Argentina, Madame was given two adorable baby ostriches, the size of spring chickens. She left the sweetly sleeping chicks in her hotel room and returned to strewn pillow feathers, torn window shades, and her belongings scattered about. After that, the babies were placed into William's care. The ostriches grew so fast, the company carpenter was constantly making bigger and bigger crates. They ate anything and everything—buttons, shoelaces, jewelry, cigarettes, drapery ornaments. Nothing was safe, and they were quick. One of the ostriches snatched a burning cigar out of the hand of one of Herrmann's guests and promptly swallowed it.

After years of financial depression, many of the theaters in South America were in disrepair. Their overgrown courtyards were the ideal place to let Madame's ostriches stretch their legs. One night, when William went to collect them, only one ostrich ran up to him. Looking around in a panic, William found a deep, open well hidden behind some tall bushes. There, at the bottom, was the second ostrich swimming frantically in circles. William called for help and the whole company gathered around the well, staring down at the poor creature. Madame was distraught. William, the smallest, volunteered to be lowered into the well by a rope. After several attempts, he managed to tie another rope around the violently thrashing ostrich, and the flailing creature was finally hoisted out. William—soaked, scratched, bruised, his clothes in tatters—was hailed as the hero of the hour.

From Brazil, the Herrmanns sailed for Portugal. The ostriches, nearly full-grown, now towered over everyone and writhed with energy in their shipping pen. Since the ship had few passengers, William often let the ostriches run around on the upper deck. The adolescent birds terrorized the deckhands, who soon learned that fleeing from an irritable ostrich assured a chase and attack in the form of a savage kick. Lying down and playing dead worked far better. A bold seaman could successfully defy an attacking ostrich by raising his arm high in the air, shaping his hand like an ostrich head, and "screaming" at the bird, seemingly face-to-face. Near the end of the voyage, a deckhand on his lunch break left behind an open can of red paint. One ostrich ran to the can, slurped up all the paint, then tried to eat the can. This would be the bird's undoing. Alexander Herrmann requested an autopsy, which reported that inside the bird's stomach were found "nails, bolts, jewelry, a thimble, and several small spoons."[15] Everybody had had enough of ostriches. To William's relief, when they arrived in Lisbon, the surviving ostrich was given to the zoo.

From Lisbon, the Herrmann company launched a two-year tour of Europe, 1885–1886, ranging from Portugal to Russia. As always, Alexander Herrmann created a sensation wherever he went. His ability to speak all the major European languages endeared him to his audiences even more. After the Spanish royal family attended Herrmann's public performance in Madrid, King Alphonso XII invited Herrmann to perform at the royal palace. This was a huge honor. Alexander had spent his childhood performing for royalty, but for Adelaide, this would be her first command performance for a European monarch. She bubbled with excitement. The afternoon of the event, William was sent ahead to set up the show. Alexander and Adelaide carefully instructed him in protocol, telling him that if he saw the King or Queen, he was to bow and address them as "Your Majesty."[16]

Some hours later, the Herrmanns arrived at the palace and were led to the performance hall. To their horror, there they saw William leaning with his elbow cocked on the mantel, his feet crossed, laughing and joking casually with Alphonso XII, the King of Spain. Adelaide was trying to catch William's attention with frantic sign language when the King turned and warmly greeted the Herrmanns.

As she would later write in her memoir, after the performance, Madame confronted William:

"'For heaven's sake, William,' I said, 'didn't you remember what I told you about the King?'

"'I sure did, Mrs. Herrmann, but I didn't see him.'

"'Why, that was the King you were talking to.'

"His eyes popped wide open.

"'For the Lord's sake!' he exclaimed. '*Dat* man de King? I reckoned he was just a waiter by his clothes. How'd I tell dat man was a king? I sure thought kings wore crowns and red robes.'"[17]

Another boss might have been angry, but the jolly Herrmanns found the episode hilarious. "*Dat* man de King?" was a company in-joke and catch phrase for the rest of the tour. It was also good for business. The tale became a stock Herrmann publicity story regularly reprinted over the years.[18] Sadly, the well-liked King Alphonzo XII died within months of the troupe's visit, at age twenty-nine.

Expectations were high in Paris, where the city's native son, Alexander Herrmann, was to appear for the first time in over twenty years. Adelaide recorded that "never—not even for Grand Opera—had a more brilliant audience assembled than on our opening night, October 1, 1885." That night at the Eden Theater, William stood onstage before Alexander's old friend from his Egyptian Hall days, the visiting Prince of Wales, the future King Edward VII of England, whose party occupied the royal box. Many Herrmann family members attended, including Alexander's older brother Carl and his wife. The performance was a triumph. At the finale, the audience rose to its feet and demanded many curtain calls. The Parisian newspapers declared Alexander Herrmann "the greatest artist in the field of magic that they had ever seen."[19] But Alexander's Paris triumph was bittersweet. Carl Herrmann could not handle his younger brother's success and left before the performance ended. Alexander was heartbroken. The brothers never spoke again; Carl died in Germany two years later.

Alexander Herrmann's company played in Paris for the next two months. After so many years away, Alexander was flooded with invitations.

The never-ending balls, receptions, and visits with Alexander's huge extended family made William's head spin as the teen rode about Paris perched aboard the Herrmanns' carriage. As fall turned to winter, the Herrmann company reluctantly packed up and set off for Russia.

The Herrmanns' train pulled into Vitebsky Rail Station in St. Petersburg in the snowy cold of December. At age eight, Alexander Herrmann had entertained Czar Alexander II. Now, at age forty-two, Alexander and his teen assistant performed for the family of his son, Czar Alexander III. Once again, William stood onstage before royalty, this time listening to his boss perform in French and Russian. Everywhere in Europe, but especially in Russia, people stared hard at William, the first Black person most had ever seen.

As a traveling superstar, Herrmann frequently carried large sums of cash, making him a tempting and highly visible target. But Alexander cleverly negotiated his own security and safe passage by constantly befriending leaders of the military and the police. In areas with organized criminal gangs, Herrmann befriended and bribed their leaders as well. He charmed and amazed everyone—making them laugh and gasp and feel happy and special—even murderous dictators, gang lords, and battle-hardened soldiers. These connections were especially important in Russia, where rampant anti-Semitism made travel risky for any Jewish person, even a star like Herrmann. As a US citizen, Herrmann had a distinct advantage over most Jewish travelers—unlike European passports, US passports did not specify one's religion.

In St. Petersburg, the Herrmanns were frequent guests of the Chief of Police and his wife. At a dinner with military officers, General Aleksey Kuropatkin, Russia's future Imperial Minister of War, made a bet with Herrmann. He dared the magician to make the dangerous mid-winter journey across the steppes to the Russian army outpost, Kayala, arriving in time for Christmas dinner.[20] Herrmann accepted the wager. For once Madame stayed behind. But Herrmann took William, his assistant and manservant. For the long sleigh ride, they were given a military escort to protect against roving bands of criminals. Once at the remote military base, after entertaining his hosts, Herrmann insisted on performing at the prison. Conditions there were horrifying. The stench was gut-churning, and the emaciated prisoners shivered in rags, their eyes hollow with despair. They instantly brightened when Herrmann spun cards throughout the cramped quarters. The prisoners snatched the cards as if they were precious treasures. As Herrmann bantered in Russian, the prisoners smiled and laughed. William could not understand the words, but as Herrmann glanced and gestured his way, and the men laughed harder, he realized his boss was talking about *him*. The Professor delivered the punch line, *"Dat* man de King?" William sighed as their ragged audience howled with laughter. Before leaving, Herrmann gave a small Christmas gift to each prisoner.[21] From Russia, the company headed west toward Herrmann's final stop on his long tour, Belgium.

In Brussels, William again encountered a European monarch, King Leopold II. William tried his best to steer clear of King Leopold, although that was not so easy. His Royal Highness liked to lurk in the wings during the show. Backstage visitors were forbidden, but Leopold was King and did as he pleased. William stole a glance at the King and caught him leering at Madame Herrmann. The famous philanderer had already propositioned Adelaide once. Now backstage, he devoured her with his eyes. Madame remained breezily cordial, ducking and spinning from Leopold, her grimace contorted into a smile, her blue eyes cold as ice.

The mood was tense. Nobody wanted to anger or, far worse, injure the impetuous dictator. As the crew moved heavy scenery around in the dark, the whole company had to work around him. It was a headache for the crew and potentially dangerous for all of them. Worse yet, Herrmann had to endure the pangs of magic secrets revealed, as his Majesty unabashedly poked around. Had the Herrmann company known of Leopold II's genocidal conquest unfolding in the African Congo and his army's unspeakable atrocities, His Majesty's backstage wanderings would have unnerved them even more. But the murderous nature of the obnoxious, narcissist Leopold would not have surprised them.

Somehow, William displeased King Leopold. Exactly what happened remains a mystery. Unlike King Alphonzo of Spain, Leopold II of Belgium was not a forgiving type and demanded the assistant's termination. In February 1886, Alexander Herrmann published a newspaper notice announcing that William Adams had left his company. The announcement, which ran two times, was an unusual gesture, designed to assure and placate the powerful despot.[22]

For William, then in his late teens, it was the end of an incredible adventure. He had been with the company for three years, working at Herrmann's elbow in seven countries on two continents. The ostrich-wrangling African American teenager had performed for the Emperor of Brazil, the King of Belgium, the Prince of Wales, the family of the Czar, and had chatted with the King of Spain and performed in a Russian prison. William Adams's teen years are the stuff of movies, yet nothing more is known of him.

Finally, the Herrmann company arrived back in the US in September 1886. For Alexander Herrmann, it was his last transatlantic voyage. He would never again leave North America.

IRVING JONES: THE BOY WHO LAUGHED

Back in New York, a new boy hanging around the stage door caught Herrmann's eye.[23] The strange-looking lad smiling back at him looked to be about eight years old. Irving Jones was thirteen and unusually small, with squinty facial features. The boy shone with personality. For good measure he showed off his singing and dancing. Herrmann hired him on the spot. Overjoyed at his luck, Irving dove into learning the magician's assistant role as his parents celebrated their family's good fortune.

Irving's father, Anderson Jones, had been born into slavery in Louisiana. After the Civil War and emancipation, he moved to New

York, where he worked as a coachman. Anderson Jones and his wife, Susan, lived in Manhattan, where their six children attended public grammar school. Irving was born in April 1873, the third of five sons.[24] His salary as Herrmann's assistant instantly doubled the family's income.

As she did with every prospective assistant, Madame Herrmann taught Irving his role. He picked up the part immediately. He was fun to be around because he was simply hilarious. Young Irving's nonstop clever commentary, delivered from his scrunched-up face, kept the company in stitches. But from the start there were problems. For one thing, Irving could not maintain his composure onstage. A comic actor must not break character and laugh at the show's jokes in the middle of the performance. Irving tried so hard, but it was such a struggle not to laugh. Herrmann was just so funny, and the audience's laughter was infectious. Irving would manage to hold himself together for nearly the whole first act. After falling and crushing a duplicate hat, a classic Herrmann routine, he hoped he looked scared and upset like he was supposed to, not like he was fighting with all his being not to laugh. But then Irving would glimpse the owner of the borrowed hat, red-faced, shaking his fists, and that was it. Irving just howled along with the rest of the audience.

There were other issues. All company members were sworn to secrecy. The secrets of the tricks and illusions were the Herrmanns' bread and butter. This fact seemed entirely lost on Irving, who happily disclosed Herrmann's secret methods to anyone who asked. Worse yet, Irving Jones borrowed some of Herrmann's magic silver dollars, only to lose them in a backstage craps game. Thankfully, the stagehands took pity on the naive thirteen-year-old and made up the loss for him. Future assistants would not be so lucky. As much as the Herrmanns liked Irving Jones, his undisciplined ways were unacceptable and, reluctantly, they fired him.[25] The talented boy landed on his feet. At age fourteen, he joined a touring show called "Scouts of the Yellowstone," where he stole the show nightly as a little singing cowboy. A year later, Irving was working variety shows as America's only "kid comedian." He would go on to a brilliant career as a singer/songwriter and comedian on the minstrel circuit before becoming one of the very few Black entertainers in mainstream vaudeville.

JAMES A. WILLIS: FLINGING PASTEBOARDS AND TICKLING THE IVORIES

In Pittsburgh, Herrmann found a new assistant, a spunky teen named James A. Willis.[26] A budding pianist, Willis would sit and plunk out tunes at any nearby piano. Herrmann's music director tutored James and taught him to read music. James was a first-rate assistant, and when it came to learning magic, he absorbed it like a sponge. He studied Herrmann intently, and quickly picked up on the master's subtle sleight-of-hand moves. He especially loved card magic, and with his musician's delicate touch, he was soon entertaining the company with his own versions of some of Herrmann's most difficult tricks. And he was funny.

After two seasons as Herrmann's sidekick, James was craving the spotlight for himself. Full of fearless, teenaged self-confidence, sixteen-year-old James Willis quit his job with Herrmann to form his own company. Calling himself "The Black Herrmann," Willis's evening of music and magic found a niche at church socials, club events, and smaller theaters.

In early 1893, Willis was a hit with the four hundred guests who attended a night of "social entertainment" at Memorial Post 141 in Cleveland. The *Cleveland Leader* reported, "The professor is a humorist, among other things, and kept his audience convulsed with laughter throughout his performance, which included the so-called 'spirit slate writing,' which he exposed. The professor responded to an encore with a piano solo."[27] As with the Herrmann company, James Willis was often the only Black person in the room. According to the *Cleveland Gazette*, "Prof. Willis of Pittsburg, professionally known as the 'Black Herman' is considered the greatest Afro-American magician and owns and manages his own troupe, which, by the way are all white performers."[28] James A. Willis would go on to a long career as a magician, music director, and piano teacher.

ARTHUR B. WILLIAMS: PROFESSOR ARTHUR, HERRMANN'S RIGHT-HAND MAN

In September 1887, the Herrmann company opened their season in Kentucky at the Louisville Exposition. Joining them was a new assistant, sixteen-year-old Arthur B. Williams.[29] Adelaide Herrmann described Arthur as "a big fellow, black as coal, with a perfect set of white teeth."[30] At five feet ten inches, he was considerably taller than any assistant that preceded or followed him.

For years, Herrmann struggled to find just the right name for his assistant's character.[31] He had addressed his previous helpers by their own first names. At first, Herrmann referred to Arthur as "Gumbo," but the magician quickly retired the derogatory name. Instead, Alexander referred to his tall young assistant as "Professor Arthur."[32]

Arthur's starting salary was $5 per week, 75 percent less than the lowest-paid white stagehand. By any standards, the Herrmanns compensated their employees well. The company manager at this time, J. E. Warner, earned the most, at $110 a week. Next was the stage manager, T. Howell, at $40. The other white crew members—stagehands and carpenters—were paid between $20 and $30 weekly. Although Arthur's performance generated some of the biggest laughs in the show, prevailing attitudes and customs ensured that African Americans were paid far less than their white counterparts.

In the tour expense ledger, listed below the company's hotel and restaurant expenses, there was a separate entry for Arthur's "board," which was seven dollars per week.[33] Segregated hotels, restaurants, and trains meant that Arthur was often housed away from the rest of the company. South of the Mason-Dixon Line, restaurants, hotels, and train cars were racially segregated.[34] In the North, segregation was not the law but was widely practiced, nonetheless. Larger towns had colored hotels and rooming houses, where the company's African Americans could stay. These lodgings lacked wake-up services, and on at least one occasion, Herrmann's Black assistant missed the morning train.[35] Sometimes a town's only colored rooming house was also its brothel.[36] If Arthur was lucky, a Pullman porter or Black stagehand might have family or friends with a spare bed.

THE PULLMAN PORTERS

America's Black Pullman porters clearly influenced Alexander Herrmann's creation of his assistant's persona. Boomsky's crisp attire resembled the porters' uniform. Brushing off a gentleman's hat—as Boomsky did before a pratfall—was a porter's signature task, a mutually understood request for a tip. Just as "Boomsky" became a generic character name, many whites called all porters "George," after George Pullman.[37]

Almost all the first Pullman porters, in the late 1860s, had been formerly enslaved. All Pullman porters were African

The Pullman company was the largest employer of African Americans, who served as porters, waiters, and cooks.

American. By the 1880s there were approximately two thousand Pullman sleeper and dining cars on the American rails, staffed by four thousand Black porters and waiters. George Pullman's target market was ordinary Americans eager to experience the luxury of having a personal butler.

The porters weren't paid a living wage. They relied on tips to make ends meet. This pay structure was intentional to ensure they were ever smiling and responsive.[38] But it was one of the few steady jobs available to African Americans, and they got to travel. Pullman was by far the largest employer of Blacks in the country.

They were dignified men doing undignified work. The Pullman porters had strict rules of conduct and took pride in their work. Always impeccably dressed, they were ever available to make up beds, shine shoes, deliver food. But they also cleaned toilets and dealt with misbehaving and drunk passengers, always with a smile. Many white passengers treated them abominably. The porters' unofficial motto was "miles of smiles," no matter what they were actually thinking.

Fraternization with white customers was strictly forbidden. To the paying passengers, the porters were supposed to blend into the scenery, unnoticed. For the African American porters, it was the opposite, as they studied every aspect of their customers in minute detail. Watching how white Americans lived was eye-opening, inspiring porters and waiters to achieve middle-class lifestyles themselves.[39] Many porters educated themselves by devouring publications—newspapers, magazines, and books—left behind by white travelers. The porters' work and sacrifice paid for thousands of homes and college educations. Children of Pullman porters would become scientists, doctors, lawyers, bankers, and even a US Supreme Court Justice.[40]

Arthur's absolute last choice would be to bed down at the theater. In the superstitious thespian realm, all theaters are haunted by the ghosts of actors who are said to play their own dramas overnight, after everyone else has gone home. In a tradition begun long before Arthur's time, just before locking up, the stage manager placed a "ghost light" center stage, supposedly to light the specters' nightly frolics. Practical types declared that the light left burning onstage was simply to prevent someone who might wander into the theater from falling into the orchestra pit, or, in the old days, to keep pressure from building up in the gas lights. But theater ghosts remain powerfully compelling. Even today, in theaters worldwide, a ghost light—now an electric floor lamp—is placed center stage just before the stage manager turns out the other lights and leaves for the night. In addition to spirits, theaters attract earthly nocturnal frolickers in the form of mice and rats. When Arthur had no other option than to curl up in a theater dressing room for the night, it is doubtful that he got much sleep.

Many nights, the company slept in Pullman sleeper cars to the rocking of the train. The Herrmanns occupied a private stateroom, while the rest of the crew slept dormitory-style with the train's other passengers. By day, Pullman sleeper cars featured normal coach seating. At night, the coach seats converted to bottom bunks, while top bunks folded down from the railcar's ceiling. Travelers slept in close quarters with little privacy, the center aisle dividing two long rows of double bunks enclosed and separated only by curtains.

No laws prevented African Americans from purchasing berths on Pullman sleepers. But in practice, vigilante defiance by white railway employees effectively banned most Blacks from sleeper cars. Station agents refused to sell tickets to Black travelers, and even when affluent African Americans had tickets in hand, conductors barred them from entering sleeper and parlor cars. Black servants were the exception. Liveried valets, maids, and nannies were waved aboard behind their employers. Traveling in uniform under Herrmann's wing, Arthur was spared from many of the perils of traveling while Black. But tall, lanky Arthur could count on having to squeeze into one of the cramped, bumpy bunks over the wheels or water cooler. The porter was required to make up Arthur's berth with blue sheets to reassure the white passengers that the white sheets in their own berths were never slept on by Black people. If the sleeper car was full, Arthur's berth could be claimed by a white traveler. In that case, a well-tipped porter might share his own sleeping sofa in the smoking lounge since most Pullman porters were kept too busy to sleep more than an hour or two per night. The seven dollars for Arthur's board was more than his five-dollar weekly salary. For a Pullman porter used to hustling for tips of ten or fifteen cents, Herrmann's one-dollar tip for looking after Arthur for the night was a bonanza.

Besides assisting the teen aboard the trains, the porters knew the lay of the land and could advise him on the particular dangers of each new town. In all-white towns, Arthur stuck close to his boss. His brass-buttoned suit clearly marked him as a servant, and his HERRMANN cap blazed his affiliation. By day he safely ran errands for his employers, but in some towns, Arthur dared not venture out alone after dark.

JIM CROW LAWS: AMERICAN APARTHEID

In the 1890s, rapidly emerging "Jim Crow" laws mandated strict racial segregation.[41] A dozen years after the Civil War and emancipation, governments of Southern states, in a backlash against Reconstruction, enacted increasingly repressive legislation regulating Black people's behavior, restricting opportunity, codifying racial segregation, and eliminating voting rights.

Some municipalities went further with even stricter local statutes. In some Southern towns, a Black person could break the law and be arrested simply by walking on the wrong side of the street. Once they were convicted, often sentenced to multiyear terms, the prisoners were forced to work on chain gangs as legally sanctioned slave labor. Some captives succumbed to vigilante violence before or after being arrested. A uniform was not necessarily protective; in Georgia a Pullman porter, accused of an unknown offense, was lynched, strung up by his own jacket.[42] Many Southern and Midwestern municipalities were "sundown towns," where Black people faced arrest if they did not leave town by sunset.

Jim Crow laws would persist in the US until the passage of the Civil Rights Act in 1964.

On payday, a few weeks after joining the company, Arthur was handed what seemed an enormous sum: thirteen dollars.[43] He had indeed been given a raise, but his original five-dollar salary had been increased by just one dollar. The Herrmanns now trusted Arthur to make his own living arrangements while touring, so his seven dollars for board was now paid directly to him in cash. Seven dollars was also the cost of a week's supply of the duplicate hats that were destroyed nightly onstage—again more than Arthur's salary. Though a pittance compared to the rest of the company, Arthur's pay, equivalent to about $195 today, was ten times that of a Black field worker and double that of a Pullman porter if board was factored in. Plus, the Herrmanns provided Arthur's uniforms, shoes, and other necessities that porters were required to buy with their own earnings.[44]

Arthur became an exemplary assistant. A company member dubbed him "Herrmann's right-hand man."[45] Yet one reviewer for the *Jersey City News* wrote that it was obvious how he did one trick. "Of course, everyone knew last night that the boy from whose mouth Herrmann appeared to take numerous eggs had only one egg in his mouth which he showed at intervals, the magician only pretending to remove it."[46] Bad review aside, after eight months touring major northern cities, Arthur got a raise to seven dollars a week.[47]

At the end of his first season, Arthur took part in a show like no other—Herrmann's exposure of the notorious spirit medium, Madame Ann O'Delia Diss Debar. In the 1890s, Americans were flocking in great numbers to spirit mediums, a profession tailor-made for con artists. For hefty sums of money, crooked mediums conducted séances for bereaved people, whose deceased loved ones would appear through supernatural manifestations and phenomena—in truth, simple magic tricks. Many people were fooled, and these spirit mediums began gaining credibility. Herrmann and other magicians detested these fraudsters.

In this den of thieves, there was none worse than Madame Diss Debar. She and her husband, a painter, moved from city to city, targeting the rich and vulnerable. In New York, retired attorney Luther Marsh, afflicted with dementia, signed over his Manhattan townhouse to Madame Diss Debar after she manifested the spirit—and willing body—of a beloved dead actress from his youth. Marsh's friends sounded the alarm. The Diss Debars were arrested and charged with fraud. Yet even as they awaited trial, the victim, Luther Marsh, and several other prominent New Yorkers still defended Madame as a genuine miracle-producing spirit medium. In rebuttal, the New York Press Club seized upon Herrmann's offer to publicly expose her methods.

The packed house at the Academy of Music included attorneys for both the prosecution and defense, as well as Luther Marsh himself. Arthur had assisted Herrmann in hundreds of shows, but this performance was completely different. Every other show had been all about protecting the magic secrets at all costs. On this night, Herrmann conjured "spirits," eerie and otherworldly, just as Madame Diss Debar did for her clients. But unlike the medium, Herrmann then showed exactly how each effect was accomplished.

Herrmann made writing magically appear on blank slates. When the Professor explained the method, Arthur watched spectators slap their heads in disbelief that they had ever been fooled. Not content with simple tricks, Herrmann even explained, just this once, the secret of the Spirit Cabinet, demonstrating how Adelaide was able to ring a bell and rattle a tambourine while she was bound hand and foot with secure ropes. Instantaneous paintings were another of Diss Debar's convincing tricks, full-canvas oils, still wet, materializing in under fifteen minutes. This was thought to be impossible. Diss Debar attributed them to spirits. But Herrmann found a speed painter, who amazed the audience by painting a finished portrait in under ten minutes. Herrmann pointed out the coincidence that Madame Diss Debar's husband was a painter. Although Luther Marsh believed in her to the end, both Diss Debar and her husband were convicted and imprisoned on what was then Blackwell's Island, later renamed Roosevelt Island.

The exposure of Madame Diss Debar was such a sensation that Herrmann put it into his regular program. It was renamed, "Exposé of So-Called Spiritualism, in which many of the methods of the fraudulent mediums are disclosed."[48] Everyone in the company, including Arthur, suddenly had a new role. Now Herrmann walked onto the stage as Mephistopheles, dressed head to toe in red satin. Two long red feather plumes trailed from the charming devil's red cowl, bouncing and dancing hilariously as Herrmann narrated the scene. He ordered the lights lowered to darkness. Unseen, just offstage, huddled a strange group, all of them dressed head to toe in black. Ominous music began, and the group secretly crept onstage in the pitch blackness, holding onto each other for safety. Everyone walked facing upstage, backs to the audience, hiding the props they held and the fronts of their costumes. When they turned around, the audience gasped as weird, faintly glowing skeletons, angels, gauzy ghosts, hands, tables, and chairs began floating and dancing about the stage. Just as the unnerved audience reached maximum anxiety, Herrmann called, "Lights up!" The spirits were caught in the act. Arthur and the rest of the Herrmann company pulled off their black hoods and displayed the floating objects and costumes, all glowing with phosphorescent paint. Herrmann soon retired most of the Spiritual Exposé, but the dancing skeletons and ghosts would return in future seasons.

Arthur stood by Herrmann's side for three years, performing in every large and medium-sized city in the US, Mexico, Cuba, and Canada.[49] Arthur's third season came with a promotion and a raise. As assistant master mechanic, Arthur Williams's name was now printed in the program.[50] That season, Herrmann hired a wondrous juggler named D'Alvini, who performed for twenty mesmerizing minutes in the middle of the show.[51] Every night, Arthur watched from the wings, spellbound. He waited for the juggler to drop something, but he never did. D'Alvini balanced a spinning top on the hilt of a sword. He then balanced the tip of the sword on the edge of a playing card, which he balanced on the edge of a plate, which he held in his mouth.[52] All his tricks were breathtaking. Herrmann had stolen D'Alvini away from magician Harry Kellar, his chief rival, seeding a bitter feud between the two conjurors.

An 1889 Herrmann program featuring Cremation with Arthur Williams listed as Assistant Master Mechanic.

Cremation was the Herrmanns' most ambitious magical drama ever. Most everyone, from stagehands to managers, had roles in the drama, including Arthur, who served as both stagehand and puppeteer. The program's only big illusion set an eerie and supernatural tone. The title alone unnerved audiences in an era when cremation was practiced only during plagues. Cremation had been legalized in England just a few years before and was still so uncommon that the Herrmann program contained an explanation of the practice.[53] Cremation was bulky and difficult to perform, and some of the Herrmanns' usual theaters were too small to accommodate it.[54]

In a performance that had already gone on for over two hours, the set-up time of Cremation was, according to the *Buffalo Evening News*, "of back-breaking and temper-trying length."[55] Normally D'Alvini would have stepped out in front of the closed curtain to entertain, but the preparations for Cremation required total darkness. Without light, the orchestra's musicians, who customarily tempered the tedium of scene changes with a few brisk tunes, could not see their sheet music and sat idle. The *Buffalo Evening News* noted that as the fatigued audience sat squirming in the dark, some declared "the scene was not worth the waiting."[56] Behind the scenes, Arthur and the rest of the crew rushed to move equipment into place. D'Alvini and another assistant, H. H. Skinner, were donning their robes to play guards. After master mechanic E. Soots saw that the equipment was properly set, he gathered an armful of gauzy white fabric and dashed down the stairs. Arthur finished moving props onstage, then grabbed a large red devil puppet called "Le Diable," or "Mr. Chese Eye,"[57] and followed Mr. Soots down to their station under the stage's trap door, where they waited for their cue.

The curtain finally rose to a murky scene of ancient catacombs, a giant iron casket, and a large cross rising from a pile of boulders. Two robed assistants carrying flaming torches dragged in the "prisoner," Madame Herrmann, and placed her into the casket. Alexander covered her with an alcohol-soaked cloth and set it on fire with a torch. Flames roared.

In no time, the casket was shown to contain a charred skeleton. Ladies gasped in horror.

Under the stage, Mr. Soots released the latch on the trap door, and Adelaide plummeted down feet first, landing in a practiced squat on the small platform that Arthur held steady just below her. As Adelaide hopped down, Mr. Soots swung the trap shut then threw the white gauze over his head. Arthur snatched up the devil puppet, and the three of them hurried to the orchestra pit.

Suddenly, the audience saw Adelaide appear upstage as a translucent ghost. Herrmann tried to grab her, but she disappeared. A little red devil appeared. It sat on Herrmann's knee. It tickled him with a feather, kicked him, punched him in the face, and finally disappeared. Then a white ghost fought with Herrmann. The magician ran his sword through the phantom and shot it with a pistol, to no avail. The ghost strangled Herrmann until he fell, exhausted, to the floor. The phantom dissolved into thin air as the curtain came down. The audience, used to Herrmann's lighthearted happy endings, sat stunned.

Reviews were mixed. The *Baltimore Sun* reported that not everyone found the "wife cremation act" deceptive.[58] "The cremation casket stands in the center of the stage. Mme. Herrmann is placed in it apparently drugged and ready to be burned, there is a noise of pounding from the wings to divert attention, and when it subsides the casket is again opened to allow the lighting of the fire. Last night anybody could see that no human form lay beneath the sheet. The lady had simply dropped out of the drama." But "the phantom apparitions following were really clever and everybody was telling everyone else how it was done." It was so unsettling that "it was a relief finally to get the old Herrmann back again in his dress suit and fine smile. He made his negro attendant lay four eggs from his mouth."[59] Early on, Arthur had noticed that Herrmann always finished his show on a happy note. The Professor enjoyed terrifying people, but in the end, he always left them laughing.

Cremation's phantom apparitions were indeed clever. Adelaide, Mr. Soots (the ghost), and Arthur Williams's devil puppet seemed to appear on the stage, but they were actually stationed in the orchestra pit. A bright spotlight on them created their reflections on a large piece of plate glass that sat onstage, its top edge angled forty-five degrees toward the audience. Curtains and dim stage lighting kept most of the audience unaware of the glass.[60]

Later that season, Herrmann antagonized chief rival Harry Kellar by hiring away Kellar's star assistants, William and Dot Robinson. Their exciting, fresh energy was a powerful addition to Herrmann's show. With them, and, importantly, away from Kellar, came William E. Robinson's stunning original stage illusions, performed by Dot, the only person able to execute them.

Another big change was just around the corner.

The Herrmann company was playing at the Lee Avenue Academy in Williamsburg, Brooklyn. Arthur's job was to set up Alexander Herrmann's props table before the show. Madame Herrmann checked it just before curtain time. Herrmann called silver dollars "cartwheels." He had a small leather case into which a stack of twenty cartwheels fit exactly. It could be seen at a glance if any coins were missing. For several nights, the case was not in place, and Madame had to remind Arthur to get it. At this show, a matinee, she had to remind him again.[61] The *Evening World* noted that the magician was onstage and had just produced a rabbit from a spectator's waistcoat when he called, "Now, Arthur, the twenty cartwheels." Arthur didn't appear. Herrmann shouted sharply, "Hurry, Arthur, don't make me keep the people guessing." Still, Arthur did not appear.

"'Where in sheol is that boy?' muttered Herrmann, mad clear to the marrow."[62] Forced to skip the coin trick, Herrmann instead flipped cards into the gallery "ever so dexterously."[63] Later, the Herrmanns discovered that for a while, Arthur had been gambling with, and slowly losing, the silver dollars. Before each show, to cover his tracks, he borrowed cartwheels from the box office. He replaced the missing coins in Herrmann's case in time for the trick, then returned them to the box office after the show. But that day, the box office had no silver dollars, and Arthur's scheme unraveled. In a panic, he took the remaining cartwheels and ran. The Herrmanns felt betrayed and angry. Alexander was especially miffed at being abandoned onstage. They went to the police, who did not act. Then they went to the press.

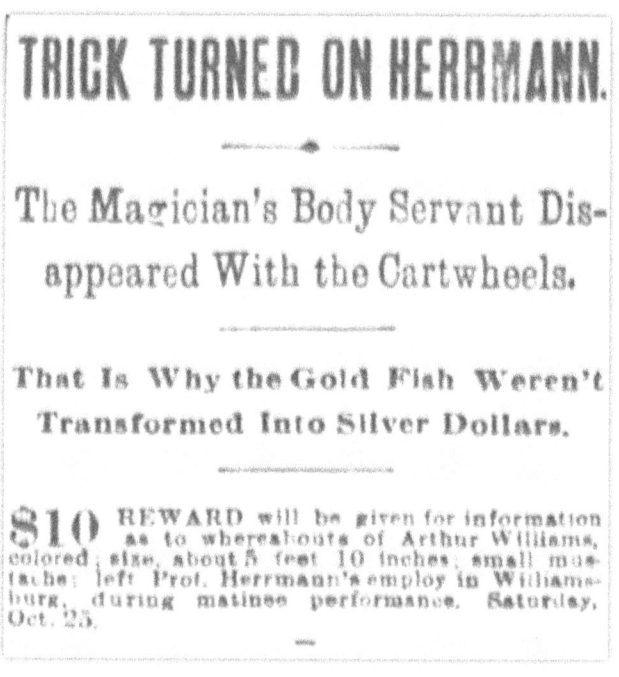

The Evening World (NY), Thursday, October 3, 1890.

"$10 REWARD will be given for information as to whereabouts of Arthur Williams, colored: size, about 5 feet 10 inches: small mustache: left Prof. Herrmann's employ in Williamsburg, during matinee performance, Saturday Oct. 25." Using a racial epithet considered acceptable in the 1890s, the theater manager told the *Evening World*, "It's a singular thing that the Professor didn't know where this 'coon' lives or hangs out. In all the three years he has worked for Mr. Herrmann, Arthur has had a great deal of his own way and has been treated like a prince. This is

Mr. Herrmann's reward. It isn't so much the twenty 'bones' as it is to catch the rascal."[64]

Herrmann never caught up with him, but eventually Arthur B. Williams did well for himself. By age thirty-one he was living in Manhattan, working as a railway porter.[65] Unlike Herrmann's other, smaller assistants, he met the physical requirements. Pullman porters had to be at least five-foot-nine, tall enough to pull down the ceiling berths, and preferably very dark-skinned, to clearly delineate them from their white passengers.[66]

The Herrmanns had difficulty replacing Arthur. One teen after another just didn't work out. In the meantime, Adelaide was back in pants, playing the boy assistant.[67] Years after Black teens took over the assistant role, Madame could still go onstage in a pinch. But her Monsieur Alexandre did not do pratfalls. Herrmann planted a crew member in the audience who volunteered for the egg trick. How many assistants came and went in the next eleven months is not known. Madame Herrmann told of one of them, a handsome young fellow "who looked brighter than he was." Unfortunately, in the hat trick, this youth forgot to switch the hat and fell on a borrowed "eight-dollar Dunlap."[68] The poor lad never got up to speed, and they had to let him go.

As they began their 1891 fall season, the Herrmanns acquired a wonderful new toy—a private Pullman railcar, which Alexander christened the *Addie Herrmann*. But they still had not replaced Arthur. Every night, Madame donned the boy's wig and squeezed herself back into Monsieur Alexandre's costume. As they headed south from Atlanta toward Americus, the Georgia landscape changed over from peach and pecan orchards to cotton and peanut fields. Herrmann gazed out at men, women, and children hunching their way down the long rows in the brutal southern sun, never imagining that his greatest assistant and comic partner would come straight from one of those very cotton fields.

~

An illustration of Alexander Herrmann and Boomsky performing the hat trick.

CHAPTER THREE

The Birth of Boomsky: Milton Hudson Everett

(1891–1893)

After being waved aboard Herrmann's midnight train, Milton Hudson Everett's head was spinning. Hutchin had never been on a train. Normally, he would have had to ride in the colored car, right behind the roaring, coal-fired steam engine, where Black passengers sat on hard wooden benches, with the windows closed to keep out smoke and cinders.

Herrmann's private car was pure opulence. Hutchin's bare feet sank into the thick oriental carpet as he followed Mr. Bloom through a wood-paneled parlor full of upholstered sofas and chairs. They went quickly through a long, narrow hallway with windows on one side and stateroom doors along the other. Mr. Bloom ushered him through a smoking room lined with bookcases, gun racks, and trophies, then through a room with a large dining table around which people sat drinking and laughing. Finally, they reached the end of the car, passing through a door into the galley and servants' quarters, where Mr. Bloom placed Hutchin into the hands of a tall Black man. Mr. Bloom introduced the man as George. Hutchin admired George's crisp Pullman porter's uniform.

Another Black man appeared, dressed all in white—the Pullman cook. As the rest of the company took to their beds, George and the cook went to work on Hutchin. They gave him a bath, scrubbed his nails, and cut his hair. They talked to him, comforting a stunned boy who had just left his whole world behind. George advised him to always remember the Pullman porters' "Three Ls"—Look, Listen, Learn. Although none too happy about sharing their already cramped quarters, George and the cook carved out a sleeping nook for Hutchin. He lay down with his eyes wide open, his mind racing. But one minute later the exhausted boy was asleep, rocked by the rhythmic swaying of the train.

A nudge to the shoulder woke him. The train had stopped, and the sun was shining. The cook handed Hutchin a plate of fried eggs, ham, and grits, which he wolfed down. Hanging by his nook was a uniform—deep royal blue, with a double row of polished brass buttons. He rushed to put it on but fumbled when he got to the shiny leather shoes. George had to help him tie the laces. He handed Hutchin a brimmed cap embroidered with gold letters. George read it to him: "HERRMANN." Hutchin had never seen anything so beautiful in his whole life.

"Thank you, George," he said.

The porter replied, "I'll take your thanks. But don't call me George." His name wasn't really George, he explained, and calling him that was an insult. Many white people, including Manager Bloom, addressed all porters as George. They never bothered to learn the porters' actual names, even though every porter wore a name tag.

As he escorted Hutchin to greet his new employers, the porter reminded him, "Look, listen, learn."

Milton Hudson Everett thrust out his chest as the Herrmanns looked him up and down. He could barely contain his excitement and beamed his biggest smile. Madame Herrmann later wrote that this crisp, uniformed page was unrecognizable from the ragamuffin of the previous evening. After living barefoot all summer, Hutchin's shoes felt like bricks squeezing his feet, but he did not care. Herrmann and his wife looked at each other and nodded. Perhaps their search was finally over. As Madame would later recount, she declared that morning in Macon that there was no prouder Black boy anywhere south of the Mason-Dixon Line.[69]

That first afternoon at the theater in Macon, Georgia, while the crew assembled the illusions, installed Herrmann's runway, hung the backdrops, freshened and repaired costumes and props, and organized the dressing rooms, Madame Herrmann began teaching Milton Hudson Everett the role of Alexander Herrmann's assistant. Although Hutchin had been with the company just a few hours, Madame would put him onstage that night. That way if he was a dud onstage or too homesick, they could send him back to Americus on the morning train.

Adelaide Herrmann was all business. Unlike the previous evening, she was no longer dressed as a boy. Madame bustled about in a finely tailored dress, her auburn hair swept up off her face. She showed Hutchin how to set out all the small props in Herrmann's dressing room. The coins, playing cards, billiard balls, handkerchiefs, and small cages containing bunnies, doves, parakeets, and guinea pigs all had to be in perfect order for Herrmann to load his pockets just before he made his entrance. The magician's assistant would deliver props to Herrmann as he bantered with the audience at the beginning and end of each show. Hutchin quickly picked up his part. Madame Herrmann was happy to see that this new boy was curious and focused.

Hutchin's first performance would be his real audition. There was just one trick he had to get right that night. The rest he could learn later, but tonight, he had to successfully execute the hat trick. The secret move was simple, but Madame knew that everything felt different in the heat of the moment in front of a theater full of people. Other new boys had frozen onstage or fled midshow. As the setup continued all around them, Madame taught Hutchin how to walk briskly and confidently onto the stage. To begin, she took a piece of chalk from her pocket and drew three bold X's on the stage. She explained that the two chalk marks closest to the audience were the spots for Herrmann and his pedestal table. She drew a circle around the X slightly behind and to the right of Herrmann's X. She directed Hutchin to the spot and told him to stand there and watch.

To rehearse, Adelaide played the role of Herrmann. She pointed at a gentleman's hat sitting on a seat out in the theater and told Hutchin to go get it. That night it would be a borrowed hat, offered up by an audience member, she explained, taking the hat from him and pointing him back to his chalked X. Madame Herrmann made strange plucking gestures. "I am taking coins from the air," she announced, tossing the imaginary coins into the hat. "And then I fling them into the audience!" She pretended to toss the contents of the hat into the empty theater.

"My assistant will brush off your hat and return it to you." Madame Herrmann handed Hutchin the hat. As he walked it back to the wings, she scurried ahead of him and was waiting behind the curtain with a brush in one hand and a different hat in the other. When Hutchin was safely out of audience view, they quickly exchanged hats and Madame handed Hutchin the brush. He turned around and walked back to center stage brushing the dummy hat. They practiced the handoff over and over until it was quick and smooth. The hat was out of sight for the briefest moment. No one would suspect that the little page now carried a different hat.

"And here is your hat, good as new!" she exclaimed. That was his cue for his big move.

Hutchin had so much more to learn. Over the previous decade, at least six other youths had already played the assistant role, several of them over multiple seasons. Over time, the role had become complex and intricate, with tasks sprinkled throughout Herrmann's act. But all that would come later. For his first night, Hutchin learned how to walk onstage with scarves draped over his arm so that nobody could see the bunny crouched in a pouch underneath. Madame showed him how to hold the squirming guinea pigs that Herrmann would hand off to him after producing them from under a spectator's collar. He learned how to listen for his cues to walk onto the stage and to walk off. Madame Herrmann assured him that she would be standing right there in the wings, whispering to him what to do.

Suddenly it was showtime! Hutchin barely recognized Madame when she emerged from her dressing room in a breathtaking gown. She sparkled with jewels from head to toe, her mane of auburn curls wild and loose, barely tamed by a diamond tiara. And suddenly there he was, Alexander Herrmann, the great magician, striding onto the stage to thunderous applause.

"I wish to borrow a gentleman's hat," Alexander announced. Madame Herrmann gave Hutchin a little push, and he walked onto the stage. Herrmann looked at him and smiled. The twinkle in his eye told Hutchin he had nothing to fear. This was all about having fun. Hutchin remembered Madame's instructions. He fetched a hat from a man in the audience and gave it to Herrmann.

The magician deftly plucked coins from the air, one after the other, tossing each one into the hat with an audible "clink." Hutchin was as astonished as the audience. After Herrmann had produced twenty silver dollars, he held the heavily laden hat and suddenly tossed its contents toward the spectators. Out flew not coins, but a fluttering cloud of confetti. Herrmann extended the confetti-speckled hat toward Hutchin. "My assistant will brush off your hat and return it to you." Hutchin took the hat and walked to the curtain's edge. Exactly as rehearsed, Madame handed him the brush as they smoothly exchanged hats. He strode back toward Herrmann, casually brushing the dummy hat.

"And here is your hat, good as new." On cue, Hutchin stumbled. He let out a shriek as he flew and—boom!—landed flat onto the hat. The audience howled with laughter.

"Boomsky! How could you?" Herrmann exclaimed.

Hutchin cowered and hung his head. That brought more laughs. Herrmann frantically apologized to the owner of the hat, while scolding

Boomsky. Two assistants rolled a small cannon onto the stage. Adding further insult, Herrmann tore the smashed hat into small pieces and proceeded to stuff them into the cannon.

"Now bring me a cannonball, one that weighs five hundred pounds!" The assistants struggled to hoist the heavy cannonball into the barrel. First Herrmann aimed the cannon at the right side of the balcony, excitedly shouting for everyone to clear those seats. No sooner had they moved, than the magician swung the cannon around, threatening the left side of the balcony. In the upper sections it was mayhem, with people in and out of their seats, bumping into each other. Herrmann lit the fuse. There was a *bang!* and a puff of smoke. A cannonball flew into the balcony, first causing screams then laughs when everyone realized it was a hollow rubber ball.

Finally, Herrmann drew everyone's attention back to the stage. There, hanging from a ribbon above the proscenium, was the borrowed hat, looking good as new. Herrmann aimed his pistol at the ribbon and fired. The hat dropped into his hands. With a flourish, he handed it to Hutchin.

"Careful now!" quipped Herrmann, as Hutchin returned the hat to its owner.

The audience applauded furiously. Madame, laughing, met her husband in the wings. "Boomsky?" she asked, eyebrows raised. "Yes. I have named him," replied Herrmann. "He fell with a boom onto the hat!"

"Boomsky" pleased Herrmann so much that all of his Black assistants, past, present, and future, would henceforth be known as Boomsky. Previous assistants who had not been called Boomsky during their tenure now referred to themselves as Boomsky in retrospect. But the name Boomsky was officially born on October 20, 1891, in Macon, Georgia, the first night that Milton Hudson Everett fell on the hat.

Hutchin had passed his audition. Madame happily packed away her boy assistant costume. Hutchin, for his part, learned that making an audience laugh felt very *very* good.

LEARNING THE ROPES

Hutchin's first days were a blur of shows, travel, and learning his role. The private railcar, the *Addie Herrmann*, was a never-ending riot of people and animals, laughing, squawking, barking, singing. Hutchin learned that the railcar had been put into service just a few weeks earlier. With their own rolling accommodations, the Herrmanns could now do one-nighters in small cities that lacked nice hotels or restaurants, small cities like Americus.

Now the animal-loving Herrmanns could travel with their pets, which were not allowed in public Pullman railcars or in hotels. During previous tours, the magical couple had usually been successful in sneaking aboard Lily, the tiny white Chihuahua, or Fidget, Adelaide's little Yorkshire terrier. But sometimes they got caught. An impromptu performance by Herrmann, or the flamboyant couple's sheer star power, might convince a railroad employee to bend the rules. But often, it was off to the baggage car for the poor pooch.

In the private car, Hutchin counted four dogs curled up sleeping—three tiny ones on the sofa and a gigantic beast sprawled on the rug.[70] He also noticed two caged birds, a parrot and a magpie; both sang and talked incessantly. Hutchin learned that cleaning up animal messes was his responsibility. When Adelaide Herrmann sighed about the destructive antics of Jimmie, her deceased monkey, Hutchin was secretly glad that Jimmie was not there. The many other animals in the show—doves, geese, chickens, rabbits, guinea pigs—traveled in crates in the baggage car.

The Herrmanns lived in jaw-dropping luxury that Hutchin could never have imagined. The Pullman car's interior was stunning, with its polished woodwork, brass fittings, stained glass windows, carved furniture, and crystal chandeliers. The Herrmanns dressed in gorgeous clothes and ate scrumptious-smelling food. Hutchin could barely believe that people could live in such comfort and finery. Money flowed from

Herrmann's fingertips as he tipped bellboys, porters, and waiters and tossed coins to the indigents who huddled at train stops.

Hutchin got to know the rest of the company. They spent much of their time on the train. Higher-level employees traveled with the Herrmanns in their private car, which slept eight passengers plus the railcar's Pullman staff. The Herrmanns' chief assistants were William Robinson and his wife, Dot. Will and Dot were younger than Alexander and Adelaide, then forty-seven and thirty-eight. Will was thirty. Like most show women, Dot, then in her mid-twenties, lied about her age. Olive Robinson's tiny size inspired her nickname, Dot. The Robinsons had just started their third season with the company. Compared to their two earlier seasons with Herrmann's rival, Harry Kellar, Herrmann's tours were a delight. Kellar ran an austere troupe, punctuated by his explosive outbursts when angered. By contrast, the Herrmanns were generally relaxed and jolly and all too happy to share their expensive tastes with their favorite assistants.

The Herrmanns' and Robinsons' relationship was warm. As illusion assistants and magicians' wives, Adelaide and Dot bonded over swapped war stories. Alexander felt fatherly toward Dot. He nicknamed her Florine, after a little princess from a French fairy tale. Alexander and Will shared a passion for magic. Like little boys, they would huddle for hours, sketching ideas and performing tricks for each other. They often called Hutchin over to show him a trick, laughing at his gaping astonishment. Madame Herrmann's sighs and sideways glances betrayed her jealousy at having to share her husband with the rough-hewn Will Robinson. She didn't trust him and warned Alexander that Will Robinson could be Harry Kellar's spy.[71] Plus, Robinson had an eye for the ladies. Adelaide loved Dot like a daughter, and Alexander adored both Robinsons. Will and Madame Herrmann tolerated each other for the sake of the show, and for Alexander.

Unknown to Hutchin, the Robinsons harbored a deep secret—Will and Dot were not legally married. Since unmarried couples were forbidden to share a hotel room, Will and Dot's pretense was crucial. They could not marry; Will already had a wife, with whom he had a son. The relationship was over, but as a Roman Catholic, William Robinson could not be divorced. Robinson also had an older child with a different woman, a daughter conceived out of wedlock, who was being raised by Robinson's parents.[72]

Edward L. Bloom, Herrmann's latest in a long string of company managers, also traveled in the private car. The financially freewheeling Herrmann was notoriously unmanageable. But young Ed Bloom was unflappable. The Herrmanns liked him because he didn't act like a suit type. Indeed, Bloom was an outrageous practical joker, and Herrmann loved people who made him laugh. Herrmann's music director, personal secretary, and business manager filled out the railcar's entourage.

Since the Professor's head was in the clouds, Madame Herrmann acted as de facto leader of the company. She officiously chided and corrected the staff and was sometimes very bossy. When angry, her cheeks flamed, and her sharp words could sting. Will Robinson and other male crew members did not hide their resentment at taking orders from her. But Adelaide Herrmann was tough. Earlier that year New York's *Evening World* declared she had shown "that a woman as well as a man can use both hands at once" after Madame Herrmann saved an elderly woman who had fallen in front of a fast-approaching horse car at Fifth Avenue and Twenty-Third Street. "Mme. Herrmann sprang to her assistance, caught the horses' heads with one hand and whisked the old lady from the track with the other."[73]

Like everyone else in the company, Hutchin had multiple responsibilities. When not performing, he was Herrmann's valet, or manservant. In addition to laying out and packing Herrmann's magic paraphernalia, he also took care of the magician's clothes and polished his shoes. He drew Herrmann's baths. He learned to shave him and trim his hair. He emptied the chain-smoking magician's ashtrays. He manned the door at both railcar and dressing room, delivering visitors' cards to Herrmann on a little silver tray. He tended to Herrmann's guests as well. From taking coats and lighting cigars to refreshing drinks and ordering carriages, Boomsky's work never ended.

Despite their lavish lifestyle, the Herrmanns themselves were rarely idle. They worked their company hard, but they demanded as much from themselves. Adelaide, an excellent seamstress, repaired costumes, drapes, and fabric props. Her hands were always in motion, either working a needle and thread or writing letters to family and friends, always with a tiny dog on her lap. At train stops she delighted in shopping for groceries in town markets "like an ordinary housewife." But she certainly did not look like an ordinary housewife. Dressed in Parisian couture, her auburn hair flaming, she was followed by a uniformed page carrying her parcels. Striding alongside Madame Herrmann was Cora, the Great Dane, who proudly carried in her mouth a small basket containing Fidget, the tiny Yorkie, and "needless to say, these two extremes of dogdom attracted no end of attention."[74]

Alexander was the more self-indulgent of the pair. He loved to wake up slowly, lounging in bed with his coffee and cigarettes, dogs by his side, the morning newspapers spread about him. But if a morning press interview, publicity stunt, or charity appearance at a school, hospital, or prison was on the schedule, he rose to the occasion with the same good-natured vigor that he put into every single performance. Whenever there was time, Herrmann had his local hosts take him hunting. The railcar's cook was frequently plucking game birds and skinning rabbits shot by the master himself.

On Hutchin's fourth day, the company headed west toward their next stop, Montgomery, Alabama. As Hutchin gazed out the window of the speeding train, mile after mile, in field after field, he saw hundreds of people picking cotton, many of them boys just like him. In the 1890s, many of America's five million Blacks still lived in the great Southern cotton belt, and the vast majority were agricultural laborers. Each picker wore a wide-brimmed straw hat, their only protection against the brutal sun. They worked their way down mile-long rows, bent nearly in half as they plucked the sharp-husked cotton bolls and tossed them into long, shoulder-slung bags they dragged behind them. When the bags were full and heavy, the pickers set them aside to be weighed later and quickly grabbed an empty bag to start all over again. A strong adult man could fill three bags in a day, over two hundred pounds total. Hutchin thought of his family and how they sang and fooled around together as they picked the soft cotton bolls with their razor-sharp husks. You could always tell a cotton picker by the scars on their wrists. Hutchin looked at his own wrists and saw that his cuts and scars were already fading. Hutchin hoped he would never have to pick cotton again.

Hutchin missed his family, his grown brothers, Daniel and Lewis, and his big sister, Polly. He missed the younger twins, Cook and Fort. He really missed his closest brother, Sidney. Their whole lives they'd never spent a day apart. More than anything Hutchin missed his parents. They were probably worried. And mad. At least they knew what happened to him. In the cotton field, there would be talk of little else. One hand short, they would keep picking cotton in the scorching sun, hour after hour, week after week.

Hutchin's parents, Ben and Leitha Everett, had both been born into slavery in Georgia.[75] They did not know where their own parents were born.[76] At forty-four, Ben was considered old for a Black man.[77] When he was Hutchin's age, Ben had still been enslaved; he was eighteen when the war ended and slavery was abolished. Ben stayed near his old plantation and became a sharecropper. Times were desperate after the war, and his family had nearly starved. In the twenty-six years since, life hadn't gotten that much easier. To be sure, emancipation had ended slavery's greatest horrors. Families were no longer split apart and sold. Black people were allowed to travel, if they had money and knew somewhere to go. But Ben still spent every day at hard labor, earning barely enough to feed his family. Leitha Everett had also been enslaved as a child. She labored in the fields while trying to care for her family. Leitha and Ben had borne much sorrow. Of Leitha's fourteen babies, only six survived to adulthood.[78] As soon as they could walk, the Everett children picked cotton alongside their parents. None of them went to school. Every day, as they headed to the fields, the Everetts saw the daughters of Humphrey Hooks, their nearest white neighbor, walking to the schoolhouse, books in hand.[79]

Most Georgia Blacks eked out a living as sharecroppers or tenant farmers, laboring in the fields in exchange for a small plot of land and a dilapidated shack to call home. A top cotton picker earned three dollars a week, minus the sharecroppers' "expenses," which included rent, use of tools, fabric for clothing, and food staples such as flour, lard, and rough cuts of meat. When expenses were totaled, they often came to more than a worker's earnings. At the end of each season, after months of his whole family picking cotton from dawn to dusk, Ben often came up short and ended up owing money to his boss.

Suddenly, Ben's thirteen-year-old son was earning double his family's weekly income. On payday, Hutchin was stunned to receive a handful of coins—*his* coins. The porter showed him how easy it was to send money back to his family using a postal money order. Introduced in 1864 as a safe way for Union soldiers to send their pay to their families, money orders were an American success story, a boon to the US Post Office and highly popular with the public.

On Friday morning, the Herrmann company arrived in Montgomery, Alabama.[80] One hundred and fifty miles from Americus, it was a different world to Hutchin. Montgomery was so much bigger and grander. Massive smoke-belching factories on the Alabama River bordered a downtown of three- and four-story buildings that to Hutchin were enormous. The first capital of the Confederacy, Montgomery was as Old South as one could get, and the color of one's skin was an inviolable divide. The porter and cook schooled Hutchin on the many rules for behavior in Southern cities, where just looking at someone the wrong way could mean deep trouble for a Black person.[81] But Hutchin didn't have time to get into trouble in Montgomery. The show opened on Friday night, and Hutchin had to be back at the theater the next morning to set up for a Saturday family matinee. The Herrmanns' newspaper ad promised that after their big finale, the Flags of All Nations, each child attending would receive a free flag.[82]

The Opera House was packed to capacity with parents and children of all ages for the Saturday matinee. The advertisements had guaranteed that no guns would be discharged during the performance. As a result, many of the children were very small. Herrmann played differently with the children—sweeter and gentler, yet still wickedly hilarious. Again and again, the children's squeals of laughter infected the whole audience. Hutchin had to fight hard not to laugh himself. After the show, Hutchin stood onstage with Herrmann handing little flags to hundreds of white children in their starched shirts and pinafores. There were no Black children.

Hutchin enjoyed the no-gunfire matinee. Normally, Herrmann fired blank rounds several times per performance, as did nearly all magicians. The noise was earsplitting, and the smoke made Hutchin cough. Many audience members, especially women, intensely disliked the practice and complained continuously. But magicians resisted giving up the effortless misdirection of a gunshot reverberating in an enclosed space. People startled out of their skins were unlikely to notice a secret move. Herrmann and others compromised by eliminating gunshots at matinees when women and children filled the house.

The next day, Sunday, October 25, the train pulled into New Orleans for a full week's run, the biggest city so far for Hutchin and a favorite stop for the Herrmanns. Here they would play to more diverse and savvy audiences.

In New Orleans, Hutchin first confronted the issue that would dog Herrmann's Black assistants throughout their careers. When they played longer runs in bigger cities, the company—but not always the Herrmanns themselves—moved off the train and into hotels. Hutchin quickly discovered that segregation laws prevented him from staying in the same hotels or eating in the same restaurants as the rest of the troupe.

Some hotels offered servants' quarters. If not, Hutchin would have to stay by himself at a colored hotel or rooming house. This would prove true across much of America, even in Northern states where segregation was not mandated by law. But the Herrmanns made sure their young charge was accommodated.

The St. Charles Theater in New Orleans was far grander than any of the small-town theaters they'd played since leaving Americus. After playing a different city nearly every night, a full week in New Orleans felt almost like a vacation. Not having to pack and unpack constantly meant time to relax a bit. The Herrmanns played New Orleans every season and had many social connections. As Professor Herrmann's valet and part of his entourage, Hutchin found himself clinging to the clattering horse carriages that whisked his employers to late-night parties and clubs. There they mingled with local socialites, artists, and civic leaders. Hutchin was used to going to bed early to be in the fields by dawn. At first, he struggled not to doze off as he stood at attention in his brass-buttoned uniform, always ready to catch Herrmann's ashes or light his next cigarette.

Herrmann was the life of every party. Into the wee hours, people crowded around as he performed trick after trick. Everyone talked about the wine glass trick. Full to the brim, Herrmann raised the glass to his lips, and it suddenly vanished! Before long, Hutchin began secretly assisting Herrmann in his party tricks. Herrmann's cigar trick was a stunner. As the Professor displayed one of his special Herrmann-banded Cuban cigars, Hutchin moved around the edges of the room, unnoticed and unremembered, lighting cigars, emptying ashtrays, and freshening drinks. With all eyes on Alexander, Hutchin could easily slip a duplicate cigar into the pocket of Herrmann's designated target. When a cigar vanished at Alexander's fingertips and reappeared in the spectator's pocket, it seemed like a miracle. It was all so much fun that the hardest part for Hutchin was keeping a smirk off his face. These were the hours when Adelaide finally relaxed. The extroverted starlet enjoyed a few glasses of Veuve Clicquot Champagne with an ever-changing cast of extremely hospitable friends. Hutchin could never relax, but he did not care one bit. He was thirteen years old, with the best job in the world. And it was still just his second week.

In the early morning, when the Herrmanns slept in, Hutchin had a chance to explore his first big city. In New Orleans he gawked at ships on the fast-moving Mississippi River—steamers, paddle-wheelers, trawlers. Out on the streets he saw colorfully dressed women walking arm in arm with sailors. Vibrant street markets displayed produce, animals, housewares, clothing—it all made Hutchin's head reel.

In the afternoons, Hutchin accompanied Herrmann on one of his favorite pastimes—visiting pawn shops. There Herrmann haggled over small pieces of diamond and gold jewelry, purchasing studs, rings, pins, buckles, and cuff links. He repeated this ritual in every city. Hutchin wondered why anyone would need so much jewelry, but soon he understood that it was Herrmann's way of converting bulky piles of tour cash into a more easily safeguarded form. Both Herrmann and Madame loved showing off their sparkly gems; even the buttons on Alexander's shirts sported precious diamonds.

As Hutchin settled in with the company, he began noticing more. Less than a month into the season, playing so many one-nighters was already starting to strain the crew. During the week in New Orleans, William and Dot Robinson had a moment to breathe. The Robinsons had brought on tour their own three dazzling stage illusions—Florine: Child of the Air, Cocoon, and Black Art, which Will and Dot performed between Herrmann's own tricks. So far, Hutchin had only seen one of these illusions, Black Art. The Robinsons' other two acts weren't well suited to one-night stands and were often cut from the show. Both illusions took a lot of time to set up and needed careful rehearsal in every new theater to be sure no one in the audience could detect the secret methods. Arriving in a new venue every afternoon, with an entire evening's show to prepare, there often wasn't enough time to rehearse the Robinsons' elaborate stage illusions, to Will and Dot's great disappointment.

As the company's chief stage mechanic, Will Robinson was responsible for all technical aspects of the performance, an enormous task in such a large-scale touring production. Night after night, Will somehow made it work. Nobody knew how. As if running the backstage operation wasn't enough, Will also performed. For his own Black Art illusion, he played the wizard Abdul Khan. In the Herrmanns' Strobeika illusion, he played Ivan Ivanhoff, a Russian prisoner. The crew was used to Robinson barking orders backstage as he glued on his wizard's beard and got into his costume. Once he stepped onstage, he instantly transformed into his character, only to go right back to issuing cues the second he was back in the wings.

Dot was a paradox. Her tiny frame and angelic face masked a tough physicality and ferocious determination. The former showgirl with a rough past was the perfect magic assistant.[83] As with Boomsky, Dot's childlike features worked as misdirection. Her small size and placid face let audiences easily believe that the magic simply happened to her. This disguised the real secret, that she was actually a rugged athlete who was *making* the magic happen.

Hutchin watched the Robinsons' illusions from backstage. From his angle and proximity, the secret methods were obvious, yet the illusions were still wondrous. When seen from the audience, they were astonishing.

Florine: Child of the Air was Herrmann's name for the Robinsons' breathtaking levitation.[84] The curtain opened to reveal Dot Robinson and Madame Herrmann standing before a black backdrop. Adelaide reached down, grasped Dot's foot and simply tossed her in the air, where she remained, floating. But then Dot moved! She swam back and forth through the air. She also rotated. She cartwheeled and somersaulted, even diving through a hoop, before descending to gently alight on the stage. Hutchin could see what the audience could not, that Florine floated not by magic but by means of a piece of heavy machinery hidden behind the back curtain, operated by Will.

The Robinsons' other featured illusion, Cocoon, also required complicated rigging and lighting, as well as a trapdoor in the center of the stage. If the theater didn't already have one, the company's carpenter would cut out a trapdoor, then patch the stage when they vacated. For one-night stands, there was rarely enough time for this. Many nights, Cocoon also stayed in its crate.

Hutchin saw Cocoon for the first time in New Orleans. Watching from the wings in his brass-buttoned uniform, he could see part of the secret, but the rest was still baffling. Herrmann began by striding onstage trailing a fluttering red ribbon behind him. The ribbon reached all the way across the stage. Herrmann draped it over high hooks at each side of the stage and attached small weights to the ends, which pulled the ribbon taut just above his head. Herrmann displayed a wooden box frame, completely open but for a piece of paper covering one side. The magician set the box on the stage, paper side toward the audience, while he reached up and pulled down the ribbon. Herrmann looped the ribbon under hooks atop the box frame and gently lifted the lightweight box onto a stool. Suddenly, something inside expanded and burst open the paper. Herrmann lifted away the box to reveal a large cocoon sitting atop the stool. Suddenly, the cocoon opened and out popped a sparkling butterfly—tiny Dot Robinson.[85]

Robinson's Black Art was presented at every performance, no matter how rushed the setup. The first time Hutchin saw Black Art, it startled and frightened him. The curtain opened to reveal a strange wizard named Abdul Khan. Robes, a turban, and a fake beard rendered Will Robinson completely unrecognizable. He gestured toward a huge rectangular box that sat on trestles, elevating it off the stage. The side facing the audience was open, and the entire inside of the box—floor, walls, and ceiling—was black. A row of bright lights on the floor was pointed toward the audience. Abdul Khan stepped up into this elevated room. As the audience squinted past the lights into the box's inky blackness, suddenly a bright white table appeared! It happened shockingly fast. Over and over items appeared and disappeared—candlesticks, tableware, a hand, a skull. Suddenly the wizard's head was gone! It reappeared in midair and floated around the stage, still speaking all the while, until finally reconnecting with his body.[86]

Eventually Hutchin discovered that the secret behind Black Art was Dot. Dressed head to toe in black, including a hood with mesh-covered eyeholes, she crept around the black-fabric-covered room. The bright stage lights, called "dazzlers," contracted the audience members' pupils, helping to make Dot completely invisible. To make an object appear, Dot simply whipped off its black cover. To make it disappear she would quickly cover it up. To make an object appear to float, she would lift it and carry it fluidly around the room, taking care that a black-gloved hand never passed in front of it, exposing the method. The effect was so astonishing that the audiences just gave up trying to figure it out.

For René Stretti, Herrmann's music director, Black Art presented a special challenge. The maestro's job was to lead the ensemble of local musicians. Large cities with their house orchestras were a pleasure. In small towns, sometimes only a pianist and drummer showed up, along with a ragtag assortment of musicians who by day might be clerks or teachers. Maestro Stretti conducted the ensemble while also playing the violin. During Black Art, the musicians were frequently so mesmerized that they forgot to keep playing, craning their necks to see the stage. One by one, instruments would drop out as the music got quieter and barer. Stretti's intrepid violin kept the tune going as the maestro refocused his ensemble with a sharp "Psst!"[87]

Strobeika and the Slave Girl's Dream, the Herrmanns' own two illusions, were in every show. Once Hutchin saw how difficult they were to do, he marveled at how effortless they looked. Strobeika was Alexander's favorite type of illusion because all he had to do was talk. The athletics were left to others.

Inspired by a Russian story, Herrmann told of Strobeika, a political prisoner's wife, who sacrificed herself for his freedom. As Herrmann narrated, the struggling prisoner, Ivan Ivanhoff—Will Robinson in striped prison garb—was dragged onstage. The prisoner was wrestled onto a plank suspended by chains. Herrmann clamped the prisoner's arms, legs, and neck into iron shackles attached to the plank. Some gentlemen from the audience locked the shackles with padlocks, closing each with an audible click. Herrmann drew a curtain, hiding the prisoner momentarily, then threw open the drapes. The prisoner was gone! Shackled to the plank in his place was his wife, Strobeika, played by Adelaide. The audience gasped, but there was more. A man's voice boomed from the back of the house. "I'm free!" shouted Will Robinson, as he ran down the aisle and back to the stage.[88]

The Herrmanns' other illusion, The Slave Girl's Dream, was Alexander and Adelaide's special moment, just the two of them, together onstage. The mesmerized audience felt like they were part of an intimate exchange between the pair. Hutchin could hear the audience's applause, but he could not see the act as he sat crammed into his tiny niche, awaiting his cue. Adelaide, dressed in a simple sheath, stood on a little stool atop a platform as Alexander waved an ether-soaked handkerchief under her nose. She relaxed into sleep, resting against a vertical pole under her arm, like a crutch. First, Herrmann removed the stool from under her feet, and she remained suspended in the air. As the music swelled, Herrmann snapped open a fan and began to gently waft air toward Adelaide. Slowly, Alexander lifted her feet off the ground, raising her into a level position, floating, touching nothing but the pole. Hutchin heard his cue—Herrmann's footsteps inches from his face—and began slowly turning a crank. Adelaide began to revolve, her arm still resting on the pole as she rotated in a slow, horizontal circle. Alexander draped her with a velvet robe and placed a crown upon her head. She seemed to partly waken from her trance, as if she dreamed of being a queen. The audience was enchanted. What they did not see, and never imagined, was Boomsky, crouched under the platform, turning the winch that slowly spun Madame around.[89]

The illusions were wonderful. But for Hutchin, and everyone else, the best part of the show was simply watching Alexander Herrmann perform. Every performance began and ended with thirty minutes of Herrmann onstage by himself, assisted by Boomsky. At each theater, Herrmann's crew installed his wooden runway, which ran from the center of the stage into the middle of the audience. It sacrificed a dozen seats but gave an intimacy with the crowd.

For his solo sets, Herrmann picked from nineteen tricks that he had honed to perfection. He could play multiweek runs, completely changing his program every week. Not every trick required Boomsky's assistance, but Hutchin had to be ready. Herrmann was famously spontaneous. On a whim, he might substitute a different trick, midshow.

Herrmann began every performance with the flying cards. Holding the deck in one hand, Herrmann sent card after card spinning into the audience in rapid succession, filling the air with twirling cards. His accuracy and distance were astonishing, bouncing cards off back walls of the largest theaters. If he spotted a uniformed officer in the front of the balcony, Herrmann would land each of the four aces in the stupefied gentleman's lap.

Boomsky watched Herrmann closely, awaiting his cue for the egg trick. Alexander Herrmann loved this trick and performed it his entire career.[90] Like the hat trick, the egg trick was a staple, season after season. The stage illusions changed every year, but the core of the show, Herrmann's solo acts, did not.

As Boomsky stood holding a plate, Herrmann thumped him on the back. The teen's eyes widened and his cheeks bulged as he finally opened his lips to reveal an egg. Herrmann took the egg and placed it on the plate. As Herrmann thumped him again, Boomsky's eyes and cheeks once again bulged. Surprised, Herrmann removed another egg from his assistant's mouth, and placed it on the plate. Over and over this happened, to Herrmann's annoyance, until the plate was precariously overloaded with eggs. Herrmann tapped Boomsky's back one more time. Out of Boomsky's mouth came a live flapping chicken. Then Boomsky himself started walking and squawking like a chicken, wing-dancing his way offstage. The chicken, trained to follow him, strutted along beside him, and the audience howled.

The egg trick required perfect coordination between the magician and assistant. Boomsky secretly pre-inserted the first egg into his mouth. It didn't have to be a whole egg, or even an egg at all. A piece of white leather worked just as well and was easier to hide. By just blowing some air behind it, Boomsky could make the white leather look just like an egg expanding inside his mouth. Herrmann never removed it. Instead, he pushed it back into his Boomsky's mouth as he revealed a palmed egg. When timed right, it was impossible to see the switch.

Each time Herrmann removed an egg from his assistant's mouth, Boomsky's wide-eyed, panicked expressions provided the distraction for Herrmann to palm another egg. Boomsky played it up, taking his time, letting maximum distortion build on his face, until—pop!—another egg appeared between his lips.

An earlier assistant had made an impression during a performance the Herrmanns gave at an insane asylum in Washington, DC. When Herrmann pulled egg after egg from the assistant's mouth, the *Washington Post* reported, "the crazy people enjoyed it."[91] The same assistant was present when

Detail from a poster showing Herrmann removing a chicken from Boomsky's mouth. Racial caricatures of African Americans were common and considered normal.

Herrmann gave a charity performance for the inmates of the Maryland penitentiary, which housed "motley" inmates, in other words, men of color. Many of them were superstitious and fearful of Herrmann's magic. But others were eager to assist Herrmann and "yelled with delight," according to the *Baltimore Sun*.[92] To Black folks, Herrmann was either a wonder or a demon. There was no middle ground; they either laughed and cheered, or they fled in terror. Herrmann often quipped that "Negroes from the South" were his favorite magic audience.

The week in New Orleans flew by, and the company was back on the road. The next two months combined full-week runs with relentless slogs of one- and two-night stands. When they arrived in Galveston on November 2, Madame Herrmann handed Hutchin some money and instructed him to go buy some cowboy hats to add to the trunk of duplicates for the hat trick. The wide-brimmed hats came in handy that week in Houston, Dallas, Fort Worth, and Tyler, Texas.

Over the following two weeks they worked their way through Arkansas and Tennessee before landing for a week in St. Louis, which Hutchin decided was both the most wonderful and the most awful place he had been so far. Magnificent municipal buildings and monuments rose up all about them, inspired by the city's grand vision of itself as Gateway to the West. America's fourth-largest city bustled with energy, but it was also filthy. Dozens of coal-fired factories belched a thick, choking smog that burned Hutchin's eyes and stung his throat. Even worse was the horrible smell from the rendering plants that processed carcasses discarded by the city's many tanneries. Yet the Herrmanns seemed not to notice or care. Each night after the show, as their local hosts ferried them to dinners and receptions, Hutchin heard music that touched his soul—St. Louis blues—spilling out from after-hours clubs and cafés.

The following week they played Cincinnati, another large, smoggy industrial city. Then they hit the road in earnest. In the first three weeks of December, they performed in Kentucky, Tennessee, Indiana, Illinois, Missouri, and Kansas. The one-nighters were rough on the crew. With

Cabinet card depicting Milton Hudson Everett at about age fourteen, photographed by José Maria Mora, circa 1892.

their fifty crates of equipment, any day they didn't have to load in and out the same night felt like a blessing. Plus, spending a night or two meant actually seeing a place. Three nights in Nashville, two nights in Indianapolis—those cities stuck in the mind. Others were a blur. In four days, from December 16 to 19, they played Kansas City and St. Joseph, Missouri, and Leavenworth and Topeka, Kansas. It was suddenly far colder than Hutchin had ever known. The Herrmanns gave him his first wool coat and socks.

This kind of touring was grueling, but it was very profitable. Herrmann was a big star. The nation was in a financial depression, but in these small cities, the whole town always turned out. They filled the theater on that one night of the year when Herrmann the Great played their town. Medium-sized cities, like Galveston, Little Rock, or Sioux City, could wait years for Herrmann to grace them again. For some small towns, like Americus, Georgia, or Peekskill, New York, a visit by Alexander Herrmann was a once-in-a-lifetime event.

These one-nighters were not nearly as draining for the Herrmanns as for the rest of the company. While the crew set up at the theater, the stars would relax on their comfortable railcar, enjoying meals prepared by their chef. Alexander would arrive at the theater just in time to apply his greasepaint, load his pockets, take his wand proffered by Boomsky, and stroll onstage.

They worked their way across the plains of Kansas and Colorado, traveling over prairies dotted with homestead farms, as newly constructed railroads extended to every corner of the US. The explosive population growth of the American Plains states would continue for nearly forty years before the droughts and dust bowls of the 1930s would force millions of family farmers off the land. But in the 1890s, burgeoning, whistle-stop prairie towns were building churches, schools, municipal buildings, and opera houses.

As they chugged west to their next destination, a small, jagged edge of horizon grew and grew until they found themselves at the foot of towering, white-capped mountains. On December 21, the Herrmann company opened a weeklong run at the Tabor Grand Opera House in Denver, at the base of the snowy peaks. On Friday, Christmas Day, just before showtime, the Herrmanns presented each member of the company with a gift and a cash bonus.[93] For Hutchin, on his first Christmas away from his family, the gesture lifted his spirits. On Monday and Tuesday, they played Pueblo and Colorado Springs. Then on Wednesday their train headed high into the Rockies, winding its way through breathtaking winter terrain to perform that night in the rough silver-mining outpost of Leadville, which had its own smaller Tabor Opera House. The next day, after a long train ride through rough mountain wilderness, they landed for four nights in Salt Lake City, their westernmost stop that season. They rang in 1892 in that strangest of cities, where, to Hutchin's astonishment, many of the men had more than one wife. Hutchin had never heard of Salt Lake City or dreamed he would be starting a new year in such a place. He could never have imagined such bitter cold. And the snow! For a boy from southern Georgia, it was marvelous and surreal.

That January, the company plied its way back east through Nebraska. They played Kearny, Lincoln, Beatrice, and Omaha in the space of six days. Over the next couple of weeks, they worked their way through Iowa and Minnesota until they landed in Minneapolis, then St. Paul.

Traveling took its toll on the crew and the equipment as they tumbled their crates across America. Ingenuity and resourcefulness were needed to keep everything working, especially the magic props, with their delicate springs and wires and complicated mechanisms. The crew constantly touched up scratches, dents, and chipped paint. Every day brought new deadlines—another train departing, another curtain going up. They encountered one crisis after another, somehow always solved before the show began. They were a team, and in a very real way, a family. Most nights, they slept while being rocked by the train.

The better Hutchin got at doing his job, the more tasks he was given to learn. While performing, he was often supposed to look clumsy to throw the audience off the scent and make him appear less skilled than he really was. But in truth, his assistant tasks, including many secret moves, required precision and perfect timing. Herrmann and Madame constantly corrected Hutchin—stand a little closer here, move a bit faster there—molding and refining his skills. Hutchin began to understand that, in the assistant role, he was Herrmann's secret weapon. He knew that other assistants had preceded him. But crew members began nudging each other, remarking that this youth was clearly Herrmann's favorite.

PRIVATE PULLMAN RAILCARS

Adelina Patti Railcar & Crew, Long View.

Opera star Adelina Patti with her private railcar and staff. Personal Pullman railcars were equivalent to today's private jets. The Pullman Company staffed each private car with a porter and a cook.

LIFE ON THE ROAD

Four months into his first season as Boomsky, Hutchin Everett from southern Georgia shivered his way through his first northern winter. By that point, Hutchin had already performed in twenty states, plus the territory of Utah.[94] And the touring season was barely half over. For the Herrmanns, with their private railcar, these breathless months of one-night stands had been a fun and profitable new adventure. For the crew, especially chief stage mechanic William Robinson, they had been totally exhausting. With so much daily setting up and packing, the Robinsons' own spectacular illusions seemed like an afterthought and were frequently cut from the program. Herrmann didn't seem to care. It was almost as though he simply didn't want his rival, Harry Kellar, to have them.

Hutchin was unaffected by Robinson's grumblings. From the very beginning, Herrmann and his young assistant got along famously. Milton Hudson Everett was now fully comfortable with his duties. The Pullman porter's words—Look, Listen, Learn—stayed with him. Those words were Hutchin's lifeline. He was only thirteen, but he already understood their power. His position with the Herrmanns was much more than a job. It was a priceless education.

Alexander and Adelaide always conversed in French. Hearing the language every day from morning to night, Hutchin quickly picked up phrases. Adelaide and Alexander were charmed when he began responding with, "Oui, Monsieur" and "Oui, Madame." Naively fearless, Hutchin mimicked Alexander's French accent and distinctive mannerisms—his toss of the head, his mincing step, his flick of the wrist. Hutchin's uncanny impersonations kept the company in stitches. Herrmann loved it. When entertaining illustrious guests, Herrmann often called upon Hutchin to mimic him. The conjuror took such glee in Hutchin's antics that the company began calling the youth "Herrmann's pet." Like his boss, Hutchin delighted in making people laugh. And he liked the attention, too.

Onstage, every show was a little different. Herrmann loved to improvise. He could talk his way out of any mistake or jam, and sometimes he liked to go off script just to make mischief. Whenever rowdy youths in the balcony, nicknamed "gallery gods," disrupted a performance, Herrmann's witty, acid insults usually put them in their place. Past assistants had been unnerved by Herrmann's unpredictability, but Hutchin loved playing along, never knowing what Herrmann might throw at him. Often the joke was at Boomsky's expense, but at least he would see it coming—Herrmann would catch his eye. There was that mischievous gleam.

"Boomsky looks very pale tonight!" the Professor would say.[95]

Hutchin acted shocked—mouth wide open as he stared at his hands. It got a big laugh.

When it came to Herrmann's constant ribbing of Boomsky, Madame Herrmann called Hutchin a good sport. In the 1890s, racial and ethnic stereotypes were fair game in comedy, and Boomsky was often the butt of the joke in ways that would become inconceivable for his generation's grandchildren. But for thirteen-year-old Hutchin, it was just how things were. He was riding high. He loved his employer, and he loved his job. He was seeing the country and sending money home to his family.

Night after night, as the company zigzagged across the American heartland, Herrmann refined his magic routines with Boomsky. If an ad-lib or mistake got a solid laugh, it stayed in the act the next night. Over the years, Herrmann's knack for spotting talent had provided him with excellent assistants. But Everett was exceptional. Whatever Herrmann's joke, Boomsky made it funnier. Sometimes Boomsky mimicked his boss behind his back, to squeals from the audience.

With Everett as Boomsky, a tired old routine became screamingly funny. Unlike his predecessors, Boomsky complained—and loudly—when things went wrong. Herrmann borrowed a gentleman's handkerchief, rolled it up, and tossed it to Boomsky. But when the assistant unrolled the handkerchief, it was in shreds. Whining and grumbling, Boomsky sewed the handkerchief back together with a needle and thread, but when he opened it up it was one long strip. Annoyed, Herrmann snatched the strip, loaded it into his pistol and fired it at a lemon. The restored handkerchief was inside the lemon. Boomsky reached for it then shrieked when it burst into flames. Herrmann and Boomsky continued blaming each other for every calamity as the audience howled with laughter. Like Herrmann, Hutchin was never at a loss. The two of them could banter forever. In the 1890s, this repartee between the famous Jewish magician and his Black teenaged assistant was utterly unique on the American stage. Their opposite stations in life made their interaction fascinating, and hilarious. The broken taboos added to the wicked fun of it.

In early February the Herrmann company played some of America's coldest cities—Detroit, Buffalo, Rochester. Finally, the weary company landed for a full week in the great metropolis of Philadelphia. In addition to the usual porters, doormen, cart drivers, waiters, and laborers, Hutchin also saw purposeful Black professional men in tailored suits. Philadelphia was so much bigger and older-looking than any of the dozens of cities and towns Hutchin had already visited. The National Theater was grand. Herrmann was determined to put on a tight, fresh-looking show, despite a company exhausted from so many months of winter schlepping.

Herrmann's show would be under the microscope in Philadelphia, the home turf of his archrival, Harry Kellar. While Herrmann dragged his big illusion show all over America, Kellar had been enjoying a long, successful run in Philadelphia at his own theater, Egyptian Hall, named after the London magic venue of Herrmann's early success. Rarely did the show business enemies play against each other. But when it happened, sparks could fly.

Herrmann had already stolen three of Kellar's star performers: the juggler D'Alvini and then the Robinsons. Now, Herrmann twisted the knife. On the day of the Herrmann company's arrival, a Philadelphia newspaper published a long account of Herrmann's adventures among the fakirs of India. Kellar instantly recognized the article as his own 1886 publication, "Magician's Tour," plagiarized nearly verbatim. Livid, Kellar replied in the *Times*, accusing Herrmann of copyright infringement and threatening a lawsuit. Kellar charged that Herrmann had never even been to India, which was true.[96] Kellar's lawsuit threat was a bluff. Behind the scenes, Herrmann's nemesis plotted a far more damaging revenge.

As March 1892 rolled in, the troupe headed to New York City. Before there were tunnels or bridges across the Hudson River, all trains arriving from the west and south terminated at the river's edge at the Jersey City depot in New Jersey. Travelers then walked to the pier and boarded ferries to Manhattan. Hutchin stared upward as his ferry passed close by the sixteen-year-old Statue of Liberty. The towering monument's brown copper surface was just slightly tinged with green.[97] In his first five months, Hutchin had seen many cities but none like New York with its incredibly tall buildings, cleverly called skyscrapers. Steel framing technology and people-lifting elevators were enabling new buildings to rise to eighteen floors and even beyond. Hutchin saw construction going on everywhere, as the city rose vertically toward the sky.

In Williamsburg, Brooklyn, Hutchin heard Herrmann's crew and the theater hands gossiping about Arthur Williams's scandalous exit two seasons earlier. With run-outs from their home base in New York, the traveling was lighter. But the crew was still worn out from the brutal winter tour. Chief mechanic Will Robinson looked run-down and haggard. Yet suddenly Herrmann loaded on the illusions, doubling the work. In New Haven, on March 9, the newspaper announcement listed six illusions on one show: Strobeika, Slave Girl's Dream, New Black Art, Florine: Child of the Air, Cocoon, and to top it off, a revival of Cremation.[98] During the second half of March, they dragged Herrmann's giant show to Baltimore, then Pittsburgh.

At the beginning of April, Milton Hudson Everett learned that in show business, everything can change in an instant. Suddenly, Will and Dot Robinson were gone! Weary and frustrated, they had jumped ship and returned to their old boss, Harry Kellar. On April 4, Will and Dot rejoined Kellar at Philadelphia's Egyptian Hall, performing Black Art, Cocoon, and Astarte: Maid of the Moon, the original name for Florine: Child of the Air.

Hutchin wondered how the show could go on without the Robinsons, but his boss did not miss a beat. Herrmann's opening night in Montreal on April 18, 1892, drew the largest audience in the history of the Queens Theater.[99] All the city's high society turned out, including the mayor and his wife. Montreal had always loved Herrmann, but this time he was even better, they thought, more "mellow." The audience never suspected that Herrmann had just lost his star assistants and their spectacular illusions.

"Astarte"

Dot Robinson performing the floating illusion, Astarte, with Harry Kellar. Alexander Herrmann renamed it Florine: Child of the Air.

Herrmann performed two new tricks in Montreal. In the first, he rubbed one live canary between his fingers, and it became two canaries, which he placed into a glass box on a table. On another table he placed an empty cage. He covered both with handkerchiefs, and when he whipped them away—voila! The birds had passed from the glass box to the cage.[100] In the second new trick, Boomsky gathered watches from four people in the audience, including the mayor's wife. Each dropped their timepiece into a small velvet bag. Boomsky handed the bag of watches to Herrmann, who tossed the borrowed watches on a table and smashed them to bits with a hammer, to the utter horror of the watch's owners. Boomsky brought a chair onto the stage as Herrmann invited a young spectator to join him. The seated man watched as Herrmann dropped the smashed pieces of the watches into the barrel of a blunderbuss pistol. The magician aimed the gun at the man, who suddenly looked alarmed.

"Mesdames et Messieurs. Do not worry!" Herrmann counted down. The largely French audience joined in. "*Trois, deux, un.*" BANG!

When the smoke cleared, the onstage spectator looked stunned. Hanging from the seat of his chair were three of the borrowed watches, good as new. But one watch was still missing. Herrmann asked the spectator onstage to check around his seat for it. When the man turned around, the last watch was hanging from his back. The audience applauded furiously. Hudson Everett suppressed a smile. Nobody suspected that Herrmann's thirteen-year-old ace assistant had switched the watches, handing Herrmann a bag of broken watch parts, then secretly delivering the borrowed watches backstage. There, Herrmann's stage mechanic quickly loaded the watches onto the gimmicked chair. It was Boomsky's job to pin the fourth watch on the spectator's back. Then, at the gunshot, he flipped a hidden lever on the chair, releasing the watches into view.

Since Boomsky's name was not listed in the program, reviewers had only Herrmann's French-accented pronunciation to go by. Some spelled his name "Bumsky" or "Bumpsky." Later reviews called him "Koomsky" and "Broomsky." Adelaide Herrmann spelled his name "Boomski." Others wrote "Boomskie," "Boumsky," or even "Boomsby." That week, in the Montreal *Gazette*, he was "Mr. Bloobs, a diminutive Ethiopian assistant to the Professor."[101]

Herrmann's spring season took them to many of their favorite haunts with full weeks in Chicago, Brooklyn, and Boston. In seven months, thirteen-year-old Milton Hudson Everett from the cotton fields had visited every major American city. After months of grueling one-night stands, whole weeks in big cities were so different. The extroverted Herrmanns took full advantage. Others might crave rest after a performance, but not the ultra-social Herrmanns, not ever. Every night after the show, after his employers had enjoyed a leisurely supper, Boomsky clung to the Herrmanns' carriage as they clattered over cobblestone streets to parties and receptions thrown by civic groups, press clubs, business leaders, socialites, and politicians, or to after-hours venues with other touring celebrities who were in town. Boomsky was ever-present, tending to Herrmann while secretly assisting in tricks. Often, the Herrmanns partied until dawn, stopping at a restaurant for breakfast before returning to their hotel or railcar to fall into bed. Hutchin loved the nonstop excitement of constantly meeting new people. He made friends in every city—stagehands, porters, waiters, boardinghouse owners and patrons—not realizing that future tours would reunite them again and again.

June arrived. Suddenly, just like that, the season was done.

HERRMANN MANOR AT WHITESTONE

Adelaide and Alexander Herrmann and their entourage arriving at Herrmann Manor circa 1894.

During the summer, most touring companies went on hiatus. Before air conditioning, sweltering theaters in summer held little appeal, and affluent patrons fled the stifling, teeming cities. The Herrmann company was ready for a break. Over the previous months they had played more than two hundred shows in thirty states. As the tour wound down, crew members talked of seeing their families and relaxing. For Milton Hudson Everett, going home to his family would mean a summer of picking cotton in the blazing Georgia sun. But at season's end, Alexander and Adelaide asked Hutchin to work at their estate, Herrmann Manor, over the vacation. Hutchin exhaled. Boomsky's magical adventure would continue.

In June, Alexander and Adelaide arrived at their grand waterfront property in Whitestone, New York.[102] Like the private railcar, Herrmann Manor was a recent acquisition, another jewel in the crown of the great magic duo who had worked so hard for so many years to attain their opulent lifestyle. Neither Alexander nor Adelaide had been born wealthy. The ostentatious trappings reminded them of how far they had come. Adelaide Herrmann would later recall those summers at Whitestone as some of her happiest memories.

After eight months with the great magician, Hudson Everett thought that nothing much could surprise him. That was before he saw Herrmann Manor. As always, Boomsky rode on the back of Herrmann's tally-ho carriage. When they arrived at the estate, Herrmann waved his hand, and the gate swung open on its own and then closed behind them. No one was in sight. On a stump near the gatehouse sat a little stuffed monkey—an odd place for a toy, thought Hutchin. As they approached, the monkey suddenly thrust its arms forward and held out a small silver tray. Herrmann, laughing, dropped his business card onto the tray.

They passed a gardener's cottage, then wound through the woods up a long driveway lined with hydrangeas and magnolia trees. Finally, an enormous house came into view. Hutchin just stared. How could two people need so much space? Soon he would see that for the Herrmanns, the manor wasn't nearly big enough.

The carriage drew up to the grand portico, and the Herrmanns excitedly climbed out. Adelaide led the way into the expansive foyer. Hutchin looked about as he trailed behind with their hand luggage. Every room was stuffed with curios and art objects the Herrmanns had collected in their travels—paintings, statues, rugs, furniture, mirrors, swords, rifles, and all sorts of knickknacks. On the road, Hutchin had watched Alexander buy all kinds of memorabilia from antique shops and pawnbrokers. Madame was far more measured in her spending, but she purchased items as well. Hutchin wondered where they would put everything. Now here it all was, filling every nook and corner and hanging from every wall all the way up to the ceiling. Alexander was especially fond of clocks, and every room had one. As soon as they arrived, Alexander sent Hutchin to wind all nineteen clocks and set each one to the same time. On the hour, the house rang with a cacophony of bells, chimes, gongs, and cuckoos.

The gregarious Herrmanns relaxed as vigorously as they worked. To Hutchin, the summer seemed like one long party, although not for him. Hutchin worked harder than ever. The three-story main house was usually filled with a dizzying array of overnight guests, including actors, opera singers, impresarios, tycoons, socialites, politicians, painters, writers, and inventors. Feeding and cleaning up after them required a bevy of house and kitchen staff, overseen by Adelaide and her widowed mother, Madame Adele Scarsez. Guests gathered on the large screened veranda, escaping the estate's swarms of mosquitoes. When the house was full, additional guests stayed in the large annex, which adjoined the summer dining room. Formerly a hunting and fishing lodge, the annex housed a billiard room, a locker room with showers, and nine single sleeping rooms. The estate featured a power plant to generate electricity, a novelty in 1892. People used to soft gas lights and candles now reveled deep into the night in rooms blazing with electric lights.

Every aspect of a guest's stay at Herrmann Manor was delightful, but the mischievous Herrmann kept everyone on their toes. Strange things happened, all the time. It was as though invisible helpers constantly moved through the house. Cigars and cigarettes silently appeared and disappeared, as did dinner dishes and cutlery. Doors and windows would open and shut on their own, and bells rang without being touched.

Everyone in the household assisted in this "house magic." Hutchin quickly learned the locations of secret pulleys, levers, and wires, as well as switches and buttons for wonderful electrical tricks. Hutchin also worked stealthily, right out in the open. When everyone's attention was on Herrmann, Boomsky made his move. His timing was perfect, and he was never caught. When guests announced their intention to depart, their horse and carriage would instantly pull in front of the house without being summoned. In an era when people routinely waited thirty minutes between alerting the stables and the arrival of their carriage, this seemed miraculous indeed. They never suspected the youth emptying ashtrays of eavesdropping on their conversations.

For exploring the property's eighteen acres and for getting around town, the estate's stable kept saddle horses for the Herrmanns and their guests, as well as carriage horses and a fleet of carriages. Alexander drove his tally-ho with two or four horses. Adelaide had a two-seat pony phaeton, which she drove around with her mother, Adele, who lived at Herrmann Manor year-round, overseeing the estate when the Herrmanns traveled.

The property was crisscrossed by carriage paths that wound through the woods to a seven-hundred-foot-wide beach on Long Island Sound. There, a large boathouse sheltered Herrmann's collection of watercrafts. A small fleet of rowboats and a naphtha launch would eventually be joined by a magnificent 107-foot, steam-powered yacht named *Fra Diavolo*.[103]

Herrmann Manor was a haven for the magical couple's pets, especially their many dogs. While the caged birds and some cats were kept indoors, the estate's acreage provided a free-roaming canine paradise. Wherever the Herrmanns and their guests went, they were followed by a large pack of pet dogs. Canine instinct trumped pedigree as the purebred dogs invariably returned home muddy, stinking, and covered in burrs. Hutchin was constantly bathing and combing filthy, smelly dogs. Hutchin liked the dogs and did not mind, usually. On bad days, he wrestled a reeking, skunk-sprayed pooch into a washtub or helped Madame extract porcupine quills from an overcurious snout.

Whenever a pet died, Adelaide Herrmann would be consumed with grief. Each animal—be it dog, cat, parakeet, dove, rabbit, duck, goose, guinea pig, or mouse—was given an elaborate funeral with an elegant satin-lined coffin. On Madame's orders, all the servants, dressed in full livery, stood alongside the path to the pet cemetery. Boomsky, sporting fresh white gloves, polished shoes, and gleaming brass buttons, stood at attention as Madame delivered an emotional graveside eulogy over the small casket.

In mid-June, a flock of children arrived from England. Childless themselves, the Herrmanns paid for the steamship passage of Adelaide's nieces and nephews to spend the summer with them. Adelaide's three older sisters, with twelve children among them, lived on the same city block on Farringdon Road in London's Clerkenwell district. Their husbands, all glass engravers, ran the business founded by their late father-in-law, Pierre Scarsez. The oldest of the children, twenty-three-year-old Hermann Pallme, had left home as a teen to join Herrmann's crew and now lived in New York. Adelaide's other nieces and nephews ranged from twenty-one-year-old Adelaide Kretschmann Madell, married with a new baby, down to one-month-old Eugenie Owles, back in London with her mother.

The children closest in age to Hutchin were brothers John and Felix Kretschmann, ages fourteen and eleven, and Adele Owles, who was thirteen—the same age as Hutchin. Everyone called Adele by her nickname, Dewey, which referred to her milky complexion.[104] Her little brother Alexander Owles, age seven, trailed behind the older children.[105] Surrounded by her grandchildren, Adelaide's mother baked cookies and relished the chaos. The Herrmanns flung open their gates to the neighborhood kids as well and delighted in the daylong squeals of children at play.

Several children had summer birthdays. Adelaide threw big parties for them, which surprised Hutchin. Back in Americus his family did not mark birthdays. In July, amidst the bustle and commotion of Herrmann Manor, Hutchin quietly turned fourteen.

That summer the Herrmanns gave a charity performance at nearby Flushing Town Hall.[106] For one enchanted day, the visiting children served as cast and crew for Herrmann the Great. Everyone buzzed with excitement. Preparing the big show was all-consuming. For several weeks, Alexander and Adelaide staged nightly rehearsals. Adolescent illusionists, assistants, mechanics, stagehands, curtain pullers, and lighting operators all learned their roles. Boomsky was suddenly the center of attention as he taught the children how to safely hold squirming guinea pigs, kicking bunnies, and delicate doves and canaries. Adelaide and her nieces sewed costumes for dancing skeletons and ghosts as the boys patched up scenery and illusions.

On show day, a sell-out crowd packed the children's matinee. The raucous audience laughed and applauded. At the end they stood up and cheered. For the Scarsez grandchildren, starry-eyed and dazzled, life would never be the same. Cold, dreary London was no match for Uncle Alexander's fairy-tale world. Nine of the twelve cousins would eventually emigrate to America. Four of them would work in the Herrmann magic companies for many years. Eleven-year-old Felix Kretschmann would grow up to become a professional magician—and a detested rival of his Aunt Adelaide.

The summer flew by. The children sailed back to London. Even as he relaxed and savored his extravagant life of leisure, Alexander Herrmann was eager to return to the spotlight. Every day, he spent hours in his workshop at the manor overseeing the carpenters, painters, and mechanics busily refurbishing old sets and properties while Madame directed seamstresses creating new costumes and drapes, all for the upcoming season.

Each week, as he had done all season from the road, Hutchin continued to send most of his salary home. With all his living expenses met, Hutchin wanted to help his parents. Since he could not read or write, every payday Hutchin would get someone at Whitestone to address an envelope for him, and he would dictate a brief letter. Then he would go to the post office and purchase a money order and a stamp.

Hutchin missed his family terribly. They missed him, too, but they were very proud of him. Since October, the blessed envelopes containing money orders had arrived every week. Once his parents could afford stationery, postage, and a scribe, Ben and Leitha Everett had tried to write back to their son. But while on tour, Hutchin had no fixed address. One day at Herrmann Manor, Professor Herrmann and Madame approached Hutchin. She held an envelope. Herrmann had that familiar twinkle in his eye. Suspicious, Hutchin furrowed his brow. "Allow me," said Alexander, lightly plucking the envelope from Adelaide's hand. Herrmann teased, "Ah, it is postmarked Americus, Georgia." Hutchin's heart jumped. Assuming a grandiose tone, Herrmann slowly read out the address on the envelope, drawing out the final words: "Mr. Milton Hudson Everett, Esq., Care of Herrmann the GREAT ALMIGHTY!"[107] Hutchin snatched the envelope from Alexander's hand and ran from the room as the Herrmanns, helpless with laughter, collapsed into each other's arms.

ALONZO MOORE: A SECOND BOOMSKY

Eleven months in, Hutchin had learned to expect surprises, and Herrmann's 1892 fall season brought plenty of them. Herrmann had a theater of his own, right in New York! Hutchin wondered why he was surprised. Herrmann was obviously rich enough to have anything he wanted. The show would open there in mid-September for a two-month run. As the Herrmanns' carriage clopped the fifteen miles from Whitestone to midtown Manhattan, the bustling city's noises and smells jarred Hutchin from the serenity of Herrmann Manor. The teen brimmed with curiosity, eager to solve a nagging mystery—namely, how would Alexander fill the gaping hole in the show left by the departure of Will and Dot Robinson?

As chief mechanic, stage manager, illusionist, and actor, Will Robinson had been the backbone of the touring company. When Will and Dot had defected the previous April to Alexander's nemesis, Harry Kellar, the Herrmanns had managed to limp through the rest of the season. But losing the Robinsons had knocked the wind out of them. It was four years since the Herrmanns had started a season without them. Now they faced another series of brutal one-night stands over the same route that had pushed Will Robinson into leaving. Yet Alexander acted unconcerned. Something was up. Hutchin wondered if a new illusionist couple might appear at the first rehearsal.

As their equipment was being loaded in, Madame Herrmann warned Hutchin about the stage door stairs. The second-floor theater's narrow, steep outside stairs ran straight up from the street to the stage entrance. Two seasons earlier, in January 1890, a huge, postshow fire had engulfed the Fifth Avenue Theater, which adjoined theirs. The blaze had then spread to Herrmann's Theater. A heroic effort by Herrmann's company had rescued their animals and magic apparatus, and firefighters had saved Herrmann's Theater, but not the Fifth Avenue. In a panic, their prior Boomsky had tumbled head-first down those stairs while carrying Alexander's jewelry box, scattering Herrmann's diamond cuff links, studs, and pins across the snow. Hours later, after a frantic, hands-and-knees search, the last jewel—a precious two-carat black diamond—was finally found. As Madame finished her story and Hutchin watched the stagehands heaving crates up the long stairway, he envisioned his predecessor somersaulting down them.

Inside the theater, Hutchin waited for his eyes to adjust, then scanned the dim backstage area for new and familiar faces, expecting to spot the illusionists who would be replacing the Robinsons. Instead, Hutchin saw much less equipment than last season but many more animals. Stacked cages held ducks, rabbits, and geese. Except for scurrying stagehands, nobody else was there except for a small Black youth who stood next to the animal cages. Hutchin scratched his head as Madame Herrmann waddled over, her arms stretched around two large fabric bundles. She led Hutchin over to the new boy. "Meet your new partner, Alonzo Moore." She tossed one bundle to Hutchin and the other to Alonzo. "Go get changed," she instructed.

The two Black teens carried the bundles into a dressing room. As they changed, Hutchin learned that Alonzo, age sixteen, had found his way east from Kansas City.[108] Ten minutes later, duplicate Chinese boys emerged. Hutchin and Alonzo now wore matching Chinese tunics, pants, and slippers, queue wigs, and caps. Masks painted with Asian features covered their faces. Madame bustled them over to the Professor, who nodded and exclaimed, "Perfect!"

Onstage sat an apparatus that Hutchin had not seen before. Herrmann's new illusion! The advertisements for Ya-Ko-Yo: Instant Chinese Immigration promised the impossible. A Chinese boy would travel invisibly through space from China to America and back again. Hutchin realized that he and Alonzo were that season's new illusionists.

The illusion apparatus was built to look like a giant Chinese grocer's scale. Two large vertical boxes were decorated as pagodas. Signs on them read "Peking" and "San Francisco." They were suspended from ropes attached to a long horizontal bar balanced on a tall fulcrum. When one pagoda sank to the stage, the other rose a few feet into the air.

Rehearsals for Ya-Ko-Yo went smoothly enough. The teen assistants quickly learned their roles. The masks' small slitted eyeholes gave Hutchin and Alonzo very limited vision, requiring extra care to avoid tripping or catching their costumes on the illusion's moving parts. First, Herrmann opened the doors of both pagodas and showed them empty. He introduced a Chinese youth, who stepped into the Peking pagoda. Slowly Peking ascended as San Francisco descended. Herrmann reached up and opened Peking's door. The pagoda was now empty! Herrmann opened San Francisco's door, and out stepped the Chinese youth! Then the

Chinese lad reversed the magical journey, traveling from San Francisco back to Peking.

Hutchin and Alonzo marveled at how simple the secret was. The illusion depended on the audience believing that there was just one assistant, not two. A vertical screen that pulled down from the top of the box divided the box in half, creating a false back and hiding the box's occupant as required. The second Chinese assistant was concealed behind the screen from the beginning of the trick. On opening night, Hutchin was surprised that audiences bought it so easily. The crowd applauded vigorously.

Herrmann presented the illusion as a lighthearted joke, which audiences of the time found acceptable. In 1892 Chinese immigration was a serious political issue. Chinese laborers had built America's transcontinental railway, and the gold rush had attracted more Chinese immigrants, prompting an anti-Chinese backlash. Beginning in 1882, with the Geary Act, any Chinese person caught without the proper identity papers could be arrested and forced to work a year at hard labor before being deported. The Geary Act would stay in effect for over sixty years until it was finally repealed in 1943.

With the Robinsons gone, Herrmann presented a greatly scaled-down show. Madame Herrmann, Hutchin, and Alonzo were the only onstage assistants. Hutchin continued all his Boomsky bits with Herrmann. Both Hutchin and Alonzo set up the magic apparatus, moved props and tables on and off stage, and wrangled the animals. Instead of a program of big illusions, the show featured eerie, supernatural effects performed by Madame—a mind-reading rapping hand and the Spirit Cabinet. Madame also performed the Mysterious Swing. Adelaide sat in a wooden chair that was hoisted by ropes high above the stage. Herrmann fired his pistol, and Madame instantly vanished into thin air as the chair fell clattering to the stage.

The show's grand finale was a macabre entertainment called Ta-ra-ra Boom-de-ay (Done to Death), which was a revival of the dancing skeletons and spectral ghosts from Herrmann's earlier Spirit Séance show.[109] In the pitch darkness, Hutchin and Alonzo played the dancing skeletons, their black, hooded costumes decorated with luminescent paint. Adelaide, herself in head-to-toe black, swung a long pole trailing luminescent fabric just over the audience's heads. The act was so ghostly and weird that some people were frightened by it. But at the end the lights would come up to reveal the black-clad culprits and to emphasize, once again, that the paranormal effects were just tricks. One night, in the darkness, Hutchin and Alonzo were startled by a small scream then a big crash coming from Adelaide's direction. When the lights came back up, Adelaide had vanished! Later they learned that an audience member sitting in a box seat had grabbed Adelaide's fabric "ghost" on a pole and had dragged her into the orchestra pit. Thankfully, Madame and the musician she landed on suffered only minor injuries.

New York audiences loved Herrmann's mysterious new show, and the company enjoyed two months of sitting in place at Herrmann's Theater. But the big money came from touring. On November 11, after their last New York performance, they packed up and headed straight for the Jersey City rail yards, where the *Addie Herrmann* and their baggage cars sat waiting. After Herrmann's crew loaded their equipment, rail yard workers coupled the company cars to a southbound express train, and they set off in the middle of the night.

Two nights later they opened their winter tour in New Orleans at the Grand Opera House. It was a whole year since Hutchin had first performed there, still fresh from the cotton fields. For Alonzo Moore, on his first tour, every stop was an incredible new adventure. Alonzo learned very quickly. Hutchin enjoyed having him along. He was a good worker and good company, funny as anything. Hutchin was proud to show Alonzo the ropes. The Herrmanns were strict when it came to work being done properly. It was the same with dress and grooming—uniforms had to be pressed, shoes shined, hair trimmed, nails clean. But as long as standards were maintained, surprises and practical jokes were part of

Herrmann company tradition. One night, when Herrmann called for Boomsky, Hutchin pushed Alonzo onstage in his place. Only a slightest arch of the eyebrow betrayed Herrmann's surprise. The Professor seemed positively giddy as this new Boomsky fell on the hat and popped eggs from his mouth. For his part, Alonzo rose to the occasion, performing all the tricks perfectly and answering Herrmann's quips with his own sharp, snappy comebacks. Hutchin felt a jealous pang.

In New Orleans, Herrmann's smaller-scale show attracted sell-out crowds and positive reviews. The New Orleans *Times-Democrat* marveled that "Herrmann is the whole show. His only assistant is his wife, and her part is merely a passive one. In fact, the only human beings that appear on the stage besides Herrmann and his spouse are two negroes, who attend to the capture of rabbits and geese, which Herrmann produces from the noses of persons in the audience."[110]

Milton Hudson Everett and Alonzo Moore shared Boomsky's duties. Both wore identical brass-buttoned uniforms. Most people called both of them Boomsky, including Manager Bloom, who also addressed every Pullman porter as George. When Herrmann entertained important guests backstage, Boomsky—either Hutchin or Alonzo—greeted the visitors and led them to the wizard's lair. Guests would crane their necks, trying to glimpse Herrmann's secrets, but black curtains shielded the stage from their view. They proceeded through a dimly lit passageway leading to Herrmann's lavishly appointed dressing room. Inside, half the dressing room was filled with sofas and chairs for receiving politicians, tycoons, and celebrities. The other half of the room, shielded from view by a curtain, held Herrmann's secret magic props, as well as the cages of rabbits, guinea pigs, and doves. Boomsky offered cigars to guests and stood by, awaiting Herrmann's bidding.[111]

In New Orleans, after the Wednesday children's matinee, a *Times-Picayune* reporter came backstage to interview Adelaide. Alexander was still onstage distributing to the children in the audience hundreds of tiny roses that he had magically produced from a paper cone. The visitor gazed in awe at the bustling backstage area. At least fifty packing cases, all marked "Herrmann," were piled around, and cages of doves, canaries, and a duck all added to the cacophony. Hutchin guarded a screen that had been set in front the magic props, while Alonzo cleaned up after the coffee trick, in which Herrmann magically produced steaming cups of Turkish coffee and served them to audience members.[112]

When the reporter finally located Adelaide in her dressing room, Madame regaled him with stories of her travels, many of them exaggerated for effect. The thirty-nine-year-old starlet gave her age as thirty-five. This would be her official age for at least the next ten years.

Sometimes things went wrong. One night, as Hutchin and Alonzo pushed the Spirit Cabinet onto the stage, the large box collapsed in a heap. The assistants' genuine shock brought screams of laughter. The collapse had been an act of sabotage. Jealous actors from a failing theater company sharing the theater had loosened the box's thumbscrews. Their scheme backfired. Herrmann added the hilarious collapsing Spirit Cabinet to the nightly bill.

Unlike the previous holiday season spent slogging across the Rocky Mountains and snow-swept plains, the company settled in for a two-week Christmas run in one of their favorite cities—Chicago. The giant lakeside city churned with new construction, commerce, factories, and people. Hutchin marveled at Chicago's many skyscrapers, grander even than New York's. As America's primary inland transportation hub, all railroads led to Chicago, carrying the exploding bounty of the heartland—livestock, grain, produce, industrial goods—to the port on Lake Michigan. By 1892, Chicago's population surpassed one million, making it the world's sixth largest metropolis. The city's many slaughterhouses lent a lingering scent of death to the air, but the Herrmanns, as always, never seemed bothered, as they flitted from one party and club to the next.

On Saturday, January 28, 1893, Herrmann and his company were on a midnight train passing through Ionia, Michigan. The train to which their company cars were coupled consisted of assorted freight, coach, and sleeper cars. A few hours into the trip, everyone was jarred awake by a series of violent jolts and the terrifying shrieks of metal crashing and twisting. A broken rail had caused a huge derailment. When it was all over, twenty freight cars and two public coaches lay piled up in the ditch. Screams of pain and terror pierced the night. The Herrmanns' private car was near the back of the train and did not derail. But closer to the front, a number of people were seriously injured, and more were trapped. As reported in the *Grand Rapids Herald*, the members of the Herrmann company, including the unnamed Milton Hudson Everett and Alonzo Moore, "lent valuable assistance rescuing the passengers from their perilous position."[113] Everyone in the company, including Herrmann himself, climbed through the wreckage to help extricate the victims. One passenger, a man from Ionia, later died of his injuries.

The Herrmann company spent a frigid February touring between Detroit, Saint Paul, and Minneapolis, circling back again to Chicago for another two weeks. As always, audiences flocked to the shows, and reviewers gushed their praise. As spring arrived, the company played full weeks in Brooklyn, Washington, DC, and Pittsburgh before swinging through smaller cities in Pennsylvania, New Jersey, and Connecticut. While they were in Hartford, a local magician named Fred Jewett took the Herrmanns around town and gave them a tour of his own collection of magic. Alexander brought Hutchin and Alonzo with him. A *Hartford Courant* reporter along for the tour wrote that Herrmann's "two darkies can perform the tricks themselves."[114]

As they took the stage with Alexander Herrmann night after night, Hudson Everett and Alonzo Moore fell hopelessly in love with magic. Working behind the scenes, they knew the secrets to all the tricks. They operated many of the show's effects themselves, while Herrmann took all the credit, acting as though he had done it all himself—a time-honored technique in the all-is-fair world of magic. Many of the mechanical tricks, such as gaffed tubes and boxes, or tables with hidden compartments, required no special sleight-of-hand expertise to operate.

Nonetheless, performing them required finesse and perfect timing for the trick to look magical.

The mechanical tricks were fun and interesting, but as the assistants watched Herrmann over hundreds of shows, they began to understand the true power of sleight-of-hand, the highest form of the magician's art. Freed from trick boxes or gimmicked props, the whole world became Herrmann's stage. Like a *real* magician, the Professor could conjure impromptu miracles anytime, anywhere, using any small object—cards, coins, jewelry, silverware, wine corks—whether on his person or borrowed. Hutchin and Alonzo watched and learned.

Alexander Herrmann was a renowned sleight-of-hand master. Every day, as he had done since childhood, Herrmann practiced dozens of secret moves with cards, coins, and billiard balls. His hand muscles were so finely developed that even with his fingers spread wide he could securely grasp objects on the palm of his relaxed-looking hand. Herrmann was happy to teach his magic-smitten assistants, Hutchin and Alonzo. The teens learned the secret language of sleight-of-hand: steal, load, ditch, switch. Although he had huge hands, Alonzo was especially good at the delicate, precise moves. Yet the moves were only one aspect of creating magic. Herrmann also masterfully controlled people's attention. Hutchin and Alonzo marveled that it was almost impossible not to look where Herrmann intended, which in turn made it almost impossible to catch him. They noticed that all of Herrmann's secret moves occurred during natural-looking gestures and on the offbeat, especially during laughs. When people were laughing, they were not really watching.

In the 1890s, the multiplying billiard balls trick was considered the most difficult sleight-of-hand to master.[115] Regular billiard balls, made of ivory, were extremely heavy and slippery. Magicians cheated with lacquered wooden balls, but these were only slightly lighter and easier to grip. The unwieldy balls took great skill to palm without dropping one or flashing a glimpse, or without the palming hand looking strained. Herrmann taught his students to roll the balls between their fingers to limber up their hands, which was also a flashy display. Hutchin and Alonzo learned ways of making a ball appear and disappear, then how to turn them into two, then three, then four balls—then, *poof*, make them all vanish.

Hutchin and Alonzo picked up not just Herrmann's magic, but also his movements, timing, flair, and his charming comic delivery. When they began performing magic themselves, they skillfully executed Herrmann's tricks, but they also moved, dressed, and spoke like Herrmann, French accent and all. Other than his assistants and his wife, Herrmann took no other students. His Boomskys would become the keepers of the Herrmann legacy and the treasured secrets and skills that had been passed down through generations.

H. H. Dennis: A Boomsky Lost, A Boomsky Found

Rival magicians often attended Herrmann's shows seeking to steal his tricks and ideas. These magicians ruthlessly purloined Herrmann's look, jokes, and repertoire. Sometimes they stole even more. One night, as Alonzo Moore emerged from the stage door, a young man approached him. He introduced himself as Maro the Magician and said he was looking to hire an assistant. Whatever Herrmann was paying, Maro, whose real name was Walter Best, would double it. Just like that, Herrmann's assistant was gone.

Soon Alonzo Moore had a new stage name, Theosis, but his tricks were the same as Boomsky's. The *Scranton Tribune* reported, "Maro performed Herrmann's old egg trick with huge success, taking three or four eggs from his colored servitor's mouth."[116] In fact, many of Maro's tricks were the same as Herrmann's. Rumors circulated in the magician community that Maro's assistant, a Black teenager, was actually Maro's teacher.[117] Years later Alonzo Moore would venture out on his own, beginning a long career as one of America's finest magicians—Alonzo Moore, Prince of Magic.

Alexander Herrmann lost no time in replacing Alonzo Moore. In March 1893, the Detroit *Plaindealer*, an African American newspaper founded ten years earlier, posted news of Herrmann's new assistant. "Mr. H. H. Dennis, of New York, was in the city last week as the assistant of Herrmann, the wonderful magician. Mr. Dennis is a young Afro-American of fine intellect, being a former associate and college chum of Prof. R. T. Greener."[118] Dennis was Herrmann's only college-educated assistant. When describing his exotic new job to his friends, Dennis did not mention that his immediate superior was a fourteen-year-old, illiterate former field hand from Georgia.

One day in late April, Madame Herrmann sought out Hudson Everett and H. H. Dennis. Again, she held two bundles of fabric. She tossed a bundle to each assistant and told them to go change. Hutchin and H. H. soon emerged wearing, none too happily, the white-and-gray-striped uniform of prison inmates. As stage carpenters hammered and sawed, Madame announced that rehearsal would begin momentarily for Herrmann's newest illusion, Escape from Sing Sing.

A recent news story had captured Herrmann's imagination. At the height of a crashing thunderstorm, two convicted murderers in New York's Sing Sing Prison had overpowered their guards and climbed over the walls. The men jumped into the Hudson River and swam away.[119] Soon the escapees, Roehl and Pallister, were household names. Herrmann immediately announced a new illusion based on the story. It would debut within a month, to capitalize on the trending story. This seemed impossible; illusions took months to build and fine-tune. Yet, on May 11, 1893, less than three weeks after the actual Sing Sing Prison escape, Herrmann introduced Escape from Sing Sing.[120] In truth, Escape from Sing Sing was not exactly new. It was Ya-Ko-Yo repackaged. The Chinese pagodas were now prison cells with vertical bars. The grocer's scale set was gone. Instead of being levered up and down, the prison cells were fixed onto a frame and suspended about a foot from the floor. Otherwise, the two illusions were nearly the same. But Escape from Sing Sing was so much better.

The curtain opened to Herrmann wrestling with a struggling young Black man wearing prison stripes. Finally, the wizard managed to thrust the prisoner into one of the cells, which Herrmann padlocked and covered with a drape. Almost immediately a shout—"I'm here!"—came from the back of the house. To everyone's astonishment, it was the prisoner, who ran down the aisle and onto the stage. Herrmann whipped away the drape, and inside the cage was a prison guard! Herrmann freed the guard and the two of them chased the prisoner all around, until they finally caught him and threw him into the second cell. Herrmann covered that cell with a drape, and when he whipped it away, the prisoner had vanished! The Professor briefly covered the empty first cell again. When he pulled the cover away, there was the prisoner, finally captured.

The story, the action, and Herrmann's hilarious commentary made Escape from Sing Sing wildly entertaining. It was baffling as well. With the constant activity, audiences never got a clear look at the prisoner. They never suspected that two different youths shared the role of the prisoner.

When Escape from Sing Sing debuted, the country desperately needed a diversion. Earlier that month the stock market had crashed, creating the Panic of 1893. Fortunes were erased, railroads failed, and the country entered a deep depression. Other than the long breadlines he saw everywhere, Hutchin was unaffected. People still lined up for Herrmann's show, despite the country's financial woes. More than ever, they sought to forget their troubles through laughter and magic.

By June 1893, the Herrmanns had wrapped up a profitable season and retreated to Whitestone for another relaxing summer of children, pets, and houseguests. Nobody noticed when Hudson Everett turned fifteen, as he worked around the estate, tending to guests, house tricks, and the dogs. Adelaide Herrmann's birthday on August 11 was celebrated with a big party. Everyone knew that it was Adelaide's fortieth birthday, but no one dared say it aloud. Delmonico's Restaurant catered the entire affair, bringing everything, including tables, chairs, linens, and dishes, so that the Herrmanns' own employees could attend as guests without having to work. Even Boomsky got the day off. The summer seemed to fly by, and all too soon the Herrmann company was back on the road.

∾

CHAPTER FOUR

M. H. Everett, Veteran Teenaged Assistant

(1893–1895)

As he began his third year with the Herrmanns, Milton Hudson Everett noticed how each season was different. Last season, they had eased in with two months at Herrmann's own theater. Now they were preparing Herrmann's newest illusion, After the Ball, for their opening week at the Harlem Opera House. Rehearsals were not going well.

After the Ball had been touted with great fanfare in Herrmann's advertisements, promising a breathtaking vanish of Madame Herrmann as she stood on a platform before a large, freestanding mirror. In truth, the illusion was still slow and clumsy. Worse yet, Madame was getting banged up. Scrapes and bruises were part of the job, and Adelaide was tough. But mishaps with After the Ball risked hair torn out by the roots and even broken bones.

Each afternoon the Herrmann company gathered to rehearse. Boomsky stood just offstage, waiting for his cue. Not one run-through of After the Ball had gone perfectly, and everyone was in a bad mood. Each failure heightened the tension. Hutchin hoped that today would be different.

The New York Dramatic Mirror, *November 4, 1893. Madame Herrmann struggled with After the Ball until finally mastering the difficult illusion.*

A platform stood center stage, topped by a full-length mirror on a stand. Adelaide walked onstage, wearing a poofy, ruffled ball gown. She ascended a small set of stairs to the platform and stood before the mirror. Boomsky marched onstage, carrying a folding screen. He handed the tall screen up to Madame and helped her unfold it around herself. Boomsky began to roll away the small stairs when he heard Madame's muffled shout, "STOP!" Boomsky grimaced. What was it this time? Had Madame's bulky gown snagged again? Did the apparatus malfunction again? Or was Adelaide simply too slow or too large to perform such an uncompromising illusion? Hutchin had rarely heard the Herrmanns argue, but now their rapid-fire French took on a sharp tone.

Despite daily rehearsals, After the Ball was still shaky the following week when the Herrmanns opened at the Harlem Opera House. Adelaide somehow managed to pull off the illusion, but just barely. Yet people never noticed After the Ball's rough edges because everyone's attention was on the show's special guest star. The world-famous serpentine dancer, Loie Fuller, had joined them for the week.[121]

On opening night, Boomsky watched from the wings, hypnotized. Loie Fuller wore a voluminous, tent-like garment of gauzy silk that gathered at her neck and draped to the floor. Underneath the dress, her hands held long, flexible bamboo poles with which she swirled a hundred yards of white fabric, creating mesmerizing flowing wave patterns. Special lighting from below created a magical effect. Searingly bright calcium lights in the theater's basement shone upwards through glass panels placed in the stage. Standing offstage in the darkness, Boomsky was captivated by the sight of the glowing silk, undulating ghost-like in the beams of light.[122] Suddenly a sharp nudge to his shoulder broke the spell. Madame sighed as Boomsky, late to his duties, tore toward Herrmann's dressing room.

Herrmann was enchanted by Loie Fuller. After the performance, in front of the whole company, he offered her a contract to tour with them. As Alexander fawned over Miss Fuller, Hutchin glanced over at Madame, who looked on coldly. Adelaide, stung and sobered by her own struggles with After the Ball, had just watched her husband offer a younger dancer a starring role without even consulting his wife and partner. Hutchin could see that Madame was spitting mad. Her cheeks burned and blue eyes blazed. Hutchin held his breath, waiting for Madame to explode. Then Miss Fuller thanked Herrmann and declined his offer, citing commitments in Europe. Hutchin exhaled.

Yet the insult to Adelaide continued. The headline in the next day's *New York World* review read, "Herrmann and Loie Fuller in Harlem." The critic marveled that "La Loie" received more curtain calls than Herrmann. Adelaide was not mentioned in the review at all.[123]

Adelaide clawed back the spotlight by announcing that she would create her own serpentine act. Alexander was shocked. Adelaide had not danced in years. Plus, manipulating so much fabric took strength and stamina. As much as she tried to deny it, Adelaide was now in her forties. Alexander, of course, did not speak these thoughts aloud. He simply ordered the lights as she instructed. Adelaide set about designing four serpentine dances, to perform one after the other.[124] As they traveled from city to city, Madame and her maid went to the theater several hours before each show to sew the dresses of capacious silk, which they spread across the stage.[125] For weeks, Adelaide devoted every spare moment to creating her new act. Hutchin tried to entertain Alexander, who complained about having to eat dinner by himself night after night.

Meanwhile, despite constant tinkering, After the Ball was still slow and rough. While rehearsing the illusion in St. Louis, the mirror fell and cut Adelaide deeply on her left shoulder.[126] Hutchin jumped to her aid and helped Madame to her dressing room. As her maid dressed the wound, Hutchin returned to the stage and cleaned up the blood. Everyone urged Madame to rest. Instead, Adelaide climbed to the catwalk above the stage to direct the painting of snakes on one of her serpentine dresses.[127] That night, during the Slave Girl's Dream, a carefully draped costume hid the bandages on her shoulder. A few days later, Madame declared herself ready to perform After the Ball. A month into the season, the troublesome illusion finally began working smoothly.

Adelaide introduced her dances in October 1893, in Washington, DC. They were a sensation. In city after city, theater managers praised her serpentine dances as the best they had ever seen.[128] Loie Fuller had many imitators, but Adelaide's dances were innovative. Fuller and the others manipulated plain white silk. Adelaide's dresses writhed with painted snakes, fluttered with butterflies, sparkled with sequins, and radiated iridescent hues as her calcium light operator switched colored gels mid-performance. Although exhausting to perform—one of the dresses weighed 125 pounds—Adelaide would present the dances in nearly every show for the next six years.

Adelaide Herrmann's Serpentine Dances.

Now almost all their fall and winter tour stops were familiar to Hutchin. At each theater, Herrmann's crew reacquainted themselves with the permanent house crew—curtain pullers, spotlight operators, stagehands—and caught up with news and theater gossip. Their familiar, welcoming faces warmed the hearts of Herrmann's company and broke the tedium of never-ending rootless travel.

Hutchin began going by just his initials, M. H., following the lead of Pullman porters, who often used only their initials on their nametags. Many people thought, wrongly, that this practice was a pretentious imitation of business tycoons, such as J. P. Morgan or E. H. Harriman. In truth, in an era when many passengers addressed porters as "Boy" and "George," being ordered around by one's actual given name felt like a painful betrayal of dignity and privacy. Going by his initials allowed a porter to depersonalize the insults somewhat.

M. H. Everett received a promotion to a crew position, a major milestone for the fifteen-year-old. His name was now listed in the program and had a title, "Properties."[129] Everett was officially in charge of the magic props, anything that was not a large illusion. With this promotion came a raise.

In Chicago that February, Alexander Herrmann threw himself a huge party to celebrate his fiftieth birthday and his thirty-fifth anniversary in show business. At a resplendent banquet at the Auditorium Hotel, hundreds of luminaries from the theater, politics, high society, and the press gathered for a multicourse feast. In typical Herrmann fashion, supper began at midnight. Will and Dot Robinson attended the celebration, two years after suddenly leaving during Hutchin's first season. Although the Robinsons were still with Kellar, the Herrmanns greeted them warmly. M. H. Everett attended the lavish event but not as a guest. As always, Boomsky scurried about, tending to Herrmann's invitees and assisting in his boss's constant chicanery. He would partake of the delicious food, but he would eat with the kitchen staff, away from the glittering guests.

Monsignor Boomsky

On Tuesday, March 13, 1894, the Herrmann company opened a five-night run in Kansas City. That night the Coates Opera House was packed. The next day at their hotel, Herrmann yawned and sat up in bed as M. H. Everett entered with a pot of coffee and a stack of morning newspapers. Madame was already dressed for the day and sat sipping her tea. As M. H. refilled her cup, she frowned at the bony wrist extending beyond his jacket sleeve. Boomsky was hard on uniforms, always outgrowing them or wearing them out. M. H. struck a match, lit Herrmann's cigarette, then set about tidying the room. Herrmann quickly found his opening night reviews. The *Kansas City Star* critic had loved the show. Alexander gleefully read aloud: "All the seats were occupied, and the people all seemed to be friends of his, for they applauded when Herrmann first came forward with his long ostrich-like strides and applauded again every time there was half a chance until the performance ended."[130]

The critic had declared After the Ball to be "marvelous." Herrmann continued reading:

The Kansas City Star, March 14, 1894. The elaborate promotion for Kenilworth Tailors was larger than the same newspaper's review of Herrmann's show, which appeared in the adjoining column.

A magnificent mirror stands in the center of the stage. There is an open space below and all around it. A lady stands on a glass shelf in front of the mirror. "Boomsky," Mr. Herrmann's black boy, hands up a screen which is placed on the shelf so as to obscure the lady from view. The mirror, however, is exposed on all sides. Herrmann says "tra la la" or "tra la lo," either one will do, and pulls down the screen. No lady. She appears presently, at the side of the stage, to bow in response to the applause of the audience.

Herrmann went on reading the review, which praised Escape from Sing Sing and Madame's dances.

Herrmann suddenly straightened up and exclaimed, "What is this!" M. H. turned toward his boss. Herrmann held the newspaper closer and began reading, slowly and deliberately: "'Monsignor Boomsky, the great Assyrian prestidigitateur and magician, original instructor of the world-renowned Herrmann.'"

Hudson Everett chuckled at the thought of Boomsky being Herrmann's instructor. His boss made such silly jokes. Herrmann turned the paper around and pointed. "No, it is written here." He tapped a large block of print that bordered the review of his show. Herrmann continued reading aloud: "'His present colleague and traveling companion is now in Kansas City. He is on his way to the Pacific coast and is billed to appear in all of the larger cities en route. Owing to the fact that all Kansas City theaters are contracted for by other attractions, Mon. Boomsky had about concluded to spend the week here without performing, thus gaining a much needed rest.'"

Hutchin's mind reeled. Who was this Boomsky? Why had he not heard of him? Herrmann continued, "'But the ever alert Kenilworth Tailors stepped to the front and offered him superior inducements to appear before the public at 719 Main Street, and he accepted. He will be assisted by Sa Ah Bra, a fin-de-siècle artist in his line. The engagement extraordinary began this morning and will continue through the week.'"

Hutchin still did not understand, but Madame had perked up. With her eyes fixed on Boomsky, she addressed her husband. "Did you say tailors?" Alexander read on: "'A word about Monsignor Boomsky—He was the first known representative of necromancy. He came from a tribe of Gypsy natives that formerly inhabited the lower valleys of the Himalayas. His early youth was spent in thought and study that caused his companions to look askance upon him, as it was known that his face at birth was covered with a caul. His first attempts at necromancy so worked upon his kinsmen that he was driven out of the country and fled to England where he created a profound sensation.'"

Herrmann paused. He looked at Adelaide and Boomsky and said, "You did not know about my old teacher, eh? And that he appears in a tailor shop window in Kansas City?" Adelaide burst out laughing. Hutchin relaxed. It was a joke after all. Alexander read on: "'The Great Herrmann, then a youth, secured the services of the magician as instructor with results well known to the civilized world. After twenty years of separation the famous preceptor and pupil are now reunited and will travel together during the remainder of the season, although they will not be seen upon the same stage in Kansas City.'"

Herrmann looked up from the paper briefly. "Ha! They will not be seen on the same stage anywhere." He looked down again and read: "'Come to the Kenilworth store and see this wonderful man. It costs you nothing and will do you worlds of good. On exhibition from 10 a.m. to 6 p.m. every day this week.'"[131]

Herrmann tossed back the covers and put his feet on the floor. He addressed his own Boomsky, "Send for my carriage. And tell Mr. Bloom to meet us in the lobby."

A small crowd milled on Main Street outside Kenilworth Importing Tailors, waiting to see Herrmann the Great's revered teacher, Monsignor Boomsky. The Kenilworth store, open for just three months, had leapt to public attention with a series of unusual promotional events, announced via large advertisements in the *Kansas City Star*. Earlier that month, a woman called Priscilla, costumed as a Pilgrim, sat in Kenilworth's window, spinning wool yarn on an old-fashioned spinning wheel.[132] The previous week, the store had hosted a party for the public. Referring to the tiny, good-natured household spirits of Scottish folklore, the advertisement promised "there will be a Brownie in the window whose antics will amuse you."[133]

Heads turned and jaws dropped as Herrmann the Great sprang from his carriage and loped toward the tailor shop. Madame Herrmann, Manager Bloom, and Boomsky scurried to catch up. The crowd parted when the four of them reached the store's front window. In the window, sitting opposite a display of men's suits, was Monsignor Boomsky. The window performer stared back through the glass at the real Boomsky, who stood arrow straight in his crisp brass-buttoned uniform and jaunty hat. Monsignor Boomsky, the Himalayan Gypsy, wore a turban and robes.

Herrmann continued into the store, followed by Madame, Bloom, and Boomsky. Behind the counter stood the smiling proprietor, F. Kerby Wilkins, tape measure around his neck and order form in his pocket. When he recognized Herrmann and the real Boomsky, the blood drained from Wilkins's face. The manager had put much time and effort into inventing Monsignor Boomsky's story. The verbose newspaper advertisement had been monstrously expensive to run since linotype printing charged by the word. Totally absorbed in his project, Wilkins had never considered that Herrmann himself might discover his hoax.

Herrmann tilted his head toward the front window. Mr. Wilkins, his face now turning beet red, summoned the robed man into the store. Herrmann spoke, "So this is Monsignor Boomsky, my instructor?" Wilkins began a stammered apology, but Herrmann held up his hand. "I could sue you for fraud. Or I could force you to print a retraction." Wilkins was sweating. "But the real Boomsky needs a new uniform." Adelaide nudged her husband. "Actually, Boomsky will require two new suits. Mr. Bloom, my manager, will take matters from here." The Herrmanns swept out as M. H. stayed behind to be measured. That afternoon, Herrmann's crew arrived with brushes, paste, and enough Herrmann posters to nearly cover the front window of Kenilworth Importing Tailors.

Boomsky's new spring uniforms received Madame's nod of approval. But M. H. Everett had not heard the last of Monsignor Boomsky. For weeks, Herrmann introduced Boomsky as "my instructor." No matter how many times Herrmann said it, Madame still laughed.[134]

BERNARD BAKER: HERRMANN'S HORSE WHISPERER

In the spring of 1894, as their train sped from Indianapolis to Cleveland, the great magician announced that next season he would combine his two passions—magic and horses. He was tired of continually riding in hired carriages, never as nice as his own, with their depressed, dispirited horses. Now they would bring their own horses and carriages on tour with them! Herrmann would commission a marvelous new railcar to carry his steeds and his beautiful carriages. But that was just the beginning. Glory on the stage was already his. Now he would seek laurels in the horse show ring as well. Herrmann excitedly unveiled his plan as he handed Manager Bloom a sheet of paper and directed him to schedule the upcoming season's tour dates to coincide with this list of horse shows. During his engagement in Pittsburgh later that month, he would purchase some stunning new steeds.

As Herrmann spoke, M. H. glanced at Madame Herrmann and Manager Bloom. Neither looked happy. Where Herrmann envisioned triumph and blue ribbons, Bloom and Madame foresaw astronomical cost and complications. Adelaide had learned long ago that objection was futile; Alexander always got what he wanted. She grimaced and stayed silent. For Manager Bloom, however, it was the last straw. After three years of on-a-whim changes of plans, out-of-control spending, and constant packing and shipping of bulky purchases to Herrmann Manor, Edward L. Bloom stood up and declared, "I quit."

Press reports marveled that Bloom had lasted so long. The *New York Times* predicted Herrmann would have trouble finding someone else who "managed him with a club."[135] But Herrmann simply promoted his assistant manager, Edward Thurnaer, and continued seamlessly.

In Pittsburgh, the blue-ribbon sale of the Arnheim Livestock Company was so packed with people that M. H. worried he would lose Herrmann in the crowd. Rows of temporary horse stalls occupied one end of the Second Avenue Pavilion, while a throng of people crowded near the auction block at the other end. Outside, an entire block of Second Avenue had been closed to traffic and served as a speeding course to exhibit the gaits of each horse put on sale. All day long, racehorses, saddle horses, carriage horses, and horse teams tore back and forth as hundreds of prospective buyers jostled for a better view. Herrmann noted several horses of interest, but as he watched the demonstrations, he couldn't take his eyes off Arnheim's head trainer and chief presenter. Sitting erect and looking confident, the young Black man was one of the best horsemen Herrmann had ever seen. Whether balancing atop speeding chargers, driving carriage teams, or demonstrating fancy gaits under the saddle, he made every horse look good. All the while he smiled and played to the crowd, tipping his distinctive bowler hat. Herrmann sent Everett to learn the man's name. M. H. returned and reported, "Bernard Baker, six years a protégé of Professor O. Gleason." Herrmann nodded knowingly. That explained everything.

Professor O. Gleason was a famous trainer and showman whose rapport with horses was legendary. Professor Gleason's show began with wonderful feats by Gleason's own horses, who performed complex gaits and spun around in coordinated dances, all with just the lightest touch of the whip. But the show's biggest draw was Gleason's guarantee that he could quickly "break" any horse, no matter how unmanageable.

Horse breakers usually used brute force. But Gleason's approach was radically different. He had an uncanny way with horses, which nobody could explain. Horses just seemed to trust him like an old friend, willing to do whatever he asked.[136] Gleason toured with a team of young Black apprentices. Now, here was one of them, right before Herrmann's eyes. The magician could not believe his luck.

Bernard Baker with Herrmann's show horse My Queen, in front of Herrmann Manor.

Herrmann bought three horses at Arnheim's auction. For the pacer, Thorndike, he paid $460. The crack carriage team, Black Dandy and Matchless, cost him another $1,000.[137] But Herrmann's proudest deal came at the end of the day when he sought out Bernard Baker and offered him a job. As Arnheim's top trainer, the twenty-two-year-old already commanded a high salary. Plus, after being on tour since age sixteen, Baker enjoyed being back home in Pittsburgh. Herrmann asked the horseman to name his price. Baker's price was high indeed, many times higher than Boomsky's wage and more than most of Herrmann's other employees. But the magician simply extended his hand and welcomed Bernard Baker to his company. The Professor watched excitedly as his new stablemaster led his sleek new horses onto the northbound train en route to the Whitestone estate, where they would await Herrmann's return at season's end two months later. Regrettably, the Professor's return home would come much sooner than expected.

Bernard Baker with Herrmann's show horses.

OFF TO CUBA

Looking back later, Adelaide would mark spring 1894 as the first real sign of trouble. It had begun well enough. In April, Herrmann gave up the lease on his New York theater. It had become a money-losing headache. Although continuously booked with plays and variety shows, the theater made a profit only when Herrmann himself played there.

In late May, the Herrmann company boarded a ship for Havana. Everyone bubbled with excitement. The Herrmanns had not visited Cuba in fourteen years and foresaw a triumphant return. As they sailed out of New York Harbor toward open ocean, M. H. Everett was excited about his first sea voyage and his first trip outside the US. When they landed in Havana, the Herrmanns were met by a boisterous official delegation who escorted them to their hotel. On opening night at the Payret Theater, Havana's high society turned out in force and cheered for one curtain call after another. The two-week run in Havana netted Herrmann an enormous $20,000.

Suddenly Herrmann's luck turned. They had just begun a tour of Cuban cities when Alexander fell ill with a tropical fever. Several shows were canceled. Adelaide tended to her husband, desperate for him to improve. But over the next week, Herrmann remained weak and feverish. Madame abruptly canceled the rest of the tour and brought Alexander home to recuperate.

Back at Whitestone, Alexander's recovery was hindered by his refusal to rest. Though still pale and listless, every morning Herrmann insisted on visiting his stables, where he spent hours watching his new stablemaster, Bernard Baker, train and work his horses. With Baker's help, Herrmann began designing a magnificent, state-of-the-art railcar for his horses and carriages. No expense would be spared.

Madame joined them after breakfast for her daily brisk ride. Alexander loved to ride, but he stuck to safe, gentle horses. Adelaide, on the other hand, was fearless in the saddle, forever leading mad charges across fields and through woods. Somewhat scandalously, she wore trousers and sat astride the horse, rather than sitting sidesaddle in a skirt, as was the custom for women. Both Herrmanns loved driving carriages, and both were reckless speed demons. M. H. Everett knew to hold tight through the violent jolts as they pounded over bumps and through ruts, but Adelaide's young nieces and nephews regularly flew off her carriage and into the ditch.

M. H. Everett's third summer at Herrmann Manor began much like his first two. Once again, he tended to house magic and dogs. With Herrmann's attention on Bernard Baker, his new stablemaster, M. H. quietly turned sixteen. Everyone's summer was about to get much more exciting.

THE HEAT WAVE AND THE BULLET CATCH

The summer of 1894 was the hottest in anyone's memory. Beginning in June, the heat and humidity were unrelenting, and this went on all season long. At Whitestone, on Long Island Sound, the Herrmanns felt an occasional limp breeze. Alexander was still recovering after falling ill in Cuba and being rushed home mid-June. By July, he was somewhat improved but still not his normal robust self. He spent each evening lounging in a hammock on the screened porch, dogs splayed around him, wilted from the heat. Adelaide sat drooped on a lounge chair, fanning herself as M. H. Everett served cold tea to the Herrmanns and their guests. Adelaide's visiting nieces and nephews, normally rambunctious, lazed about sluggishly.

One sweltering night, Herrmann was smoking a cigarette on the veranda when M. H. brought him the evening newspapers. The news of late was not good. The heat was merciless. On many days, the temperature never dipped below 90 degrees Fahrenheit, even at night. In the teeming tenements of New York's Lower East Side, indoor temperatures reached as high as 130 degrees. The situation turned deadly. Unlike a disastrous heat wave two years later, which would claim roughly 1,500 lives in just ten days, 1894's heat killed slowly, striking a handful of victims every day.[138] Each morning the newspapers published the names of the previous day's heatstroke fatalities. The crisis hit the poor much harder. Affluent citizens could afford ice to cool themselves. The hundreds of ice houses that bordered New York's rivers and lakes had more than enough supply, stored from the previous winter, but only for those who could pay.

Herrmann shook his head as he read the evening edition of the *New York Herald*. Stories of suffering always tugged at him. New York City's government was disgraceful! Despite the appalling death rate, the city did nothing. Indeed, most officials believed that helping the poor was not the government's job. Suddenly Herrmann sat up and tapped the newspaper with his finger. Here was some good news. The *Herald* had established a Free Ice Fund for the poor. The magician exclaimed, "We will give a benefit!"

Adelaide stopped fanning herself and shot her husband a doubtful look. "In this heat?" she exclaimed. "Who will come? Even for you?"

Alexander paused a moment, then declared, "They will come." He drew a breath, then added, "I will perform the bullet catch."

Adelaide's gaze hardened. Everett's ears pricked up. He kept moving—emptying ashtrays, lighting cigars, pouring drinks—while he listened intently.

Madame exploded into furious French. M. H. had trouble following the words, but the meaning was clear. She vehemently objected to her husband performing the bullet catch. It was too dangerous. She would not allow it.

M. H. did not know this trick, the bullet catch, but the name certainly sounded dangerous. Indeed, M. H. would learn that more than a dozen magicians had died attempting the feat. He also learned that years earlier, Alexander had performed the bullet catch in huge arenas in Cuba, Mexico, and Portugal, so terrifying his wife that he had agreed to present it again only with Adelaide's permission. Here she was, fervently protesting, but M. H. already knew the outcome. Madame could stand up to anyone except her husband. In the end, Alexander always got his way.

Gradually, Madame calmed down and admitted defeat. She nodded her permission. Alexander called for his secretary and dictated a letter to the publisher of the *New York Herald*, offering a benefit performance for the Free Ice Fund. The *Herald* immediately accepted. The performance was scheduled for August 1, at the Metropolitan Opera House.

With the show less than a month away, there was no time to lose. Now, instead of spending his days with his horses and new stablemaster, every morning Herrmann headed straight to his workshop. As the magician and his mechanic hunched over the workbench, tinkering, M. H. Everett stood at Herrmann's elbow, ready to grab whatever they might need—tools, wire, glue, paint, a bit of leather or cork. M. H. began to understand exactly why the bullet catch was so dangerous, especially Herrmann's presentation. Instead of one gunman shooting at Herrmann, there would be six marksmen, all active-duty soldiers, each firing his own military-issued Springfield rifle. Their sergeant would serve as an accomplice, but M. H. was shocked to learn that the gunmen themselves would not be in on the trick. In the workshop, Alexander and his mechanic were building two different magic devices on which the trick relied. If either of them malfunctioned, Herrmann could die.

Madame usually avoided the workshop, but now she dropped in frequently with pitchers of lemonade. She eyed Alexander closely. He was still pale and not well. Adelaide leaned in close to inspect the work in progress. The little switching tray was Alexander's design. A hidden lever on the side would switch real bullets for fakes. The prop had to be completely foolproof because it would be operated by a real soldier, not a trained magic assistant.

The fake bullets had to be perfect enough to fool the six military marksmen.[139] Instead of heavy lead slugs, the fake bullets were hollow and light. Formed from a mercury-based amalgam, they would disintegrate upon firing. The soldiers would notice the weight difference, so Herrmann and his mechanic carefully weighted the cartridges with lead. Herrmann was eager to test his fake bullets. He grabbed his gun and told M. H. to fetch Madame. They all headed for the estate's shooting range. Herrmann loaded a fake bullet into his Springfield rifle and pulled back the bolt. He took aim at the target twenty feet away. BANG! The smoke cleared. The target and wall behind it showed no marks. Herrmann reloaded and halved the distance. BANG! The target and wall remained unmarked. The magician moved to within five feet, barely more than an arm's length, and fired again. BANG! Again, nothing. Three more times he loaded and fired. Alexander looked at Madame, who shrugged a solemn nod. Satisfied, Herrmann began rehearsals.

M. H. Everett focused on learning his part in the bullet catch. He was just sixteen, yet Herrmann was entrusting Boomsky with a crucial role. M. H. would not let his boss down. Madame Herrmann hovered at every rehearsal. She had her own role in the trick, but she also fussed over Alexander, who remained unwell. She constantly urged him to sit down or take breaks, counseling he ignored.

Soon, the big day arrived, along with wilting heat and humidity. Clinging to Herrmann's carriage as it bounced through New York's sweltering streets, M. H. wondered who would sit in a theater in this heat. But neither Alexander nor Adelaide seemed worried. Sure enough, that evening, August 1, a standing-room-only audience packed into the Metropolitan Opera House. Inside, the theater was like an oven. The fashion constraints of the day assured maximum discomfort for everyone. Gentlemen wore suit jackets, high-collared shirts with bow ties, and vests. Ladies' dresses were long-sleeved and floor-length, and even indoors, ladies did not remove their hats. Many women carried large fans, some tipped with fur or feathers to better waft the oppressive air.

Backstage the mood was tense. The bullet catch had everyone on edge. But worse, Herrmann was visibly unwell. All day he had seemed feverish and not himself. When the overture began, he was still in his dressing room, as Madame nervously paced the hallway just outside. Herrmann finally emerged, pale even through his greasepaint, and slowly walked to the wings. At the orchestra's final chords, Herrmann mustered his energy, summoned a beaming smile, and marched onto the stage with his usual determined stride. That night the audience would never suspect that Herrmann was ill. Reviewers would note his pallor but attribute it to the emotional stress of facing death onstage.

The evening began with excerpts from Herrmann's show. Alexander started off with his usual small tricks and the flying cards. He conjured silver dollars, and Boomsky fell on the hat. The audience warmly applauded for After the Ball, then Adelaide brought down the house with two of her new serpentine dances. But it was the promised finale that kept the perspiring crowd in their seats—the bullet catch.

Finally, everyone's patience was rewarded. A squad of six United States soldiers from Governor's Island marched onto the stage, accompanied by the 7th Regiment Band. Herrmann directed the proceedings from the opposite side of the stage. The magician never went near the rifles or the bullets. One by one, each soldier dropped a bullet onto a small tray held by their sergeant, who then went into the audience. Distinguished audience members examined the cartridges and lead bullets and marked them with identifying scratches. The sergeant then returned to the stage. As he climbed the steps, with his back turned to the audience, the sergeant secretly pulled the lever on the tray, stealthily switching the real bullets for the fakes. Each soldier plucked a bullet off the tray and held it over his head. The sergeant handed the empty tray to Boomsky to remove. At the order of their commander, the soldiers loaded the bullets into their rifles and began to march in single file toward the end of the long runway extending from the stage into the audience.

As the audience watched the soldiers, just offstage Boomsky and Madame Herrmann worked furiously. Boomsky flipped the tray's lever and dumped the real bullets and cartridges into a shallow pan that Madame had dusted with gunpowder. Working together, they quickly pried the six lead bullets loose and discarded the cartridges. Madame struck a match and dropped it in the pan, causing a quick flash of fire. Boomsky, holding a china plate in one hand, snatched up the burning hot bullets with his other hand. He flinched slightly as he palmed the bullets.

Upon reaching the end of the runway, the soldiers turned to face Herrmann, who had stepped to center stage. Boomsky walked out and handed Herrmann the plate. Nobody saw Boomsky drop the bullets down Herrmann's sleeve. The magician and assistant had practiced the move dozens of times, until it was smooth and fail-safe. The magician set the plate on a low table in front of him as the soldiers took their formation, four standing and two kneeling in front. They aimed their rifles at Herrmann, who extended his hands in front of him, palms forward.

The stress was too much for some in the audience. A number of women, and even a few men, left the theater. Several other women fainted from the heat and frayed nerves. Backstage, Adelaide trembled with nervousness. True, the trick had already been accomplished. The real bullets had been switched for harmless fakes. Herrmann had the marked bullets in his sleeve, warm against his elbow. Yet the danger was still very real. An unpredicted malfunction could be deadly. A blank cartridge could still maim or kill if an object, such as a button or a tack, had been dropped into the barrel. Magicians had died that way. Or perhaps an armed spectator would simply stand up and shoot his own gun at Herrmann, since the magician was claiming invulnerability.

The command was shouted, "Fire!" BOOM! The report from the six rifles was deafening. Some women screamed. Everyone's ears rang. Through the cloud of smoke Herrmann was seen making a grasping gesture. As the smoke cleared, he remained perfectly still. Many wondered if he had been hit but had not yet fallen. The tension was electrifying. Then Herrmann stepped forward, opened his hands, and dropped six bullets, clattering onto the china plate. The audience exploded with applause. Adelaide ran onstage and threw herself into her husband's arms. The bullets, still warm, were distributed for examination and their etchings were verified, proving that these were the original marked bullets.[140]

Everyone exhaled when the trick was over. Herrmann briefly bathed in the glow of his triumph. The publisher of the *Herald*, James Gordon

Bennett, ran backstage to report that the performance had raised nearly two thousand dollars for the Free Ice Fund. Many lives would surely be saved. A parade of dignitaries congratulated Herrmann in his dressing room. As Boomsky closed the door after the last visitor, Herrmann collapsed with exhaustion and fever. Alarmed, Adelaide enlisted several strong men to help Alexander into their carriage for the two-hour ride back to Herrmann Manor. Perhaps now he would finally rest.

DOG DAYS AND HERRMANN'S ILLNESS

That sweltering August, Herrmann was not a cooperative patient. He insisted on keeping the house open to guests, many of them friends escaping the blistering city. People flowed in and kept the Whitestone party rolling. Every day, the entire group traipsed down to the estate's private beach. Adelaide's nieces and nephews cooled off in the water, as did many of the adults. Alexander, who was never much of a swimmer, still looked pale and ill. Each day he sat in a lounge chair by the shore, wrapped in his bathrobe, the hood hanging over his head like a monk's cowl.

M. H. Everett was back to his dog-tending duties. This had become more difficult with the recent addition of Queenie, a huge mastiff. M. H. liked the dogs, but this one scared him. She growled when anyone went near her food dish or any toy in her view. M. H. didn't trust Queenie, who outweighed him, and he kept his distance.

Just a week after the Free Ice Fund show, the Herrmanns, their guests, and the dogs were lounging on the beach. Adelaide was admiring her new mastiff and decided to see if Queenie would swim to fetch a stick. She had M. H. throw a stick out into the water. Instead, Strobeika, the Great Dane, jumped into the water and snatched it. When Strobeika dropped the stick at Adelaide's feet, Queenie attacked, burying her fangs in the Great Dane's neck. Strobeika shrieked in agony, but Queenie would not release her. The dogs thrashed violently as Strobeika screamed. M. H. and several of the men tried to separate them. Adelaide tried to pry open Queenie's jaws. Then, as her horrified guests watched, Adelaide seized the enormous dogs by their collars. Fully dressed, she heaved the writhing beasts into the water to the level of her shoulders. Madame Herrmann then dunked the dogs' heads repeatedly until Queenie let go. Witnesses expected Madame to be "torn to pieces," but both Adelaide and Strobeika emerged mostly unscathed.[141]

Over the next two weeks the brutal heat persisted, and Alexander's condition worsened. A doctor diagnosed his ongoing illness as rheumatic fever. Adelaide finally put her foot down and sent the guests home. All but one of the children sailed back to England. Adelaide's sixteen-year-old niece, Adele "Dewey" Owles, stayed on at the estate, ready to join the Herrmann company in the fall. Madame's birthday arrived, but this year there was no party. M. H. had never heard the house so quiet. Without the gales of laughter and constant chatter, the hourly outburst of the mansion's nineteen clocks—chimes, bells, gongs, cuck-oos—echoed eerily throughout the empty house. A skeletal household staff supported Adelaide and her mother and niece, the two Adeles. The three generations of Scarsez women worked with grim determination to nurse Herrmann back to health. M. H. stayed within earshot, ready to dash for the doctor. By Sunday of the second week, Herrmann's fever was alarming. Physicians came and went. The newspapers printed rumors that Alexander was near death. At Herrmann Manor, everyone was desperately worried. Adelaide prepared to postpone the fall tour.

Finally, Alexander's fever broke. By Monday he was up and walking around the house.[142] M. H. was astonished. Suddenly, his boss looked better than he had in months. Herrmann the Great announced that he would open his new season in less than two weeks, on September 3, in Montreal. It was a last-minute booking. Herrmann had learned that Harry Kellar was playing Montreal, and he had a rivalry to pursue.

ᵀHE ᴿOBINSONS ᴿETURN

As the *Addie Herrmann* sped north toward Montreal, sixteen-year-old M. H. Everett felt like he was thirteen again. In many ways, it was just like the first day he climbed aboard the railcar. Will and Dot Robinson were back! After two and a half years with Kellar, the star assistants had defected back to Herrmann. Manager Bloom had returned as well, four months after quitting in a huff. M. H. wondered how Herrmann had managed to lure him back.

Adelaide's niece, Adele Owles, was new to the company. M. H. had known Adele for three years, since they were both thirteen, during summers at Herrmann Manor. Adele was blond and very pretty, with porcelain skin that inspired her nickname, Dewey. Aunt Adelaide's hands were full, warding off constant inappropriate attention from older males toward her lovely niece.

Although she remained firmly the star, Adelaide was happy to have the two younger women along. She was fond of Dot, a good-natured, industrious trouper who understood like no one else the punishments endured by illusionists. Dot's illusion work took the heat off Adelaide. Now older and stockier, Madame retired from the most difficult illusions. In her day, Adelaide had been a great illusionist, but Dot was even better. Tiny, strong, and lightning fast, Dot was hands down the best illusionist anywhere. Dewey, Adelaide's teenage niece, was like a breath of fresh air. Tall for an illusionist, Dewey was strong and flexible as well as blond and beautiful.

After two pared-down seasons, Herrmann had gone big again. Now they carried nine different stage illusions. M. H. already knew many of them—Strobeika, Escape from Sing Sing, After the Ball, Black Art—but others were new, including The Artist's Dream and The Asiatic Trunk Mystery.

As they traveled northward, Herrmann's new horse car attracted admiring stares. Stablemaster Bernard Baker had overseen its design, and it was magnificent. A painted filigree pattern adorned the corners of the car's face. Two-foot-tall letters boasted, "Herrmann Special Car 3" and "Herrmann the Great." The sixty-eight-foot car was fitted with pivot stalls, giving the horses space to lie down and to turn in any direction, which helped them compensate for the movement of the train. The rest of the show's performing animals enjoyed equally comfortable quarters in their own section of the car. Even with Herrmann's fancy horse carriages aboard, there was space to spare. The railcar had its own stove, running water, and six sleeping berths for company members.

At every stop, Manager Bloom invited members of the press to tour the fancy new horse car. Bernard Baker, a natural showman, guided guests through the car before giving a training demonstration with one of Herrmann's horses. A reporter was impressed by Baker's command of Herrmann's saddle mare, My Queen. Although Baker had worked with her for just three weeks, My Queen bowed upon request and stamped her foot on the ground to accurately answer questions such as, "How many working days in a week?" As a crowd gathered on the street in front of the stables, Baker climbed into the saddle and "made My Queen trot, lope and canter very nicely. Among the other accomplishments she displayed were single foot, running trot, side march, counter march, see-saw, and Spanish trot, all under the saddle."[143]

With the Robinsons back onboard, Herrmann chuckled over one-upping his opponent, Harry Kellar. Historians have theorized that the bitter Herrmann/Kellar rivalry was just an elaborate publicity stunt. But Herrmann's and Kellar's words and actions expressed true disdain for each other. The two great magicians could not have been more different—Herrmann, the educated, genteel, multilingual Frenchman, and Kellar, the hardscrabble, working-class American. Their performance styles also contrasted—Herrmann's devilish, lighthearted banter versus Kellar's mesmerizing focus on the mysterious.

After two challenging seasons with Kellar, Will and Dot were thrilled to be back with the more relaxed Herrmann company. Will and

Dot told stories of Harry Kellar, a true professional in every other way, being completely thrown by onstage mistakes. He would fly into violent rages midshow, cursing his assistants and at times throwing or kicking a malfunctioning prop offstage. Later, the normally sweet-tempered Kellar would be horrified at his own behavior and would apologize profusely. But in the moment when things went wrong, the magician was always a flustered hothead.

Herrmann scoffed at these tales of Kellar. For Herrmann, mishaps were opportunities for hilarity. One night, Herrmann reached under a wafting silk scarf and removed a brimming bowl of water. As he stepped forward triumphantly, something wet and floppy splattered onto the stage beside him. In grabbing for the falling object, Alexander spilled the bowl of water, soaking himself from the knees down. Even his shoes were full of water. On the stage sat something the audience was never supposed to see—the stretchy rubber cover that had enabled the magician to hide the full bowl of water under his coat. Herrmann calmly picked up the wet disk of rubber, placed the dripping circle on his head, and struck a pose, exclaiming, "Do you like my new beret?" His quip brought down the house.

Now, just before facing off with his rival in Montreal, Herrmann had stolen away Kellar's star assistants. As they chugged northward, M. H. Everett saw Herrmann smiling smugly, twirling the end of his mustache.

Once in Montreal, Herrmann quickly got the upper hand over his nemesis. The *Gazette* ran a column on the competing magicians' upcoming performances. Herrmann's profile was above Kellar's, with two pictures of Herrmann and none of Kellar.[144] Furious, Kellar sent an overnight crew into Montreal to paper over Herrmann's posters with his own. The next night Herrmann retaliated, sending his own crew to paper over Kellar's posters. Night after night, the two magicians alternated this expensive and childish game, as Manager Bloom shook his head and groaned.

HERRMANN, SCOURGE OF BLACK WAITERS

In a promotion for Herrmann's Montreal run, the *Gazette* ran a story that was completely acceptable by the racist standards of 1894. Much is made of Herrmann's legendary kindness, but many Black waiters did not find him so nice. Herrmann constantly made them the butt of the joke with his impromptu tricks. The waiters' reactions, from confusion to unabashed terror, were unceasingly hilarious to Herrmann's guests. Ridiculing Black people's superstitions, naïveté, and presumed lack of intelligence was considered fair game. Newspaper accounts presented these degrading stunts as lighthearted amusements, disregarding the waiters' insult, humiliation, and trauma.

The *Gazette* article told of Herrmann dining with friends at a restaurant in Cincinnati. When a Black waiter came to take the order, the dishes on the table "commenced to disappear. Some seemed to go down Herrmann's throat, others flew in the air, and in less than half a minute the table was cleared. The startled waiter looked at Mr. Herrmann, then at the door which he made a wild rush for, yelling at the top of his lungs . . . , 'Dat man got devils. I'se done with him.'" Another waiter who said he was not afraid provided Herrmann with a steel knife to cut his meat. "Just as the colored man handed it to him, Mr. Herrmann pulled it across his wrist, seemingly cutting an artery. The blood squirted over the waiter and the floor. The colored man was scared almost to death." He ran for help, and when he returned with several other waiters, there was no blood on Herrmann's wrist. The waiter who witnessed the cutting said, "'Dat man's a witch,' . . . and he refused to serve the magician."[145] Herrmann always left generous tips for his victims, assuaging his conscience and, in his own mind, making things right.

Noah's Ark Animal Riot

Bernard Baker had a way with all animals, not just horses, which may have influenced Herrmann to program Noah's Ark, After the Flood for the 1894 fall season. Suddenly Herrmann's touring menagerie quadrupled in size. Several additional dogs now squeezed into the private railcar's already close quarters. Madame Herrmann obsessively combed and groomed her dogs. She adorned them with bows and outfits and spritzed them with French cologne. Still, they shed everywhere. Sweeping and brushing dog hair from clothes and furniture was a never-ending chore for M. H. Everett. In the new horse car, Bernard Baker contended with a traveling barnyard. A section of the car was occupied by a dozen wire pens and crates containing doves, geese, ducks, turkeys, chickens, rabbits, and a small pig.

With so many animals involved, rehearsals of Noah's Ark had been chaotic. Yet Herrmann was not worried. New illusions always had kinks to work out. The illusion principle for Noah's Ark was sound—classic and time-tested. On opening night, his assistants were not so confident.

The complicated illusion required three assistants—M. H. Everett, Bernard Baker, and Adele Dewey. The assistants prepared and performed all the magic; Herrmann was simply a delightful front man—talking, pointing, firing guns (his favorite part), and of course taking all the credit for the trick. Behind the closed curtain the preparations were frantic and rushed as the three assistants lifted the animals from their cages into the ark's secret load chambers. Tricks with livestock had to be loaded at the very last moment to prevent suffocation. M. H. and Bernard worked quickly, but Adele's mermaid costume slowed her down. M. H. and Bernard lifted Adele into the ark. As she wriggled into her hiding place, M. H. and Bernard loaded the last few creatures, closed the illusion's doors, and cleared the empty cages from the stage.

When the curtain opened, the audience saw a three-dimensional model of an ark sitting center stage, supported by trestles. The vessel's hull was about the size of a rowboat. Its cabin had small windows all along the sides. Herrmann directed his assistants to lower the boat's hinged sides and open the bow and stern, displaying a completely empty interior. The sides of the ark folded down easily enough, but when M. H. and Bernard lifted the rear panel to close it they struggled a bit. They strained to lift the bow and stern sections as well.

Herrmann waved his wand and fired his pistol. He reached into one of the ark's windows and pulled out a dove, which he handed to Everett. Herrmann removed a half-dozen more doves. From different windows of the ark, Herrmann extracted ducks, geese, chickens, and turkeys, placing each one onto the stage. Bunnies appeared next, followed by the dogs. Finally, Herrmann extracted a squirming pig. But that was not all. M. H. and Bernard again lowered the front of the ark. Inside was a beautiful mermaid—Miss Adele Dewey.

Audiences loved Noah's Ark. A chorus of "awwws" echoed in the theater as each new animal emerged, especially at matinees and on Friday nights, when the house was full of children. But the illusion was not deceptive. A *San Francisco Examiner* reporter observed, "This trick did not impress the onlookers to any extent, for while the preliminary letting down of the sides of the ark proved that there was nothing in the 'hold,' the muscular force exerted by the attendants in putting the bulkhead bow and stern back into position suggested that the extremities of 'Noah's Ark' served as lurking places for the farmyard layout."[146] Displeased by the criticism, Herrmann moved to cut Noah's Ark from the program. But Adelaide adored the illusion and convinced him to keep it in the show, at least for the rest of the season.

One night, hilarious calamity struck Noah's Ark. Herrmann had just placed the little pig on the stage, and the animals were all milling around. Suddenly a goose attacked the pig, chasing the squealing animal around the stage, biting its ears and tail. Panic spread among the animals, and pandemonium ensued. Dogs, chickens, rabbits, ducks, and geese flapped, flew, and ran about the stage and into the footlights trough. As they scrambled around, the pig and goose almost fell into the orchestra pit, but the drummer managed to push them back onto the stage. The audience was paralyzed with laughter. The chaos lasted five long minutes. Finally, Boomsky saved the day. With a broom, he shooed away the attacking goose and herded all the other animals into the wings.[147] Starting the next night, the pig wore leather ear protectors and a strange leather cap on his tail, hurriedly fashioned by Madame Herrmann.

At the end of January 1895, they reached the season's prized destination—San Francisco. It was the Herrmanns' first time in California in four years and the first time ever for M. H. Everett. He marveled at the vibrant young city with its steep hills, rolling fog, and spectacular bay views. The hammering and sawing of new construction sounded throughout streets teeming with miners, speculators, importers, entrepreneurs, seamen, and Chinese people wearing robes and queues. San Francisco eagerly awaited Herrmann the Great. The newspapers ran splashy preview articles alongside large advertisements. A *San Francisco Examiner* advertisement on January 20, 1895, featured a sketch of Herrmann taking a live chicken from Boomsky's mouth.

When the Herrmanns arrived in San Francisco, they were greeted at the train station by hundreds of admirers. Locals braved a ferocious storm on opening night to completely pack the house. The show ran for three weeks, with a change of program each week. The crowds were so dense that even the standing-room section sold out, and patrons were turned away. Matinee performances were added to handle the overflow.[148] The company spent a month in California, traveling south to the frontier mission outposts of Los Angeles and San Diego before heading back up to Oakland. The New York–based Herrmann company loved touring balmy California in January. Alexander announced that they would return the following winter.

They were working their way back east, playing towns in Nebraska and Iowa, when they received terrible news. Adelaide's mother, Adele Scarsez, had died at their home in Whitestone at age eighty-six. They canceled the week and rushed back to New York. It was a tremendous blow to Adelaide. Her mother had lived with them for years, and they were very close. A native of Belgium, Adele's lilting French had reverberated through the halls as she managed the household and made the estate feel like home. The Herrmanns purchased a family plot in Woodlawn Cemetery in the Bronx, where Madame Scarsez was laid to rest. Exactly one week after Adele's death, they resumed their tour in Saint Paul. As Adelaide would write, "It is among the most pathetic aspects of the stage—of which the public knows little—that it allows no time for the indulgence of private sorrows."[149]

The Handsome Amateur Magician

In Saint Paul, a good-looking young man sought Herrmann out and introduced himself as a magician. Frederick Bancroft had not performed professionally, but he was passionate and knowledgeable about magic. He charmed and flattered Alexander and hung on the Professor's every word. Though not yet thirty, Bancroft had amassed a fortune in Saint Paul, working as an insurance agent, inventor, and real estate speculator. When the company finished their week in Saint Paul, Frederick Bancroft surprised the Herrmanns by buying himself train tickets and traveling along with them to Wisconsin. From March 25 to 27, the Herrmanns hammered out consecutive nights in Winona, Eau Claire, and Oshkosh, where the magical couple celebrated their twentieth wedding anniversary.[150]

When they opened in Milwaukee for four nights, Bancroft was still hanging around, attending every show and taking copious notes. He was curious about all aspects of the show and was frequently spotted deep in conversation with Manager Bloom as well as with Herrmann's crew members. M. H. noticed that Will Robinson remained aloof. As the newcomer bandied about, Robinson's eyes narrowed and his jaw clenched. Bancroft finally took his leave when the company departed for Cleveland. A month later, a small-town Minnesota newspaper printed an announcement that the Herrmanns would likely have missed. The article advertised the first professional performance of twenty-eight-year-old local magician Frederick Bancroft.[151] It would take a year for the Herrmanns—and M. H. Everett—to feel the impact of Bancroft's raging ambition, newly unleashed.

MADAME HERRMANN'S ARREST AND TRIAL

In mid-April, the Herrmann company began what should have been an easy home-turf month in and around New York City. It started out with exciting news: Herrmann's acquisition of his huge, 107-foot yacht, *Fra Diavolo*, was complete.[152] The company's two weeks playing the Academy in New York City were marred only by the news that a tame deer at Whitestone, around which Alexander was designing a trick, had been stolen or had wandered off.[153] Their week at the Academy of Music in Jersey City began well, with a gushing review in the *Jersey City News*.[154] Then things quickly went downhill.

After the Thursday night show, the Herrmann entourage was returning to Manhattan at about 10:30 p.m. It was a short walk from the Jersey City train terminal to the New York–bound ferry dock. Bernard Baker walked a few steps ahead, carrying a small bundle. Behind him walked Alexander and Adelaide, Manager Bloom, and Madame's maid,

Nora Cuthbert.[155] Without warning, a police officer named Christopher Bruene approached. The policeman seized Baker's arm and grabbed for the bundle. Adelaide ran up and tried to pull the officer's hand away, exclaiming that the bundle was hers. The policeman grasped Adelaide by the wrist, and Madame slapped the officer, scratching his face with her fingernails. Officer Bruene placed Madame under arrest. Herrmann and Ed Bloom joined in the fray, and the entire Herrmann party was escorted to the First Precinct station.

At the police station, the desk sergeant booked Adelaide on the charge of assaulting an officer of the law. The manager of the Academy of Music posted a $200 bond, sparing Madame a night in jail. She was ordered to appear in court in Jersey City first thing Saturday morning. The story hit newsstands Friday. When the Herrmanns arrived at the courthouse on Saturday, the waiting throng included a bevy of reporters.

Madame Herrmann was arraigned before Police Justice Potts of the First Criminal Court. Policeman Bruene testified first. He stated that just before the incident, police had received a report of a theft from the Salvation Army by a Black man. He claimed he was just doing his job by stopping Baker and that Madame Herrmann had assaulted him. Bruene pointed out the still-visible fingernail scratches raked across his cheek. Adelaide marched defiantly to the witness stand. She gestured toward Bernard Baker, sitting crisply uniformed, with a cap that read "HERRMANN" tucked under his arm. Clearly, Herrmann's valet had not robbed the Salvation Army. The policeman had targeted him simply because of his race. Madame testified that Bruene seized her wrist roughly when she simply tried to claim her property. His grip was so painful that she screamed. Not only that, he bent her body backwards, almost to the ground, so that her only recourse was to strike him to make him let go. She added that she also believed that the policeman was drunk. Cheers and applause accompanied her walk back to her seat. Justice Potts announced his ruling. "I find that Policeman Bruene did not exceed his authority. Madame Herrmann committed a 'technical assault.'" Boos erupted in the courtroom. Potts pounded his gavel and called for order. The Justice spoke again. "However, considering the circumstances, I have decided not to pursue the matter further."[156]

It was not a vindication, but at least it was over. The rowdy crowd cheered the Herrmann entourage as they left the courthouse and proceeded directly to the Academy of Music to prepare for the Saturday matinee. Still, the episode had soured everyone's mood, and company spirits were low. Before the show, both Herrmanns looked exhausted. But once Alexander stepped onstage, to the giggles and applause of hundreds of children, he instantly revived. Adelaide pulled herself together, vigorously swirling the heavy serpentine skirts just as she did at every performance. Before the evening show, the afternoon edition of the *Jersey City News* appeared with an editorial, "The Outrage Against Mrs. Herrmann," condemning Jersey City's heavy-handed treatment of their illustrious guests.[157] At the evening performance, Herrmann quipped about his wife's upper cut before introducing Adelaide, who walked on to thunderous cheers and applause. When the final curtain fell, the Herrmanns staggered to their dressing rooms.

For Alexander and Adelaide, it was the last straw. With Adele Scarsez's death and Adelaide's assault trial, all in the space of six weeks, they needed a break. They were less than two weeks into May, but the Herrmanns finished up in Jersey City and declared their season done. It had been a good season, overall profitable. While Boomsky had surfaced in the press only a few times—when herding panicked animals in the Noah's Ark illusion, demonstrating fancy horse gaits, and being seized by a policeman—behind the scenes, unseen and unreported, Herrmann's African American assistants were important cogs in the Herrmann machine, loyally tending to their much-loved employer day after day.

≈

CHAPTER FIVE

EVERETT AT SEVENTEEN, HERRMANN'S PENULTIMATE SEASON

(1895–1896)

ALL SUMMER ALEXANDER HAD BEEN TEASING at a splendid surprise. When the company finally saw it, they all gasped. A Pullman Palace Car!

The P.P.C. was the top-of-the-line replica of George Pullman's own private railcar, preferred by kings, presidents, and the ultra-wealthy. Herrmann justified the extra expense, pointing out that their old railcar, the *Addie Herrmann*, had started showing wear after four grueling seasons and several wrecks.

The new car was christened simply *Herrmann*. Alexander first showed off the car's exterior. The chassis sported twelve wheels instead of the usual eight, promising a much smoother ride. A large storage area under the carriage could serve either as a rolling wine cellar or as an icebox for cooling the car in summer.

As Alexander brought his company inside for a tour, jaws dropped. It was almost too much to take in. The car was a rolling mini-mansion.

Breathtaking arched ceilings bordered by intricately carved woodwork stretched the length of each room. The company members admired the embossed leather-covered walls, Tiffany glass windows, polished brass fixtures, and marble sinks. Madame Herrmann's chamber featured a silver bathtub that pulled out from beneath the bed. The car had a nebulous connection to royalty. It had been custom-designed for the infamous British-American beauty Lily Langtry, an actress most famous for her liaisons with the Prince of Wales and other powerful men. No expense had been spared. As he toured the car, M. H. Everett wondered if the lavish upgrades also extended to the car's servants' quarters. He would soon discover that they did not.

As they kicked off the 1895 fall season, Herrmann traveled with the biggest entourage ever. In addition to his new palace car, the Herrmann fleet included the fancy horse car, a baggage car, and seventeen assistants. A *Salt Lake City Herald* reporter remarked that Herrmann "has a whole train to himself."[158] Rumors spread that Alexander was arranging to purchase a locomotive, as well, which would relieve the never-ending headache of hitching and unhitching his private cars to regularly scheduled trains.[159]

They loaded up the railcars, and for the second year in a row, Herrmann the Great and his company chugged north toward Montreal. Again, the company included Will and Dot Robinson, manager Edward Bloom, Adelaide's niece Adele Dewey, M. H. Everett as Boomsky, and stablemaster Bernard Baker.

They opened with a bang in Montreal, continuing through Quebec and to Ottawa and upstate New York. A week in Pittsburgh brought in a record $10,398.50 for seven performances. Ed Bloom said it was Herrmann's highest weekly dollar receipt ever.[160]

But behind the scenes, all was not well. Unknown to audiences, Herrmann was frequently ill with severe chest pain and alarming shortness of breath. Usually, he would push through and do the show, but when he was too ill to perform, Will Robinson filled in.

William E. Robinson was a terrific character actor. He was Herrmann's match in sleight-of-hand, revered among magicians as an inventor, illusionist, and mechanic. Robinson imitated his boss's act so well that small-town audiences did not even realize they were not seeing the master. Robinson's other characters—Abdul Khan in Black Art, the Russian prisoner Ivan Ivanhoff in Strobeika, and Barney, an Irishman, in The Artist's Dream—were equally convincing.

The only character William Robinson seemed unable to successfully sell was himself. One major obstacle was his strong New York accent, which undermined Robinson's elegant stage demeanor and vast skills the instant he began to speak. Every summer, as the Herrmanns relaxed at Whitestone, Will and Dot peddled their act called "Robinson, Man of Mystery." While theater managers liked his magic, Robinson himself just seemed so . . . average. Summer after summer Will and Dot tried and failed to get a toehold of their own in the business. Every fall found them back on tour as assistants.

Alexander mentioned in an interview that he was considering his nephew Léon Herrmann as his successor.[161] Previously, Léon had succeeded Alexander as the boy assistant of Carl Herrmann. At twenty-seven, freshly discharged after four years in the French Army, Léon had just debuted his own full-evening show in Belgium, assisted by his wife, Marie.[162]

The company zigzagged across the US. Crossing through Nebraska, the Herrmanns' train was in another wreck. Fortunately, the only damage to Herrmann was to his pocketbook—the company missed their performance in Lincoln that night.[163] By the time they arrived in San Francisco, Herrmann was feeling tired. The fifty-one-year-old magician told a reporter from the *San Francisco Call*, "I am getting old."[164] But there was no time to rest. Herrmann had big plans in San Francisco. It irked him to be greeted by an article in the *San Francisco Chronicle* describing in great detail the secret of his bullet catch, which he would be performing on a return trip in a few weeks.[165] Although the reporter was guessing, the method he disclosed was mostly correct. But it did not affect Herrmann's crowds or his reception. The season's new levitation illusion, Trilby, was a hit with both audiences and critics. The company also performed the Spray of Life, the Columbian Transformation, and the Asiatic Trunk Mystery.[166] The constant program changes kept the cast and crew busy. Backstage, M. H. Everett often saw more of Will Robinson's feet than his face, as Herrmann's chief mechanic sprawled inside or under various apparatus, tinkering on his illusions.

Herrmann Appears in Two Places at Once

Herrmann's two-week engagement in San Francisco coincided with the Second Annual Pacific Coast Horse Show at the expansive Mechanic's Pavilion. The magician registered to compete in three ribbon events. For weeks, Herrmann had talked of little else. At train stops, he often popped aboard the horse car to ride the next leg with his beauties. Herrmann's company was used to his animated personality, but now their boss's nervous energy was exhausting. Everyone longed for the horse show to be done. Finally, the day arrived. The Pacific Coast Horse Show opened on Monday, December 2, and Bernard Baker got the horses settled into their temporary stalls. Herrmann checked on them in the afternoon before his performance. The next day, buzzing with excitement, Herrmann drove in the four-in-hand exhibition. He cut a fine figure atop his fancy carriage pulled by four thoroughbred horses. But then Herrmann blundered. His two sets of reins tangled, causing his horses to veer wildly off the track. A reporter noted that "it was apparent from the fumble Herrmann made that he is not an artist at handling the double thong."[167]

Mortified, Herrmann wanted a chance to redeem himself in the evening exhibition of tandem carriages. However, he had an insurmountable scheduling conflict. The horse show's evening exhibition and Herrmann's magic show began at the same time. Therefore, horse show attendees were flummoxed that night when, forty-five minutes into the exhibition, Alexander Herrmann burst into the arena, driving his tally-ho carriage pulled by his two finest horses. Herrmann circled the ring, waved to the audience, and exited. People furrowed their brows and scratched their heads. Wasn't Professor Herrmann appearing at the California Theater tonight?

Herrmann was indeed at the California that night. As soon as he had finished his opening magic set, Herrmann ran out the stage door and jumped into a waiting carriage, leaving the company to carry on with the show. It was less than half a mile to Mechanic's Pavilion, where Baker stood by the entrance with Herrmann's show horses and carriage. Back at the theater, Adelaide performed her serpentine dances, then Will Robinson impersonated Herrmann in the illusions. Disguised like the Professor, Robinson mimicked Herrmann's mannerisms and French accent so perfectly that few, if any, caught on to the charade.[168] Herrmann raced back from the horse show and dashed onstage just in time for his closing set.

The following day, Herrmann strutted into Mechanic's Pavilion with the morning newspapers under his arm. His miraculous trick of appearing in two places at the same time was headline news, but the Professor had not come merely to share his accolades. Herrmann headed to the stalls, where Bernard Baker was readying Herrmann's steeds for the saddle horse competition. Presently, eight riders and horses entered the arena for the judging. Herrmann rode My Queen, and Baker rode Perfection, winning third place and the yellow ribbon, respectively.[169] During lunch, Herrmann was, as always, the center of attention, producing mandarin oranges, eggs, and rabbits from the cravats of those seated near him.[170] The tandem competition was that afternoon. Bernard Baker, driving Cock Robin and Addie, won the third-place ribbon. In the four-in-hand judging, this time Herrmann did not fumble. The magician took third place with his team of Matchless, My Queen, Cock Robin, and Addie.[171] Between them, Herrmann and Baker won eleven ribbons.[172] Herrmann chuckled with delight as he watched Baker tack the colorful ribbons above the horse car's traveling stalls. As their train left San Francisco, M. H. Everett and the rest of Alexander's company members exhaled with relief.

The company spent the next two weeks appearing at California's burgeoning frontier towns—San Bernardino, Riverside, San Diego, Los Angeles, Santa Rosa, Sacramento, and Oakland. *Omaha Bee* reporter Max Meyer traveled with them, sending chatty stories back to his newspaper. For the New York–based Herrmann company, California's mild winter was a delight. Flowers scented the air everywhere they went. They landed in Portland, Oregon, for Christmas, where it rained the entire week and they saw "five minutes of sunshine."[173] On Christmas Day, when the mail was distributed, each member of the company, including M. H., received an envelope containing a twenty-dollar gold piece and a card with compliments of the season from the Herrmanns. M. H. stared at the heavy coin in his hand. Worth the modern equivalent of $700, Everett's Christmas bonus was more than his entire family earned in a whole year. He smiled, imagining their excitement at receiving his large money order. At the end of the matinee performance that day, Alexander Herrmann's company presented the magician with a beautiful ivory and gold wand. He was taken completely by surprise and was very moved by the gesture.[174]

Before leaving the West Coast, the Herrmann company returned to San Francisco for another week. Each night after the show, the Herrmanns socialized with popular comic actor and amateur magician Henry E. Dixey, whose gift for improvisation rivaled Herrmann's. Back and forth they bantered, each remark funnier than the next. Like Herrmann, Dixey could be silly. Adonis, Dixey's stage character, was a paunchy sad sack dressed in baggy tights. M. H. Everett would never have thought anyone could be funnier than Herrmann, but he decided that Dixey came close. Infatuated by the comedian, Herrmann offered to train Dixey to be his successor. But the proposal fizzled.[175]

During that final run in San Francisco, Herrmann did something he had never done before; he performed the bullet catch at eight shows in a row.[176] Herrmann drew the attention of Colonel "Buffalo Bill" Cody, then encamped with his Wild West show at Ambrose Park near San Francisco. Regarding Herrmann, Colonel Cody told the *San Francisco Call*, "He takes his life into his own hands."[177] Under the careful watch of his chief mechanic, Will Robinson, Herrmann's performances of the bullet catch went off without a hitch. But by the end of the week, Adelaide was a nervous wreck. She demanded that Alexander promise never to perform the trick again. But M. H. Everett knew her plea was weightless and his promise empty. If Alexander wanted to do the bullet catch again, he would.

A New Rival Emerges: Frederick Bancroft

After five weeks on the West Coast, the company departed San Francisco on Monday, January 6, 1896. Their special train traveled ninety hours straight through. They arrived in Milwaukee at two o'clock on Friday afternoon and performed that night.[178] While the Herrmanns were traveling, the young magician Frederick Bancroft appeared in Logansport, Indiana. Seemingly overnight, Bancroft had greatly expanded his company and was now performing a full-evening show. The Herrmanns, amused, chuckled at a pronouncement naming Bancroft "the king of amateur magicians."

In Chicago, the Herrmanns lived in their palace car, which was parked in the yards of the Chicago, Milwaukee, St. Paul, and Pacific Railroad. Curious friends came out to visit them every day.[179] Adelaide and Alexander enjoyed entertaining their guests, driving them around the city in their fancy carriages. It was a lovely way to repay many social debts accrued over years of visits.

M. H. Everett and Bernard Baker were always close at hand. While high-level assistants like the Robinsons stayed in downtown hotels, others lived at the rail yard with the Herrmanns, tending and guarding their charges, as well as the horses and carriages. The assistants were the Herrmanns' liaisons to a constant stream of visitors. Nobody got to see the Professor without first presenting a calling card to Boomsky, his uniformed valet.

As always, Herrmann's shows in Chicago drew capacity crowds. The *Chicago Tribune* praised the new Trilby levitation illusion, as well as the "enjoyable eccentric humor of Herrmann."[180] From Chicago, the company headed south for familiar stomping grounds, opening their yearly New Orleans run on February 9.

During that week, Herrmann finally took notice of Frederick Bancroft. The Eau Claire *Daily Telegram* reported that Herrmann was furious at an article in the *New York Mail* that stated, "The magician of the future is Bancroft." The *Daily Telegram* also reported that Herrmann was "considerably exercised" over Bancroft's "rapid and substantial success," with his "phenomenal tricks and gorgeous stage settings."[181]

In fact, Herrmann had been caught completely off guard by the newly minted conjuror, whose first professional season was proving to be a triumph. Out of nowhere, the recent amateur had put together the most spectacular magic show money could buy. Bancroft's initial investment had been $30,000, the equivalent of about $750,000 today. His cast included twenty-two colorfully costumed assistants and specialty performers, including "many beautiful women."[182] Bancroft's posters, created by the prestigious Strobridge Lithography Company, were gigantic and stunning.

Herrmann put Bancroft out of his mind as they left New Orleans and zigzagged their way north, through Nashville and Memphis, back down to Atlanta and Savannah, up to Washington DC, where they played for a week and Boomsky destroyed hats nightly.[183]

But Herrmann was slowing down. In a *Morning News* article entitled "Herrmann's Home on Wheels," the Professor announced that next season he would perform thirty weeks, instead of the current forty.[184]

Everett's Review: "Genuine Comic Talent"

M. H. Everett was in his fifth season with the Herrmanns. His work as Boomsky convulsed audiences, yet he was rarely mentioned in reviews. Critics were so spellbound by Alexander and Adelaide that all others were obscured in their incandescence. But that was only part of it. Unless he broke the law or committed some sort of outrage, it was rare for a Black person to be granted space in a mainstream newspaper.

One morning in March, as he sipped his coffee and read his reviews, Herrmann gestured M. H. over, exclaiming, "Look here. It's about you!" Alexander then read aloud from the newspaper, *Brooklyn Life*. "The negro who assists Prof. Herrmann at the Montauk is not starred on the program, but he ought to be. The man has a genuine comedic talent, and if it was not for his look of contrite and sorrowing amazement when he stumbles over and crushes the hat he has borrowed in the audience, the old trick of shooting the crushed tile to the ceiling and restoring it as good as new would lose half its effectiveness.'" [185]

For a week, M. H. walked around with his ego puffed up. He hoped Herrmann might take the hint and put his name on the program's cast list. Everett's name was already printed in the program under his crew position, "properties." But neither he nor any other assistant portraying Boomsky would ever be credited by name in Herrmann's printed program.

The Bullet Catch (Again) and Bloom's Bombshell

Herrmann took off most of April, normally one of his prime touring months. The usually social Herrmanns kept to themselves that month, due to Alexander's ill health. He was tired and needed to rest. Alexander had been suffering bouts of severe chest pain for nearly a year. He had seen several doctors. To Adelaide's frustration, most physicians pandered to Herrmann's excuses and dismissals when they brought attention to his heavy smoking. However, one doctor diagnosed him with "smoker's heart" and told him that unless he stopped smoking, he would die within two years. But like so many other smokers, Herrmann would not, or could not, give up his cigarettes and cigars.[186]

On April 27, 1896, after a month-long hiatus, Herrmann prepared to start up again with three weeks at Palmer's Theater in New York, capped off with another benefit performance of the bullet catch. But the break in his schedule proved consequential for Herrmann.

Two days before the Palmer's opening, shocking news hit the theatrical pages. Edward L. Bloom, Herrmann's manager of eight years, was defecting to a competitor—the handsome young insurance-agent-turned-magician, Frederick Bancroft. In the Eau Claire *Daily Telegram*, Bloom declared Bancroft to be "the greatest magician the world has ever seen."[187] This bridge-burning quote was particularly audacious, considering that Bloom still had three weeks remaining on his contract with Herrmann.

The Professor opened at Palmer's Theater to a reliably large and enthusiastic crowd. Herrmann's timeless appeal was summed up in the *New York Times* review of opening night at Palmer's: "While that magnetic and irresistible public entertainer who calls himself Herrmann . . . is no stranger to New-Yorkers, and his repertory of tricks of legerdemain does not grow much with years, people do not tire of him . . . Herrmann's personality is all in his favor. He suggests the occult and is also a humorist. He makes you almost shiver, and he makes you laugh in the same moment. . . . It would be trite to say that Herrmann is worth seeing. It is more to the point to say that one never gets tired of seeing him."[188]

On the final night at Palmer's, the bullet catch, overseen by Will Robinson, with all its pomp and drama, went off flawlessly. At the end of the trick, Herrmann told Boomsky to take the tray of bullets into the audience for examination. Within seconds, M. H. Everett was overwhelmed by a mob of eager souvenir seekers who snatched away all the bullets.[189] This performance raised $1,400 for the *New York Herald*'s Free Ice Fund.[190]

After one more Bullet Catch performance on June 18 to benefit the Sick Babies Fund, Herrmann ended his illness-dampened season.[191] No sooner had the Herrmanns settled in to enjoy their summer at Whitestone, than Adelaide severely sprained her foot while bicycling. She hobbled aboard the *Fra Diavolo* to spend a glorious late June boating around New York's waterways, with Alexander at the helm. Boomsky, as valet, was always close at hand, tending to the needs of Herrmann and his guests.

Up the River to Sing Sing

One lovely June day, as the *Fra Diavolo* cruised up the Hudson River, they passed Sing Sing Prison, the inspiration for Herrmann's favorite illusion. Alexander decided to dock his yacht and drop in on the warden with an offer to present a performance for the prisoners on Independence Day, a few weeks later. Or so the newspapers reported.[192] In truth, Herrmann had been seeking formal permission to perform at Sing Sing for nearly a year, and the visit was prearranged.[193]

M. H. Everett had performed the illusion Escape from Sing Sing many times. But as he stood by the towering prison walls that seemed to rise right out of the river, he wondered how anyone could ever escape such a fortress. Although the June day was balmy, M. H. suddenly felt a chill.

Prior to Herrmann, no entertainers had ever been allowed within the walls of New York's most notorious prison. With its newly constructed prison chapel, Sing Sing now had a single space that could hold all 1,400 inmates. Warden Omar V. Sage was intrigued by Herrmann, who insisted that a magic show would be good for prisoner morale. Warden Sage agreed to the Independence Day show.

All the New York newspapers publicized Herrmann's Sing Sing Prison Independence Day show. Members of the public were invited to join seven newspaper reporters who accompanied the Herrmanns and their entourage on their special 8:35 a.m. train to Sing Sing.[194] They departed Grand Central Station on Saturday, July 4, 1896, for the thirty-six-mile trip, traveling north, "up the river," along the scenic east shore of the Hudson.[195]

Herrmann's large party included Will and Dot Robinson; Adelaide's nephew Hermann Pallme and his wife; Herrmann's manager, Edward Thurnaer; music director, René Stretti; and the reporter Max Meyer from the *Omaha Bee*, who had previously traveled with and reported extensively on the Herrmanns. The name of each member of the party would be noted in nearly every review. Even Adelaide's tiny black-and-tan terrier, Fidget, was mentioned, prancing around in her orange ribbon collar with purple bells.[196] Never named in any review was "the small colored boy" noted by the *New York Times*, carrying a dress suitcase on the special train—seventeen-year-old M. H. Everett.

Sing Sing Prison was already in gala mode when the Herrmann party arrived. Warden Sage had issued a directive to the inmates just after breakfast to pick up their cell stools and march in lockstep to the new chapel, which was unfinished and still lacked seats. All but the most incorrigible prisoners were allowed to attend. A makeshift stage at one end was festooned with American flags. As they settled onto their stools, Warden Sage announced to the inmates that just for this one special Independence Day, if they behaved, they could make as much noise as they wanted.

The festivities began with music, comedy skits, and songs performed by inmates themselves before the Herrmanns arrived. The concert was still going on as the Herrmann entourage took seats in the front rows, all except Maestro Stretti, who pulled out his violin and joined the prison orchestra onstage, his finely tailored suit contrasting with the black-and-gray stripes of the ensemble.

When Herrmann took the stage, the room erupted in cheers. The many guards standing along the walls joined in. This time Adelaide was just a spectator, with tiny Fidget on her lap. Will and Dot Robinson also enjoyed the rare treat of sitting back to watch their boss. The venue was basic—just the flag-draped platform with a curtained backstage area to the side—and not suitable for large tricks or illusions. But for Herrmann that was no matter. With just one long table holding a few props at the back of the stage, and assisted by Boomsky, he entertained his bestriped audience for over an hour.

Herrmann first removed his white gloves. Suddenly they vanished! The audience cheered. The Professor then threw cards all over the room, to the very last row of the cavernous space. Eager hands grabbed for the cards spinning overhead. Over and over, Herrmann would point at a faraway inmate then shoot a card right into the man's waiting hand. The *Brooklyn Times Union* reporter noted, "Then from an empty hat, the wizard took oranges, handkerchiefs, live rabbits and about a dozen silver wheels." Boomsky's whining and complaining over the mangled handkerchief had the audience wiping away tears of laughter. The Professor then removed "eggs from the little black boy's mouth."[197]

Following Herrmann's instructions, Warden Sage had installed a runway from the stage into the audience. The magician strode out casually among the thieves, forgers, and murderers and announced, "Would some gentleman in the audience kindly loan me his silk hat?" Thunderous laughter reverberated through the chapel. "Then will somebody loan me a gold watch?" More laughter. Five of the prison's office staff volunteered their watches. A voice from the audience jabbed, "Youse fellers take long chances."[198] Herrmann spoke again. "Will some gentleman in the audience come up and hold one of these watches?" Dozens of hands shot up. As the chosen convict made his way to the stage, the wisecracks continued. "Nail down his feet!" came a shout from the corner. "Watch him!" someone yelled. "He's a slick one!" shouted another.

Herrmann asked the inmate to sit in a chair that Boomsky had placed center stage. Herrmann placed the watches in a pistol with a funnel muzzle. He handed Boomsky the gun and told him to shoot the inmate. The room fell silent and the prisoners leaned forward eagerly. They had expected the magician to produce bunnies and scarves, but a firearm pointed at one of their own, and in the hands of a Black teenager, was a shock. All eyes were riveted. When Boomsky fired, there was no report. Instead, a silk scarf printed with the word "BANG!" appeared, hanging below the gun's barrel. Relieved laughs and a few jeers rose from the audience.

Herrmann then pointed his own gun at the inmate's head and fired. This time there was a very real, very loud BANG, accompanied by shocked gasps from the crowd. When the smoke cleared, the inmate was still sitting onstage, unharmed but confused. Four of the five watches were now seen hanging from the front of his chair. Herrmann told the man he could return to his seat but stopped him as he walked away. The magician reached into the man's pocket and extracted the missing watch.[199] The prisoners howled with laughter.

For his finale, Herrmann "asked that some man would come forward who was a dead shot and knew how to load an old-fashioned horse pistol."[200] "I'm yer man," said a prisoner, smiling grimly. There was much murmuring as convicted murderer Luke Hannigan took the stage. Three bullets were passed to the audience and marked with identifying scratches. Everyone, including all seven reporters, watched Hannigan load the three marked bullets into the revolver.

"You are a sure shot?" asked the magician. The man with the pistol in his hand smiled again and nodded his head. The professor had a small plate in his hand. "When I say 'three,' fire," he said. The room suddenly went silent.

The *Brooklyn Times Union* reported, "The man took deliberate aim, his hand was perfectly steady, but his face whitened. 'One, two three!' There were three reports and flashes, and the magician had the three marked bullets on the plate. The audience went wild."[201] This ended the performance. The inmates were told to pick up their stools and were marched back to their cells. The Herrmann company was served lunch and given a tour of the prison. At 2:46 p.m. their special train departed for Grand Central Station.

Everyone agreed that the show was an enormous success. As news of Herrmann's Sing Sing performance spread, so did its mythology, with several papers reporting that he had included the illusion Escape from Sing Sing. In truth, the illusion was the one trick that Warden Sage had instructed Herrmann not to perform. Herrmann's magical Independence Day show would begin a tradition of entertainers at Sing Sing. Twenty years later Harry Houdini would perform there, by then the most famous magician in the world. But in July 1896, the young Houdini, still unknown and struggling, was by chance appearing at Herrmann's very next stop.

NOVA SCOTIA, CANADA, AND A MISSED DATE WITH HOUDINI

A few weeks after Sing Sing, the Herrmann company, including the Robinsons and M. H. Everett, boarded the SS *Olivetti* in Boston, sailing for Nova Scotia. The Herrmanns were interrupting their summer at Whitestone for a week of performances in Halifax. Herrmann had wanted to pilot the *Fra Diavolo* to Halifax, but experienced sailors warned him that the rough, unpredictable Gulf of Maine was no place for his shallow-draft pleasure yacht. As the steamship *Olivetti* lurched and rolled through the choppy sea, M. H. was grateful that Alexander had listened to reason.

Scores of people greeted the Herrmanns' ship when it docked. The annual Halifax Carnival was in full swing. As visitors poured into town, Halifax's hotels soon filled to capacity, prompting city officials to ask residents to open their homes to the overflow of guests. Even though tickets were priced at the outrageous sum of one dollar (about twenty-five dollars today), Herrmann's shows sold so fast that Manager Clark of the Academy of Music took the unheard-of step of restricting ticket sales to four tickets per person.

Just a few weeks earlier, another magic show at the same Halifax theater had failed disastrously, stranding a struggling young couple—Harry and Bess Houdini. The couple had hoped the Marco Magic Company would provide their desperately needed show business break. Instead, the company had collapsed, leaving Harry and Bess with nothing to their names but their trunk illusion. The rest of the show's properties had been seized by the sheriff.

At age twenty-two, Harry Houdini had never performed on his own. But with no money for passage back to New York, Harry and Bess now moved from town to town in Nova Scotia, hawking and performing their own full-evening show. To fill out the program leading up to their big finale—the trunk illusion Metamorphosis—Houdini manipulated cards and escaped from ropes, and Bessie sang several popular songs. Ticket sales eked out barely enough for food and shelter. When the Herrmanns arrived in Halifax, the Houdinis were vacillating between success and failure, at one point so broke they slept on the floor of a hotel lobby.[202] Harry Houdini idolized Alexander Herrmann and reportedly wrote to him asking for a job as an assistant.[203] But Houdini received no response.

Herrmann opened on July 27. Each night, the theater was packed to the rafters for the three-hour show. For Alexander and Adelaide, the week provided a welcome infusion of cash after an expensive summer of yachting and relaxing at their estate. Haligonians swooned over Alexander Herrmann. Adelaide, her foot sufficiently healed, "caused a furor" with her dances.[204] When Boomsky fell on the hat, howls of laughter shook the theater. Even with the nightly shows, the week in Halifax felt almost like a vacation. It was the most beautiful week of summer, and during the day, the city's dignitaries showed the Herrmanns around the charming parts of their city, including the magnificent Citadel Hill, with its star-shaped fortress and expansive view of the seaport city's scenic, island-dotted harbor. Boomsky accompanied the Herrmanns everywhere, perched on the back of the horse carriage or next to the driver. M. H. closed his eyes and deeply inhaled the sea air as a gentle summer breeze wafted over him. What a lovely place, he thought. Years later, a different Boomsky would fall in love with Nova

Scotia and never leave. Looking back later, M. H. Everett would mark that blissful week in Halifax as the end of an era.

EVERETT SAYS GOODBYE

A month later, on September 1, Herrmann opened his new season in Newark. As he emerged from the stage door, M. H. Everett was surprised to see Herrmann's old manager, Edward L. Bloom, standing in the shadows. Bloom no longer worked for Herrmann, so why was he there? During four years of touring with him, M. H. had learned to be wary of Bloom, whose practical jokes could be mean and his ethics questionable. Renowned as a brilliant theatrical manager, Bloom would undergo numerous arrests, lawsuits, and bankruptcies, each time returning yet again to manage top performers and productions.

Bloom motioned M. H. over. Keeping his voice low, Bloom quickly got to the point. "Come work for Bancroft at double your current salary."

Everett was startled. He had never considered leaving Herrmann. The money sounded good, though.

Bloom pressed him. He reminded Everett that Herrmann's health was poor. The Professor had missed a full month the previous spring and had already cut his new season by 25 percent. The manager appealed to M. H.'s sense of adventure. "You have had only one job. Get out and see the world! You can always come back!"

Everett turned toward Bloom, his interest now piqued. Theatrical employees moved between companies all the time. When they returned, their old colleagues gathered around to hear of their adventures. Still, M. H. loved his job and the Herrmanns. He did not want to abandon them.

Reading his mind, Bloom said, "The groom can do your part. You won't even be missed."

That stung. But Bloom was Bloom.

As M. H. hesitated, Manager Bloom delivered his zinger. Drawing close, he whispered to M. H., "You could be the Professor's spy!"

Now Everett was listening. The Robinsons had returned from their latest stint with Harry Kellar brimming with secrets. Herrmann had been delighted. Now Everett would do the same! Bloom held out a contract, and M. H. Everett signed his name as Madame Herrmann had taught him.

Bloom disappeared into the shadows. Almost instantly, M. H. began to regret his decision. He needed to talk to his boss right away. As he approached Herrmann's dressing room, his resolve faded with each step. When he walked in, Herrmann was sitting at his makeup table looking old, pale, and utterly defeated.

"Not you, too," said Herrmann. Until that moment, M. H. had not considered that Bloom had hired away other employees in addition to him. Before Everett could speak, Herrmann said, "It is alright. You are so young. Wider experience will improve you. You can always come back. There will be a job for you."

M. H. spoke, "I will be your spy."

Herrmann gave a wry chuckle. "Mr. Bloom wants you to think that Bancroft has secrets I would want. He does not. Bloom wishes you to act as *Bancroft's* spy, revealing *my* secrets to *him*."

"No, I won't!" cried M. H.

"You will make Bancroft look good, better than he really is. But no matter." Herrmann stood and extended his hand. "In the theater, we never say goodbye. We say au revoir, until we meet again."

Milton Hudson Everett felt a lump in his throat as he shook Herrmann's hand. "Au revoir, Boss."

Out in the hallway, Madame Herrmann approached from the opposite direction, her elderly Chihuahua Lily tucked under her arm. The anger in Adelaide's ice-blue eyes told M. H. that she had heard the news. M. H. wanted to flee, but there was nowhere to go. He braced himself. Madame's fits of rage were like thunderstorms, brief, intense, and violent. But this time she did not explode. She fixed her withering stare on M. H. and said just one word as she passed him. "Goodbye."

Lily craned her neck around Madame's arm and glanced back at M. H., her eyes wide and sorrowful.

Milton Hudson Everett felt stunned. At eighteen, he had known no other employer besides the kind and brilliant conjuror who had plucked him from the cotton fields. For five seasons, he had stood beside the world's greatest magician on every major stage in America. He had taken the calling cards of politicians, tycoons, and theatrical legends. He had served the Herrmanns loyally through thick and thin, with good spirits and lots of laughs. He had been more than just an employee. In a very real way, he had been part of the family. Now, suddenly, it was over, and he was on his own.

∾

CHAPTER SIX

The Master's Final Bow

Herrmann Is Hobbled

As he scrambled to replace his crew, Alexander Herrmann lurched forward. The raid by Bancroft was a huge blow. In addition, Herrmann was feeling quite ill, with increasingly frequent bouts of chest pain. Still, the fifty-two-year-old magician had no choice but to perform. Unknown to the public, Herrmann's wealth and lavish lifestyle were his biggest illusions, a house of cards, balanced as delicately as the coins he fanned at his fingertips.

Alexander Herrmann was popular his entire career, reliably filling theaters wherever he went. He earned vast sums of money, but he spent it as fast as he made it. A series of unwise investments over the years had wiped out his savings. Close friends noted that the famous magician was perpetually short of cash. Herrmann frequently asked them for loans to tide him over, loans he sometimes had to be reminded to repay. The Herrmanns' luxurious lifestyle was a constant drain. The Whitestone estate was expensive, as were the railcars, the yacht, the servants, the show horses, and all the rest. No bauble or trinket that caught Herrmann's eye went unbought. Then there was his famous generosity. Anyone in need pulled at his heartstrings and in turn caused Herrmann to pull out his pocketbook.

The engine that kept it all going was Herrmann's unfailing ability to attract paying audiences. Each autumn the cash-poor conjuror found a way to fund the start of his tour through a series of strung-together loans and mortgages on properties. As the tour progressed, the money flowed in like a yearly monsoon, only to be depleted again by the end of the following summer. This system had worked for many years. But it meant that Herrmann could not retire. If he stopped, so did the money.

With M. H. Everett's surprise departure and no time to train a new actor, Bernard Baker took on the Boomsky role. In addition to his duties as Herrmann's stablemaster and valet, Baker now fell on hats and regurgitated eggs. With his newly promoted manager, Edward Thurnaer, Herrmann played a full schedule, sticking to the Northeast, ranging between Boston and Philadelphia. Although he'd lost many crew members to Bancroft, Herrmann still had his most formidable assistants, Will and Dot Robinson, as well as Adelaide's niece and nephew, cousins Adele Dewey and John Kretschmann.[205]

This year's touring show was Herrmann's biggest production ever. The *Sunday Leader* reported that the "show takes eight men five hours to set up."[206] Despite everything, they got off to a strong start. Herrmann still packed in crowds. In Jersey City, "the house was filled from the stage to the roof."[207] At the Harlem Opera House, four hundred members of the Harlem Social Club attended en masse and presented Adelaide with a "monster" floral arrangement in the shape of the letter *H*.[208]

Onstage, Alexander was still his wonderful self. In Wilkes-Barre, Pennsylvania, the *Sunday Leader* reported that "the audience was constantly convulsed with laughter."[209] Adelaide shared in the accolades. The *Jersey City News* gushed that "Madame Herrmann comes very near carrying off the lion's share of the honors."[210] Madame revealed that she would soon debut a new dance—"la danse des nuages"—which she said would be "like rolling in clouds."[211] Herrmann announced that he had accepted a future tour of Mexico.[212]

At the end of September, the company joyously welcomed many new members when Madame Herrmann's St. Bernard, Cora, gave birth to thirteen puppies. According to the *Butte Miner*, "It is the magician's lucky number, and both Mr. and Mrs. Herrmann look upon the event as a lucky omen."[213] However, hanging over everyone was the specter of Alexander's ill health—his hacking cough, his difficulty in catching his breath, his chest-clutching angina attacks.

Unwisely, Herrmann had skipped a few payments on his yacht, *Fra Diavolo*, knowing he could easily catch up in a month or two. On October 21, in New Haven, just before showtime, Herrmann's entire show was seized by the sheriff on a warrant obtained by Ed Stokes, the yacht's previous owner. As deputies assembled and company members grew frantic, Herrmann and his manager settled with Stokes, just prior to curtain time.[214] Herrmann funded the payment to Stokes by mortgaging his life insurance policies, risky for a man in such ill health. But the season was young, theaters were full, and the money spigot was open.[215] Herrmann would be out of debt by year's end.

BANCROFT HAS BOOMSKY

With Milton Hudson Everett at his side, Frederick Bancroft opened his second professional season in late September 1896, in Norfolk, Virginia, a month later than Alexander Herrmann. At the first rehearsal, M. H. spotted familiar faces in the large company. Edward Bloom stood out. Now eighteen years old, M. H. tried to avoid Bloom's line of sight, lest the famously tactless manager launch into the story of the barefoot boy from the cotton fields. Shuffling papers in the corner was William Cubitt, Herrmann's longtime business manager, with his wife and small daughter looking on. M. H. nodded to a man kneeling by the footlights—the electrician who had operated the calcium lights for Adelaide Herrmann's serpentine dances. As the company members bustled about, M. H. recognized several others from Herrmann's business staff and stage crew.[216]

Frederick Bancroft began his show by descending a giant staircase.

Bancroft's elaborate stage settings elicited gasps from his audiences.

Bancroft's troupe was even bigger than Herrmann's. Everett's pulse quickened when he realized that more than half of them were young, pretty women. He also noted four small Black teens among the men heaving and hauling Bancroft's trunks, hampers, and weird electrical paraphernalia into the theater.

Everett had wondered how the newcomer Bancroft would pull off a full-length evening of magic. Alexander Herrmann filled an entire hour with his two thirty-minute solo sets, which bookended each show. Alone onstage, with Boomsky at the ready, Herrmann teased and played with his charmed audience, performing his brilliant tricks honed over decades. Clearly, a beginner like Frederick Bancroft did not possess Herrmann's mastery. Nobody did. As the crew scurried around, from the hampers emerged stunning, hand-painted backdrops and drapes, as well as dozens of dazzling costumes trimmed with satin, velvet, feathers, and fur. From what M. H. could see, there were no big illusions being unloaded and assembled, but the crates disgorged enough furniture and stage decor to fill a museum. Notably absent was the menagerie of animals that had accompanied the Herrmanns. M. H. spotted crates containing just a few bunnies and pigeons, but no dogs, geese, ducks, or squawking parrots.

Everett directed the cases with magic properties and Bancroft's wardrobe trunk to the star's dressing room. As he had done so many times for Herrmann, he hung up the magician's costumes and placed his toiletries case by the makeup mirror. M. H. unpacked Bancroft's magic cases with utmost care and discovered that he was already familiar with most of the contents, including gimmicked billiard balls and special holders for cards, coins, and scarves. He recognized the props for the rice, orange, and cone trick, a specialty of Herrmann's in which an orange and a pile of rice changed places underneath two metal cones. M. H. confidently set up the pocket tricks and mechanical gimmicks and laid them out just as he had for Herrmann. The few props he did not recognize he carefully set aside.

The stage manager called for the specialty performers to take the stage. Hiring variety acts was a smart move, M. H. thought. Good specialty acts would liven up and fill out the show and cover up where Bancroft was lacking. As the performers rehearsed their acts, M. H. was impressed. A Miss Madison performed a serpentine dance, "Spirits of the Storm," that a *Norfolk Virginian* reviewer would later find "very very beautiful."[217] One dared not look away as Satsuma, a Japanese juggler, sent razor-edged swords and knives spinning through the air. Some troupe members exchanged doubtful looks as the new business manager's tiny daughter, Miss We We Cubitt, bounded onto the stage. The scent of nepotism kept expectations low. But when the pianist started playing and the sassy toddler danced adorably, smiling and blowing kisses, everyone smelled a hit.

The company snapped to attention as the star of the show, Frederick Bancroft, swept in. All eyes fastened onto his extraordinarily good-looking face. Blond and blue-eyed with chiseled features, Bancroft's appearance inspired frequent admiring commentary. The *Detroit Free Press* called him "the handsomest man that ever waved a wand."[218] The *Houston Post* observed, "He is quite a beau in the manner of dress. . . . He is five feet nine inches tall, is well proportioned, and has a graceful carriage."[219]

Bancroft was a young upstart from rugged Minnesota who had pursued a successful business career. M. H. Everett's new employer could not have been more different from the urbane, debonair, multilingual Herrmann, who had descended from a European magic dynasty. The thirty-year-old Bancroft had no theatrical background but had studied magic since childhood. Up until launching his spectacular production the previous year, his performing experience had been limited to church socials and fundraisers around Eau Claire, Wisconsin.

To Bancroft, his inexperience mattered not a whit. While others struggled and starved for years trying to make it in show business, Frederick Bancroft simply bought his way to the top. He had not come from money but had built his fortune selling life insurance.[220] He also earned windfall profits from real estate investments. Some whispered that Bancroft had a big financial backer, a relative in the lumber business. In addition, Frederick Bancroft held the registered patents for three inventions. He also had a gift for writing, as well as formidable marketing instincts. M. H. Everett would observe that Bancroft was not a spendthrift like Herrmann. Although the businessman invested heavily in his show, he lived modestly and counted every penny.

As they rehearsed, M. H. sized up his new boss. The newcomer's sleight-of-hand skills were adequate, though not masterful. Like Harry Kellar, he relied more on mechanical tricks, which Bancroft executed quite well. M. H. privately thought Bancroft should talk less. The magician sorely wanted to be funny like his hero Herrmann, but with his stiff, poorly timed delivery, Bancroft's jokes elicited polite chuckles at best. The previous season, an *Evening Star* reviewer had noted, "Mr. Bancroft does not improve his magic by the wit and humor he introduces into his talk."[221] Nonetheless, M. H. could not help but admire how cleverly the novice magician distracted attention from his shortcomings by surrounding himself with breathtaking stage settings and beautiful women. Everyone agreed that Bancroft's greatest talent was dreaming up these wondrous displays. Even hard-to-impress theater managers reported that Bancroft's show was "spectacular."[222] Each of his three acts opened to a different elaborately detailed scene.

The audience gasped when the curtain opened upon Act One, "The Magician's Palace," with its fantastical painted backdrop, ornate statuary, and tables hand-carved into the shapes of elephants, devils, and snakes. Dressed in elegant evening wear, swirling a satin-lined cape, Bancroft made a dramatic entrance descending a grand staircase at the rear of the stage, which required nearly an entire baggage car to transport it between theaters. Waiting at the bottom of the stairs were two pages, played by two ladies in lavender satin court costumes and powdered wigs. M. H. Everett, dressed as a footman, stood nearby. As Bancroft approached, all three assistants bowed to the magician.

M. H. Everett played a larger role in Bancroft's show than he ever had in Herrmann's. Now he was an actor as well, with many lines to speak in Bancroft's elaborate magical dramas. As chief assistant, he was onstage most of the show.

Not content to steal just Herrmann's manager and crew, Bancroft also purloined much of Herrmann's magic. M. H. Everett had performed the first trick of the show hundreds of times with his old boss. Standing far apart, Bancroft and his assistant each displayed a carafe of liquid. The magician's contained black ink while Everett's held clear water. The two of them simultaneously dropped handkerchiefs over the carafes then whipped them away to reveal Everett's carafe now full of ink and Bancroft's holding clear water and several swimming goldfish. Bancroft added his own twist for other Herrmann routines, especially those involving Herrmann's former Boomsky. While Herrmann had played on racial stereotypes in a lighthearted way, Bancroft was far more pointed. The hat trick began exactly as with Herrmann, with the borrowed hat and the multiplying coins. But after M. H. Everett fell on the hat, the pieces of the hat were wrapped in newspaper. Bancroft opened the package to discover "a large negro doll."[223]

Bancroft asked an audience member for a handkerchief, which he stuffed into the barrel of a pistol. The magician rolled a long candle in paper and handed the paper tube to M. H. The magician then aimed the pistol at his assistant. Staring down the barrel of the gun always made M. H. nervous, even though he knew the stage pistol fired only blanks. He held his breath. BANG! The shot was earsplitting. Bancroft snatched and broke the cylinder of paper. The candle was gone! In its place was the borrowed handkerchief. Bancroft turned his assistant around. There was the candle, hanging from Everett's back, "instead of his golden hair," quipped Bancroft. The audience applauded warmly.

Bancroft picked up a basket and displayed it to the audience, saying that it was full of eggs. But when he looked inside, his face fell. Puzzled, Bancroft showed the basket was empty. Then he fixed his gaze on his assistant. Hanging his head, M. H. confessed, "I ate them." Bancroft displayed an empty stew pan and placed it on a stand. The magician thumped his assistant on the back. As he had done thousands of times since age thirteen, M. H. Everett puffed his cheeks, clenched his eyes, and popped an egg into view at his lips. Over and over, Bancroft removed another egg from his assistant's mouth and put it in the stew pan. Bancroft tossed a match into the pan. Flames shot three feet into the air as Bancroft slammed down the lid. When he lifted the cover, the pan contained three large cooing pigeons.

Act Two of Bancroft's show, the "Sultan's Visitor," opened to another magnificent scene. The Sultan, with a long beard and scepter, was played by a male assistant. Ladies in harem costumes reclined on couches. Behind the Sultan stood four boys in grass skirts, waving long fans. These were the same teens who had earlier loaded in the heavy equipment crates. In the drama, M. H. Everett played a slave—a speaking role—in a convoluted rendition of the Scheherazade tale, in which the namesake character did a club swinging act. Bancroft played an old man who transformed into a young, handsome hero. None of it made much sense, but the overwhelming jumble of exoticism was impressively grand.

Act Three opened onto an exquisite fairy-tale world, full of costumed imps, pixies, and butterflies who watched admiringly as Bancroft performed his final set of tricks. Although Everett had already fallen on a borrowed hat in Act One, he stumbled again in Act Three, this time dropping and smashing a plate holding borrowed watches, which Bancroft then restored. Reviewers liked Bancroft's extravaganza. And they liked his youthful energy. "His face lights up and his eyes sparkle," gushed the *Atlanta Constitution* review.[224] Beyond the stunning scenery, the dancers, and the specialty acts, Bancroft himself was "the life and soul of the show."[225]

That fall, as Alexander Herrmann played the Northeast and Bancroft worked his way South, critics constantly compared the newcomer to his famous rival. As the *Savannah Morning News* expounded, "One cannot help realizing that at last the redoubtable Frenchman has found a foeman worthy of his steel. And still, two entirely different types of men and style of entertainment could scarcely be conceived. While Herrmann looks like the accepted pictures of Mephistopheles, Bancroft has the look of a gentleman of leisure who is on the stage simply for the purpose of entertaining his friends with no idea of pecuniary recompense. While Herrmann's stronghold consists of what might be termed a comedy vein, Bancroft's work is of the 'kid glove' order. In pure slight [*sic*] of hand work, he is the peer of any magician."[226]

Bancroft borrowed ideas and tricks from both Herrmann and Kellar.[227] He imitated Herrmann's sleight-of-hand with cards and billiard balls. However, Bancroft's easygoing presentation aligned more with fellow homespun American Harry Kellar. Unlike either of his idols, Bancroft relied on splendid tableaux and variety acts, performed by attractive women, to supplement his meager repertoire.

Although Frederick Bancroft had studied and practiced magic for years, rival magicians resented his self-financed beginner's success and his stolen tricks. Bancroft's appearance out of nowhere, suddenly headlining in major theaters, was a bitter pill for young Houdini and his wife, Bess, who were still nobodies after years in the business. Frederick Bancroft had never even carried his own luggage, much less had his act seized by a sheriff—a fate experienced by both Herrmann and Houdini, and many more. Moreover, with so little experience, how could Bancroft possibly give a polished performance? Jealous competitors portrayed Frederick Bancroft as a third-rate Herrmann imitator who did shopworn tricks for largely unimpressed audiences.[228]

But newspaper reviews told a different story. Critics found his show fresh and original. Audiences liked the pomp and spectacle. In Washington, DC, the *Morning Times* reported, "Bancroft is a very clever prestidigitateur and completely mystified the audience with his clever tricks, many of which are his own invention and have never been used by any other entertainer."[229] Even the critics were fooled. Bancroft's "inventions" were in fact Herrmann's old tricks, but Bancroft restaged them so that audiences did not recognize them. Night after night, as M. H. Everett stood on the same stages as he had with Herrmann, assisting in the same tricks, he was surprised at how easily some paint and gaily colored trim could dupe an audience into believing they were seeing a breathtaking new trick. With Manager Bloom firmly at the helm, the tour got off to a strong start, first following Herrmann's well-established southern route from Atlanta on to New Orleans then Texas. But before New Orleans, they landed for a week in Savannah.

At the Savannah Theater, where M. H. Everett had performed with Herrmann many times, Bancroft played a practical joke at the expense of the Black stagehands and loading crew. The theater's balcony was open to Black patrons, and the theater manager often allowed his workers to go up to watch the show when they were not needed.

"Diablo," Bancroft's talking skull, was a highlight of his performance. The skull did not actually speak. Instead, the skull was placed on an open table. Bancroft would talk to it by calling out the letters of the alphabet one by one, much like a conversation with a Ouija board. The skull's jaw would clatter alarmingly on its solid glass platform when a certain letter was reached. Thus, the skull spelled out a ghastly story of how he had been murdered in Boston.

One day Bancroft noticed a commotion in the balcony and saw several men run for the doors. It was the Black stagehands, and when they came back down to resume their duties, they huddled around discussing the eeriness of the talking skull. Bancroft decided that it would be fun to frighten them even more.[230]

In those early days of electricity, Bancroft incorporated his skills as an inventor and his knowledge of electricity into his magic acts. He carried a full outfit of electric lighting apparatus and was one of the earliest magicians to employ electricity in the workings of his tricks. At that time, few people knew that a small current of electricity passed through resistance coils would produce a sound like "the moan of a person in great distress."[231] On Bancroft's orders, his stage carpenter fastened resistance coils to the bottom of two of his trunks.

When the crew arrived to carry the equipment out of the theater, the electricity was turned on, "and there was emitted from the trunks a blood curdling, sepulchral sound, like a wail from the tomb, whereupon Bancroft, assuming great anger, exclaimed in loud tones to the property man: 'There you go again! You forgot to strap those skulls down to the bottom of the trunks, and they are raising merry h-ll. Don't you hear them?'" The stagehands "bolted from the stage in a wild stampede, falling over one another in their mad effort to get out of the house."[232] M. H. stood back and chuckled. As a veteran showman, he was well used to backstage practical jokes, often at the expense of superstitious African Americans.

Bancroft slowly gained popularity, attracting respectable, though not full houses. Critics praised the show and often mentioned Bancroft's assistants. "He is attended by two young ladies prettily dressed as pages and by a colored boy attired as a footman."[233]

However, things didn't always go smoothly. A reviewer from the *Fort Wayne News* witnessed a performance riddled with "inexcusable technical problems."[234] Lucky for Bancroft, his eighteen-year-old assistant, after five seasons with Herrmann, was unfazed by errors, malfunctions, and other inevitable midshow surprises. Everett's trove of magic knowledge was put to constant use. He was often able to save Bancroft's tricks from failure with his repertoire of "outs," the magicians' term for methods of covering up mistakes, with the audience none the wiser.

Bancroft's company spent the fall of 1896 touring the South and Midwest. In early December, in Port Huron, Michigan, they encountered the sad vestiges of Robinson's Circus. The small company had just gone out of business, forcing the immediate sale of their main attraction, a majestic-yet-bedraggled African lion named Wallacker. The creature was old, toothless, and clearly terrified, cringing in the corner of its cage.[235] Standing next to the caged beast, M. H. Everett could barely believe a cat could be so big. He chuckled thinking of how much the Herrmanns would love to own a lion. As Frederick Bancroft and Manager Bloom inspected the huge creature, the glint in their eyes told M. H. that soon he would be traveling with the king of beasts. Bancroft ordered the construction of a new illusion to feature Wallacker. A few weeks later, a gigantic crate arrived containing Bancroft's new illusion, Leonii.

At the first rehearsal, M. H. saw that his boss was in over his head. Bancroft had never performed an illusion of any sort, much less one featuring an animal of this size. Teaser ads promised an instant magical transformation of a lion into a woman, who would then transform back into a lion. In reality, Leonii was creakingly slow and far from magical. When M. H. saw the poster for the illusion, he laughed. The open-sided, thin-bottomed cage illustrated on the poster had nowhere to hide a lion, unlike the actual clunky illusion cage, which backed right up to the stage curtain. It was obvious to everyone where the lion came from. An *Oshkosh Northwestern* critic was not impressed. "The so-called illusion 'Leonii,' as shown in this city, had but little merit and could hardly be called an illusion in any sense of the term."[236] Despite Leonii's bad reviews, a live lion was a major draw.[237] In every new city, starting in Oshkosh, then Madison, Wisconsin, Wallacker was put on display in a downtown store window on the day of the show. Townspeople could come view the lion all day, but one o'clock feeding time was always most popular.[238]

M. H. noticed how differently Wallacker was treated compared to the Herrmanns' performing animals, who were considered beloved family members. Wallacker received no such kindness, as he was prodded, poked, and whipped into compliance. During the performance, Bancroft repeatedly fired his gun near the lion's head to provoke a reaction. The magician also electrified the bottom of his cage, shocking Wallacker to make him roar.[239] M. H. felt sorry for the poor creature.[240] He often thought about the Herrmanns, wondering how their tour was going. He missed both Herrmann and Madame. He truly missed Alexander's twinkle, that little spark between them just before Herrmann launched into his next mischief. M. H. sighed. Frederick Bancroft had never once looked him directly in the eye.

Bancroft is believed to be the first magician to use a big cat in an illusion. After Bancroft's death, a reworked version of the illusion, renamed The Lion's Bride, was made famous by the Great Lafayette.

OMINOUS SIGNS

By November 1896, Adelaide was growing alarmed over Alexander's health. But illness would not keep Herrmann from the world's largest horse show at Madison Square Garden, which coincided with his two-week run at New York's Palmer's Theater. Herrmann entered his two finest saddle horses. But amid overwhelming competition, the Professor won no ribbons. On a whim, during an intermission, Herrmann leapt aboard his four-in-hand carriage and charged his horses into the arena, intending to rouse the crowd with one galloping circuit. However, Herrmann had given Bernard Baker insufficient time to prepare his rig. Within seconds, the horses separated from the carriage and ran away. Herrmann let go of the reins barely in time to avoid being pulled flying from the front of the carriage. Herrmann's embarrassing accident at the horse show was front-page news the next day.[241]

In early December, the Herrmanns finally set forth from their home environs, with dates scheduled through Pennsylvania and western New York state leading up to their traditional Christmas week in Chicago. By now it was clear even to audiences that Alexander was not well. A reviewer from the *Scranton Tribune* observed, "Herrmann has aged and his face has grown several shades paler."[242] From Scranton, the Herrmanns crossed into New York, playing Elmira, Oswego, and Syracuse before landing for two days in Rochester.

Upon arriving in Rochester on Tuesday afternoon, December 15, Alexander accepted an invitation to visit the State Industrial School, a reformatory for boys. He was feeling quite unwell, but he would not think of disappointing the children. He thought his appearance was to be just a quick visit, but when he arrived, he found the entire school assembled in the auditorium, expecting a full show. Herrmann quickly sent word to the theater, and soon his crew arrived with props and apparatus, including, according to the *Rochester Democrat*, "a very black man carrying a cage of white doves."[243] After his performance, in typical Herrmann fashion,

Alexander invited the entire school to attend the matinee the following afternoon as his guests. The crew then raced back to the Academy of Music to quickly set up for that evening's performance.

The next day, Alexander was feeling even worse, but he pushed his way through his two shows at the Lyceum. Between performances, he encountered a stranded theater company. They had played the previous week to empty houses and now had no funds to get home to New York. Herrmann bought train tickets for the entire group and gave them some spending money. And since their train wasn't leaving until late that night, he also gave them passes for his evening performance.

After the evening show, the Genesee Valley Club threw a supper reception for Herrmann. He considered canceling, but again, he did not want to disappoint his fans. As always, the gathering was just an excuse for another performance by Herrmann, who regaled his hosts with close-up magic and stories. By the time they escorted him to his railcar at midnight, Herrmann was both ill and exhausted. Yet still, the inveterate host could not let them leave without giving a tour of the magnificent palace car as well as the horse and carriage car.

DEATH ON THE RAILS

The next morning, the train sailed toward their next destination, Bradford, Pennsylvania. After breakfast, Adelaide took the opportunity to wash her hair. As she pulled back the bath curtain, she was surprised to see Alexander lying on her bed. He was very pale and said he was having trouble breathing. She helped him to his own compartment. On her orders, his valet, Bernard Baker, brought him water and bicarbonate of soda. Alexander took one swallow, his arms dropped, and he lost consciousness. The train was stopped in Ashford Junction just long enough to wire ahead to Ellicottville, where a physician, Dr. Johnson, boarded the train.

The Rochester *Democrat and Chronicle* reported that "Dr. Johnson did everything in his power to relieve his patient, but before reaching

Salamanca, the great conjurer and magician expired, resting in the arms of his grief-stricken wife."[244]

Herrmann's last words to Adelaide were, "It looks like I'm not going to get over this. Take the company back to New York. Be certain of it."[245]

At Salamanca, New York, the Herrmanns' cars were detached from the rest of the train. A railway worker reported that "his wife and assistants were almost beside themselves with grief."[246] Adelaide, in her shock and distress, was grateful to have her niece Adele Dewey by her side. As Dewey and Dot tried to comfort Adelaide, Will Robinson wired out the news of Alexander's death, and Manager Thurnaer arranged for their train cars to be rerouted back to New York.

When the stunned company arrived at Jersey City at eight o'clock the next morning, a large group of friends stood waiting at the station. Adelaide did not want to leave the railcar, which was parked at the Erie Railroad depot. Friends implored her to come stay with them, and she finally agreed. As the company made their way to New York, newsboys from coast to coast shouted the front-page headline of the day, crying "Herrmann is Dead!"

Herrmann's funeral was a grand affair, overflowing with grief-stricken friends and admirers. Rabbi Silverman of the Temple Emanu-El conducted the religious rites, and Chas. H. Heyzer led a simple Masonic Service. A sea of standing floral arrangements blocked many attendees' view of the speakers. As reported in the *New York Times*, "The hall was crowded to the doors, and on the marble steps that lead to the street a dense gathering stood. The sidewalks, the street and the elevated railroad stairs were blocked with humanity. Men of wealth were there and men of fame, managers and owners of theatres, actors and actresses whose names are loved by the public, and side by side with them sat servants from the magician's Whitestone home, colored people who have been his servants and beneficiaries on his travels, poor people who have partaken of his bounty."[247]

At the end of the service, the casket was opened to allow a final look at the great magician. The mourners included his "colored assistants and

Whitestone staff." A special train carried Herrmann's casket to Woodlawn Cemetery in the Bronx, where it was interred in a temporary vault. In the spring, when the ground thawed, Alexander Herrmann would be buried in the family plot next to Adelaide's mother, Adele Scarsez.

Adelaide Herrmann places flowers on her mother's grave at Woodlawn Cemetery in the Bronx. Alexander Herrmann's grave is on the left.

Consumed with grief and utterly exhausted, Adelaide retreated to the home of friends. But urgent decisions loomed, and the clock was ticking. Within days, Madame Herrmann was plotting her next move.

~

Interlude

Bancroft's Company Gets the News

Bancroft's company was in Michigan when word of Alexander Herrmann's death reached them. Herrmann's old crew members were devastated, none more so than M. H. Everett. He was stricken by the news. His performer's grit, developed over many years, kept him from falling apart onstage that night. He regretted being unable to attend Alexander's funeral. When a sympathy card for Madame Herrmann went around the Bancroft company, M. H. wished he could write more than just his signature.

Frederick Bancroft responded to Herrmann's passing in a respectful interview in the *Oshkosh Northwestern*. "Bancroft states that he was intimately acquainted with Herrmann, the dead magician. 'I deeply regret his death,' said he, 'as no one realizes perhaps more than I do that the world has lost a great master.'"[248]

Manager Edward Bloom, on the other hand, seized the opportunity to advance his young American client over the dead European master with a statement to a newsman from the Waterloo, Iowa, *Courier*: "The king is dead. Long live the king!" He finished with a parting sting, "America for Americans!"[249] Bloom's callous remarks were condemned within the tight-knit theatrical community. Yet Bloom stood by them.

The *Detroit Free Press* reported that "Bloom credits himself with all of magic's best catch phrases."[250]

Bancroft's crew had little time to mourn their old boss. The company had its hands full with the addition of Wallacker the lion, who had to be kept fed and safely contained. And soon after Herrmann's death, Manager Bloom fell seriously ill. It took him weeks to recover. Then at the end of December, Frederick Bancroft's mother-in-law died.

Battling winter weather, the massive production lurched across the Midwest. Each day, M. H. Everett and the rest of the crew unloaded trunks and hampers and set up illusions, props, set decorations, backdrops, furniture, lights, electrical equipment, and Bancroft's massive staircase. The cast set up their dressing rooms, unpacking dozens of costumes, wigs, headpieces, accessories, and shoes. After the show, the company packed up, performing the entire operation in reverse, only to repeat it all over again the next day, and the day after that.

They traveled in three rented railcars, one for the company, and two for baggage.[251] In the company car, Bancroft and Bloom occupied private staterooms. The rest of the troupe slept in rows of upper and lower berths separated only by curtains, creating easy opportunity for the youthful road troupe's inevitable liaisons. Spending every moment together, the company grew close, laughing and joking their way through the hard work and grueling travel.

Newspaper reviews were mixed. The audience responded to Bancroft with "generous applause," but compared to Herrmann or Kellar, "Bancroft was not as satisfactory," although his scenery did outrank that of the two great magicians. As often happens with magic shows, reviewers frequently liked the juggler the best.[252]

For the first two months of 1897, Bancroft hauled his massive show, Wallacker included, through small cities in Missouri, Kansas, Nebraska, and Iowa. It was the same winter route that M. H. Everett had played during his first season with the Herrmanns, six years earlier. Three months after Alexander Herrmann's death, the Bancroft company had the eerie experience of playing at the Lyceum in Rochester, the site of Herrmann's final show. All of Herrmann's former employees had worked there previously with the great master. For M. H. Everett, standing there onstage next to Bancroft felt surreal and unnerving. Everett remained very shaken by Herrmann's death. He tried to keep up a good front for his colleagues, but at night his pillow was wet with tears.

News traveled fast in the theater world, and gossip spread through the Bancroft company. M. H. learned that Madame Herrmann had reopened the Herrmann show just a month after Alexander's death. To draw a crowd, Adelaide had performed the bullet catch at the Metropolitan Opera House, just as Alexander had done four years earlier. M. H. wished he had seen that. He could hardly imagine Adelaide performing the dangerous stunt. She had always acted so fearful when Alexander did it. Now the big Herrmann show was back on the road with Alexander's twenty-nine-year-old nephew in the leading role. Léon Herrmann was said to be the spitting image of his uncle Alexander as well as a brilliant sleight-of-hand artist. But word was Léon was stiff onstage, and his French-accented English was almost impossible to understand. Will Robinson told everyone who would listen that Herrmann's nephew was a dolt and was impossible to coach. M. H. wondered how Bernard Baker was dealing with all of this.

In the spring, Bancroft's touring schedule fell off. He played a few isolated shows in upstate New York in March. Several upcoming performances were canceled, and the season petered out with a whimper.[253] Bancroft returned to Saint Paul for the summer to resume his life insurance business. Jobless for the first time in six years, M. H. Everett had time to visit his family in Georgia. M. H. was overjoyed to see his parents and siblings. Because of him, his family no longer had to pick cotton. His parents, Ben and Leitha, now worked as cooks at their own tiny restaurant. Over the next decade, the Everett family would leave Georgia and join the Great Migration northward.

BANCROFT'S TRAGIC END

When Frederick Bancroft's tour started up again at the end of August 1897, Herrmann's former Boomsky, M. H. Everett, joined him again.[254] So did Wallacker the lion.

Expectations were high for Bancroft's heavily promoted New York debut at the Harlem Opera House on Saturday, August 28. As M. H. Everett stood onstage behind the closed curtain, he heard a large, animated crowd filling the house. For a moment, he was fifteen-year-old Hutchin, standing next to Alexander Herrmann on that same stage, watching Madame Herrmann nearly explode with rage over Alexander's infatuation with serpentine dancer Loie Fuller. Suddenly Everett's keen nose for trouble yanked him into the present. Nervous backstage whispers spread the news. Something was wrong with Frederick Bancroft.

Everett ran to his boss's dressing room where Bancroft sat listless and pale, his usual spark and swagger gone. The orchestra played the overture, and the magician slowly rose to his feet, summoned his strength, and walked toward the stage. Bancroft remained ill for the entire week, yet each night he somehow pulled himself together to perform, just as Herrmann had done. As his worried company swirled around him, Bancroft impressed them with his steely resolve—a true showman after all. The audience never suspected. An astute theater manager noted that Bancroft's voice was weak but blamed performance nerves.[255] When the closing night curtain came down, everyone in the company exhaled with relief. Their next performance, in Delaware, was five days off, plenty of time for Bancroft to rest and recover.

On Thursday, September 9, a full house eagerly awaited Bancroft's opening at the Bijou Theater in Wilmington, Delaware. Manager Bloom had spent lavishly on advertising, and local newspapers had responded in kind with flattering teaser articles. Just that day, the *Morning News* had declared that "Bancroft has practically taken the place of Herrmann in the public eye."[256] But on opening night, as the audience sat waiting, curtain time came and went. The orchestra played the overture and then another tune. Yet the curtain did not open. More minutes passed. The orchestra played on as the audience murmured impatiently.

Meanwhile, the scene backstage was utter chaos. At showtime, Frederick Bancroft had failed to emerge from his dressing room. Manager Bloom entered to find the star burning with fever and doubled over with cramps, clearly unable to perform. The quick-thinking Bloom emerged, clapped his hands, and called, "Places!" As the cast and crew exchanged bewildered looks and scrambled to their positions, Edward Bloom marched onstage in front of the curtain and addressed the audience. Apologizing for the delay, Bloom explained that a carload of Bancroft's special magic equipment was held up in transit and had not arrived. Sadly, the magician would be unable to perform that evening and the performance was postponed. Tonight's tickets would be honored at tomorrow's performance. In the meantime, he invited the audience to feast their eyes on a preview of Bancroft's wonderful show. The curtain opened and, as always, the scene of Bancroft's magnificent Palace of Magic drew gasps. M. H. Everett and the two female pages in their shiny satin costumes stood before the majestic staircase, awaiting the magician's grand entrance. But Bancroft did not appear. Instead, the curtain closed, and after a brief concert by the theater's orchestra, the audience went home.[257]

The next night, Friday, September 10, was quite hot, yet once again the theater was full. This time, the curtain rose without delay and Frederick Bancroft appeared at the top of his staircase to warm applause. Normally, he marched confidently to the stage, twirling his cape. That night, the magician gingerly picked his way down the steps, revealing from the start that he was not well.[258] Yet the audience stuck with him. Bancroft gave them everything he had, and they rewarded him with fervent applause. As the show progressed, Bancroft became weaker and less steady. By the end of the performance, the magician was hanging onto tables just to stay standing. M. H. Everett moved closer to his boss, ready to catch him if he fell. But Bancroft somehow made it to the end, rendering a performance that, according to the *Evening Journal*, "has never been surpassed in this city."[259]

Thoroughly spent, Bancroft staggered offstage and collapsed in a heap. On the orders of his physician, the rest of the week's shows were canceled and rescheduled for the following week.[260] As the tour ground to a halt, M. H. Everett and the rest of the company were suddenly at loose ends. Worried and anxious, they awaited news. Over the weekend the magician's condition worsened. Bancroft's fever rose to 104 degrees, and he was diagnosed with typhoid fever. Manager Bloom was forced to cancel scheduled performances in Virginia and North Carolina. Gradually Bancroft's fever came down, and he appeared to be improving.[261] On Monday, the *Philadelphia Enquirer* announced that the magician was at Clayton House in Philadelphia recovering from nervous prostration.[262] The *Morning News* stated that he would resume his run in Wilmington that Thursday.[263] On Wednesday, the *Daily Republican* confirmed that Bancroft would be well enough to perform the following night.[264] Indeed, on Thursday, the morning newspapers advertised Bancroft's rescheduled performances would begin that night and continue through Saturday.[265]

But when Bancroft again took the stage at Wilmington's Bijou Theater on Thursday evening, he did not look well at all. He was pale, his voice was weak, and he remained unsteady on his feet. As Bancroft's large company gathered around their boss, M. H. Everett smiled at the audience and desperately pretended nothing was wrong. But gossip began spreading around town, and ticket sales dropped. The theater manager published a statement denying that Bancroft was sick and assured that Saturday's shows would go on.[266] Though feverish and practically stumbling, the magician somehow forced himself through his final Wilmington shows. Desperately hoping that he would improve, the company boarded a train for South Carolina.[267]

In Charleston, on Tuesday, September 22, the magician made it through the show but collapsed immediately following the performance.

He was taken to a hospital where his condition worsened. Urgent telegrams were sent to his immediate family. On Friday, his wife, Eva Bancroft, left for Charleston, as did Mr. Bloom, who was not traveling with the company. Mrs. Bancroft arrived on Sunday, September 27, but she was met with devastating news. She was too late. Her thirty-one-year-old husband, Frederick Bancroft, had died a few hours earlier.

Bancroft's death was a great shock to the magic world but especially to the many friends of the young magician in his home communities of Saint Paul, Minnesota, and Eau Claire, Wisconsin. Unlike the financially irresponsible Herrmann, the insurance-agent-turned-magician left his widow and young son, Herbert, a life insurance policy in the amount of $50,000. Frederick's grief-stricken father, Edward Bancroft, traveled to Charleston from his home in New York to claim his son's body. Frederick Bancroft was buried at Greenwood Cemetery in Brooklyn.[268]

At Bancroft's untimely death, his rivals rushed in to sculpt his legacy, portraying him in magic books and periodicals as a failed, embittered Herrmann imitator, ignoring the innovations that would inspire Bancroft's successors to create grand-scale magic extravaganzas featuring beautiful women and big cats. As a final indignity to Frederick Bancroft and his grieving family, two theatrical newspapers—the *New York Clipper* and the *New York Dramatic Mirror*—printed an obituary that falsely stated that Bancroft's real name was Bronson and that he was a dentist. For the next 125 years, every article about Bancroft printed in magicians' publications would repeat these untruths, skewing the memory of Frederick Bancroft.

With Bancroft's passing, M. H. Everett and the rest of the company were suddenly unemployed. Manager Edward Bloom obtained the rights to Bancroft's properties, and just a few weeks after Bancroft's death, Bloom signed on another performer to take over Bancroft's show, none other than Herrmann's old friend Henry Dixey.[269] A ten-year contract falling in his lap was lucky timing for Dixey. The comedian's own show was failing, and Dixey was scheduled to appear in bankruptcy court in

Indianapolis a few days later.[270] Dixey performed Bancroft's show over the next few months, but his heart wasn't in it. Just five months into his ten-year contract, the *Washington Times* of April 17, 1897, announced that Dixey would cease as a magician at the end of the season, noting, "Apparently Mr. Dixey is not a wiz."

None of Dixey's woes affected M. H. Everett. Immediately after Bancroft's death, M. H. had received a telegram from Will Robinson with a job offer from the Herrmann the Great Company, at that time in San Francisco. M. H. had caught the next train west.

∾

Act Two

Boomsky with Herrmann's Successors

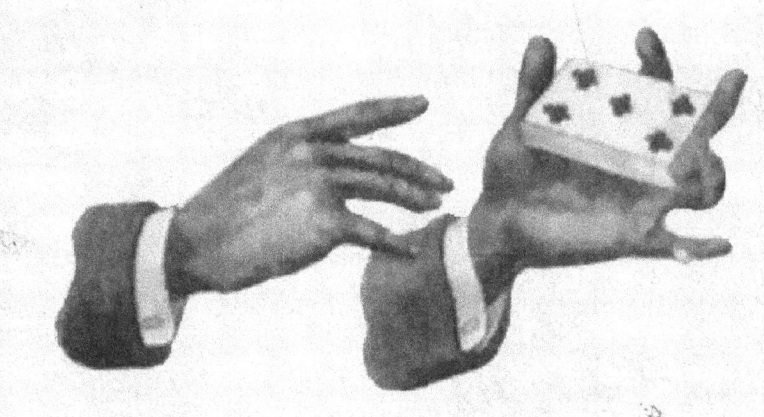

Three-sheet lithograph from the third and final season of the Herrmann the Great Company.

CHAPTER SEVEN

The Herrmann the Great Company

(1897–1899)

M. H. Everett Returns, Fall 1897

When M. H. Everett walked through the stage door of San Francisco's Columbia Theater, the Herrmann show's backstage setup was exactly as he remembered. In the wings sat the Trilby and Artist's Dream illusions. Madame Herrmann's voluminous serpentine dresses hung just offstage on their special rack. Here was Alexander's show. How could the great magician possibly be gone?

The Herrmann illusions and costumes were the same, but otherwise, everything had changed. Just over a year had passed, but it seemed like a lifetime. Alexander Herrmann's absence was jarring. In his place was a man who looked uncannily like him but was younger, shorter, and stockier—thirty-year-old Léon Herrmann. When M. H. drew close, he hid his surprise at how short Léon was. M. H. estimated that Léon would have barely cleared Alexander's shoulder.

Adelaide Herrmann, now forty-four, had aged. Her face was hollow and gaunt, with dark circles under her eyes. She was sad beyond measure. She missed Alexander with all her being. When not onstage, she wore fashionable black mourning dresses she had sewn herself.[271] Her breezy lightheartedness was absent. She had always been quick-tempered, but now her fuse was even shorter. In the past Adelaide's staff had called her either Mrs. or Madame Herrmann. M. H. quickly learned that she had instructed everyone to address her as Madame Herrmann and Léon's wife, Marie, as Mrs. Herrmann. The younger Herrmanns had not been consulted on this decision and did not like it. The two Madame Herrmanns quibbled constantly in rapid French. M. H. could not follow the words, but their disdain for each other was clear.

Several old friends welcomed Everett. Will and Dot Robinson were still with the company. M. H. quickly observed that Will, as chief mechanic, was single-handedly holding the road-worn illusions together. M. H. was happy to see his old friend Adele Dewey. Adelaide's nineteen-year-old niece was more beautiful than ever. Another old friend greeted M. H.: Adelaide's nephew John Kretschmann, now going by Ketchum, had found his calling as a mechanic and carpenter. The twenty-year-old was now apprenticing as an assistant illusionist to Will Robinson. There was a familiar dark face in the company as well. Bernard Baker had been playing Boomsky for over a year, but soon after Everett's return, he resigned. Herrmann's horses, carriages, and horse car had been sold, and Baker was eager to leave the fractious company and return to his family in Pennsylvania.

The Herrmann company traveled more roughly now. Gone was the custom palace railcar. They overnighted on Pullman sleeper cars or stayed in hotels and caught early morning trains. Without private rolling accommodations, the company's African Americans were once again subject to Jim Crow laws on the trains, as well as at segregated restaurants and hotels. M. H. Everett generally found himself assigned to the Pullman sleeper's cramped, noisy berths above the wheels.

Léon Herrmann was now the star, but the show itself remained largely unchanged.[272] The *Chicago Tribune* noted that the illusions were "all well known to lovers of the magic art and remained as inscrutable as ever."[273] Léon's feats of palming were breathtaking. Reviewers praised Adelaide, especially her dances.

Léon Herrmann had not warmed to Bernard Baker in the role of Boomsky. Nobody mentioned the obvious. Onstage, Bernard Baker was noticeably taller than Léon Herrmann. Madame now assigned M. H. Everett to the role, in the hope that working with Alexander's favorite Boomsky might improve Léon's comic timing. Léon initially resisted working with Everett as well. In his year away, M. H. had grown. At five-foot-five, he was shorter than Bernard Baker, but still a few inches taller than Léon.

Escape from Sing Sing. From left to right: William E. Robinson, M. H. Everett, Léon Herrmann

The press started taking greater notice of Boomsky. In Chicago, at least three reviews singled him out. The *Chicago Tribune* reported that "'Boomsky,' the dusky attendant who served so many years with Herrmann the Great, acts in the same capacity for his nephew."[274] A reviewer from the *Dispatch* waxed nostalgically, "The curtain goes up, and Boomsky stands there just as with Alexander."[275] When the company reached California, the *San Francisco Call* critic noticed the "ever-faithful Boomsky."[276] The *Sacramento Daily Union* reported, "There are twenty in the company, including dusky Boomsky, the faithful attendant who used to be so awkward as to fall on hats loaned to Herrmann."[277] In a later review, the same paper noted of the company, "Every one, including Boomsky, have been with the Herrmanns for many years."[278]

Boomsky's recognition continued in Texas, as a reviewer from *Galveston News* observed, "One pleasing feature of the first part is the presence of 'Boomsky,' the older Herrmann's colored assistant. As long as he travels with the company, they may really claim to be the only successors to Herrmann the Great."[279]

On Christmas Day in New Orleans, "Mme. Adelaide Herrmann presented each member of the company with jeweled scarf pins, cuff buttons, match and cigaret [*sic*] cases, all of which had been worn and admired by her late husband, Herrmann the Great."[280] M. H. choked up as Adelaide told the company of his first days with Herrmann right there in New Orleans, when he was still fresh from the cotton fields. M. H. glanced over at Will and Dot, recalling the wonder of seeing their illusions for the first time. As Adelaide distributed the precious Christmas gifts, the Robinsons held each other close, their eyes glistening.

M. H. noticed that Léon's wife, Marie, never performed in the show. He learned that this was the source of many arguments. Back in France, Marie had been Léon's onstage partner, performing Second Sight, the Spirit Cabinet, and several illusions.[281] For Adelaide, having two Madame Herrmanns traveling with the company was bad enough. Onstage there could be just one Madame Herrmann. Adelaide scheduled a photo session for the company, onstage, in costume. Adelaide Herrmann, Dot Robinson, and Adele Dewey all posed center stage flanked by William

Robinson, M. H. Everett, and the company's other male assistants. Léon, the costar, stood at the very edge of the photo, near the wings. Marie Herrmann was conspicuously absent. In subsequent years, Léon would himself be erased. Adelaide would have a photo retoucher replace Léon's image with a potted plant.

The Herrmann the Great Company in A Night in Japan. From left to right: unidentified assistant, Adelaide Herrmann, M. H. Everett, Dot Robinson, Adele Dewey, John Kretschmann, William E. Robinson, Léon Herrmann.

The company pushed through the spring, working their way back through the Midwest and Northeast. M. H. Everett, along with everyone else, noticed that audiences, while warm, were smaller and not as effusive as before. All the theaters that Alexander had sold out for years suddenly had empty seats. When they finally finished in May, the tour had barely made a profit.

189

Over the summer, all the Herrmanns—Adelaide, Léon, and Marie, as well as Dewey and John—went to Europe to visit their families. While they were away, a small staff tended to Herrmann Manor at Whitestone. Alexander's old workshop sat empty and unused. One day M. H. stepped inside. Suddenly memories of Alexander washed over him. M. H. recalled all the times he had stood by as Herrmann tinkered, waiting to fetch whatever his boss needed. About the shop sat road-worn magical apparatus, including tricks that M. H. had performed with Herrmann thousands of times. In the workshop, Herrmann felt nearby, and M. H. visited daily. He began resurrecting some of Herrmann's old, battered magic props and tables with glue, sandpaper, paint, and varnish, then with fabric, ribbon, and tassels. Inspired, he ordered a costume, white tie and tails, tailored exactly like Herrmann's, for nobody knew better the locations of the secret pockets. He invested in a professional publicity photo and began billing himself as Everett the Magician.[282] As Alexander's greatest mimic, the twenty-year-old Black man from Georgia presented an uncanny, spot-on impression of Herrmann the Great.

IRVING & SADIE JONES'S JIM CROW PROTEST

In 1898, Irving Jones was riding high. In the twelve years since getting fired by the Herrmanns at age thirteen for laughing onstage, Jones had become a star. He was now a famous songwriter with over one hundred published songs. His latest, "Let Me Bring My Clothes Back Home," was number three on the charts, following up on his earlier hit, "Take Your Clothes and Go."[283] For the previous five years he had performed with Sam T. Jack's Creole Company, an all-Black comedy and music review show, where Irving had met his wife and partner, Sadie. The couple's comedic song-and-dance act was a hit, and now the Joneses were about to start an exciting new job. They dropped off their two-year-old son, William, with Irving's parents in New York and hit the road.

Irving Jones signed photo.

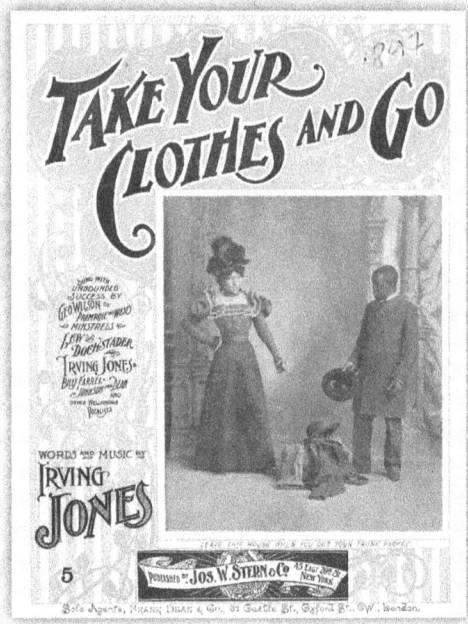

Sheet music cover of "Take Your Clothes and Go," words and music by Irving Jones, who wrote over 100 published songs.

Irving and Sadie had signed on with the Black Patti Troubadours. The hugely popular show combined minstrelsy and majestic grand opera and toured with a large chorus and full orchestra. Its star and founder, Sisieretta Jones (no relation to Irving), was called "the Black Patti," after superstar soprano Adelina Patti. Rejected by the opera world, Jones had formed her own company. Now Sisieretta Jones was the world's highest-paid Black entertainer, earning far more than any opera diva.

Irving and Sadie would join up with the Black Patti Troubadours en route. Once with the troupe they would travel in a private company railcar. But now, traveling on their own, they were subject to Jim Crow segregation laws. Irving and Sadie girded themselves for the trip. The chance of getting a Pullman berth was practically nil, which meant traveling in the colored car. Located right behind the loud, smoky, coal-fired steam locomotive, the colored car was dirty, uncomfortable, and dangerous, especially for women. While technically off-limits to all white people, colored cars were the dumping ground for drunk and belligerent male passengers who had worn out their welcome in the whites-only cars. Irving and Sadie prayed for a peaceful trip. Eating was another worry. Dining cars admitted only whites. Black travelers had to pack their own food or buy expensive but bad meals at train stops. Black travelers feared for their safety and worried about where they would eat and sleep each night. For Black entertainers in small troupes lacking private cars, the never-ending stress could feel overwhelming. It was bad enough for the majority of African Americans, who traveled infrequently. Touring performers endured these conditions every single day, growing ever more frustrated. As Irving and Sadie lurched westward, tossed about on the malodorous colored car's hard wooden bench seats, they plotted a risky stunt. A bevy of reporters had boarded at the last stop, which meant someone important was on the train. Ideal conditions for a Jim Crow protest.

WOULD NOT EAT WITH NEGROES.

Governor and Mrs. Stephens of Missouri Changed Their Seats.

ST. LOUIS, Oct. 4.—Gov. and Mrs. Stephens have returned from the East. An incident occurred coming west that politicians are talking about. The Governor and his wife had just taken seats in the dining car, when a negro, accompanied by a woman, came and sat down opposite them. The Governor glanced around for a moment and then, speaking low to Mrs. Stephens, arose and the two took seats at another table.

The negro was Irving Jones, a colored comedian and author and composer of songs. The woman was his wife. According to other occupants of the car, the comedian and his wife did not seem to notice the act of the Governor and his wife.

The New York Times, *October 5, 1898.*

Black entertainers regularly staged Jim Crow protests aboard trains, calculated actions intended to maximize visibility while minimizing personal risk. The presence of a reporter was critical. Train and streetcar protests were often carried out by women, who were somewhat less likely to be physically attacked. Usually, the protestor would simply take a seat in a whites-only car until told to leave. Protestors were invariably peaceful. But the response could be violent. In extreme instances, Blacks refusing to comply with Jim Crow laws had been thrown from moving trains.

That October, on their westbound train headed to St. Louis, Irving and Sadie Jones entered the whites-only dining car. A few tables down, a reporter spotted them and took a notebook from his pocket and a pencil from behind his ear. Moving quickly, Irving and Sadie plopped themselves down at a table opposite a well-dressed white couple who happened to be Missouri Governor Lon Vest Stephens and his wife. Shocked at finding themselves seated with Black people, the governor and his wife immediately moved to another table. All the while, Irving and Sadie perused menus and blithely appeared not to notice any of it. The next morning, the story appeared on the front page of the *New York Times*. Entitled, "Would Not Eat with Negroes," the article would be reprinted in newspapers across America.[284] This time, Irving and Sadie made their point and escaped unscathed. Black entertainers and many others would continue these flash protests for another fifty-seven years, right up to the time when a woman named Rosa Parks would refuse to move to the back of a bus in Montgomery, Alabama.

Making History: A Biracial Illusion

When the Herrmann the Great Company set out in the fall of 1898, M. H. Everett's career was advancing. While still playing Boomsky onstage, he had been promoted to the position of assistant electrician on the crew.[285] He was also cast in a new role performing one of the Herrmanns' most baffling illusions.

For the two previous seasons, the Asiatic Trunk Mystery had been performed by Adele Dewey and Dot Robinson. It was crucial that the two performers contrast in appearance, so their fast exchange immediately registered with spectators. Reviewers had noted the startling transposition of tall blond Dewey and short brunette Dot.

Adelaide thought of a way to make the transposition even more surprising. This season she replaced Dot with M. H. Everett.[286] To begin, M. H. bound Dewey's wrists, placed her inside a cloth bag, tied the top of the bag closed, and padlocked her inside a trunk. A curtain briefly dropped in front of the trunk. M. H. ducked behind the curtain and instantly Dewey ran out from the other side. The curtain was raised, the trunk unlocked, and there was M. H., inside the sealed bag, his wrists bound. The lightning-fast transposition of a fair blond woman and a Black man was shocking.

It was the first biracial illusion ever performed in America and perhaps in the entire world. Audiences loved it. M. H. and Dewey brought down the house every night. Adelaide took credit for her progressive casting. But putting M. H. into the role was also a slight to Léon's wife. Marie Herrmann was short and dark-haired and could have easily stepped into Dot's role if Adelaide had been inclined to allow the other Mrs. Herrmann anywhere near the stage.

The onstage pairing of M. H. Everett and Adele Dewey raised eyebrows, especially in the South. In 1899, any presentation that merely hinted at interracial coupling was considered taboo on the American stage. Five years later, Harry Houdini would comment from England

195

on a controversy stirred after the *New York Dramatic Mirror* published a photo of a mixed-race couple performing together.

> Just a few lines referring to your article appearing Sept. 24, in which you reproduce a cut of a team called Cline and Clark, in which a white woman is doing a sketch with a colored man. That is nothing unusual on this side of the pond and were I a colored man I would never leave this country. They are all looked upon here just as amicably as if they were white. The color line is unknown here, and many a team I've seen in which the man is colored and his partner white. The colored race over here has made a great big hit, and certainly are making good with their ability.[287]

There was another big change that season. Adelaide Herrmann began performing magic herself, conjuring flowers and handkerchiefs—most unusual for a woman. In the fall of 1898, Léon and Adelaide debuted their new act, A Night in Japan. Madame herself performed most of the magic. Billed for the first time as "the only woman magician in the world," Adelaide performed her tricks while wearing a kimono.[288] Set in a Japanese garden, the act was performed entirely in pantomime. Adelaide never spoke.[289] The act was an instant hit. In Washington, DC, a reviewer from the *Evening Times* raved. "Everyone was surprised when a woman came onstage and began the work of a trickster. Everyone would have been willing to remain another hour."[290] After seeing A Night in Japan, a reporter for the *St. Louis Post Dispatch* would declare Léon and Adelaide "joint successors of the late Alexander Herrmann."[291]

The third season of the Herrmann the Great Company had started strong but began to falter. Ticket sales fell. The stars became thin-skinned and irritable. M. H. sighed, wistfully recalling Alexander's happy troupe. Now he heard constant bickering, in French, between Adelaide and Léon and between the two Madame Herrmanns. Adelaide owned the show; Léon was her employee. Léon felt constrained. He had his own ideas, which Adelaide refused to consider. And Marie Herrmann was still not allowed to perform. Audiences liked the show, but without Alexander's magnetic personality to draw them in, they were not as compelled to attend. After six continuous seasons, even Adelaide's spectacular dances began to lose their drawing power.[292] And Madame was losing steam. She was tired. Adelaide again advertised the new act in which she would do fifty costume changes in ten minutes, each time closing then opening an opera cloak to reveal a new outfit. But for undisclosed reasons, she abandoned the act after just a few performances.[293]

In early October, the fractious company had a rare day off between dates in Lincoln and Kearny, Nebraska. It was a short hop to Omaha, where the company could enjoy an autumn Sunday at the Trans-Mississippi and International Exposition. The Exposition was on the scale of a world's fair. The endless midway featured one grand amusement after another, including the South African Ostrich Farm, the Moorish Palace, Hagenback's five hundred trained wild animals, and The Old Plantation, where M. H. Everett witnessed a hundred African Americans acting out a revisionist history of slavery.[294]

The Herrmann company rushed past all these attractions and headed straight for the Chinese Village and Theater, eager to see a new magician that had set the magic world agog—the marvelous Chinese conjuror, Ching Ling Foo.

The performance started off more like a circus than a magic display, with Ching Ling Foo's family troupe of musicians, acrobats, and jugglers kicking off the show. The richly costumed performers exhibited extraordinary skills. A juggler tossed huge porcelain pots into the air and caught them, spinning, on his head. A woman with tiny feet, even smaller than Dot's, sang songs with a tiny girl, a mere toddler, who beamed with personality. The acrobats, one of them just a small boy, prompted gasps with their flying leaps and flips.

Finally, Ching Ling Foo took the stage. He was dark-skinned and tall—much taller than most Chinese men—wearing a beautiful embroidered robe and a big, welcoming smile. He took command with astonishing never-before-seen tricks. He waved a silk cloth slowly and deliberately, building up tension and expectations. Suddenly, like a flash of lightning, the smiling Foo whipped away the cloth to reveal an enormous bowl of water sitting on the stage.

Every trick was new and different. Foo spit flames. He produced more bowls of water. Nobody in the Herrmann company knew how he did it. Foo's Chinese linking rings, tossed and linked in midair, made Léon Herrmann's mannered version seem pallid and dull. As his finale, Foo dispensed with the robes and appeared in tight-fitting shirt and pants. He ran across the stage, executed a diving somersault, and stood up holding a bowl of water containing swimming goldfish.

As the cheering audience rose to its feet, the Herrmann company members sat stunned. Unlike the Herrmann show, Foo's show was seamless, with no stage waits to set up illusions. Every time Foo left the stage to reset his tricks, another performer rushed on to entertain. Foo never spoke, performing entirely in pantomime—an unheard-of way to present magic.

After the performance, M. H. glanced at Will Robinson, who sat frozen, staring off into space. From that moment on, Robinson was different. He became distant and even more surly.[295]

A week later, at Denver's Tabor Grand Opera House, Robinson enraged his bosses by secretly helping a young, unknown magician named Howard Thurston fool the Herrmanns with a rising card trick. Léon and Adelaide were humiliated by the subsequent *Denver Post* article entitled, "Herrmann, the Magician, Mystified by Another Magician." For the next few weeks, the Herrmanns paused their internal squabbling to focus their scorn on Will Robinson.[296]

EVERETT IS HONORED IN *MAHATMA*

While company turmoil swirled around him, M. H. Everett received the greatest recognition of his magical career. In December 1898, his dashing publicity photo, in white tie and tails, appeared in the distinguished magician's magazine *Mahatma*. A rare honor for any magician, an African American prominently featured in *Mahatma* was unheard-of.

M. H. Everett, known professionally as "Boomskie," is a well-known and clever assistant to Herrmann the III. Mr. Everett has all the qualifications that go to make up the quick-witted assistant who at all times is able to cover up and help out in case of an accident in the workings of the professor's problems. He was an assistant to the late Bancroft, and was with him until his death last winter, he then joined Herrmann III and was given the name of "Boomskie," and Herrmann's entertainment was not complete without seeing Boomskie, who is a clever comedian in the part he plays upon the stage. His mimicry is perfect and his actions were all so natural that he became a great favorite with the "Herrmann the Great Co." Mr. Everett fills in his idle time in the summer in giving magical entertainments at which he is exceedingly clever.[297]

M. H. Everett was featured in the December 1898 issue of Mahatma.

Everett's *Mahatma* profile did not mention that he had been Alexander Herrmann's Boomsky for five seasons, starting at age thirteen. Future magic history books and articles that mentioned Milton Hudson Everett would omit this information as well.

ISAAC WILLIS: WHITE HOUSE BOOMSKY

During the company's yearly Washington, DC run, Léon and Marie Herrmann took a sightseeing tour of the White House. There Léon spotted a vivacious, smiling youth wearing a messenger's uniform. Isaac Willis looked to be about fourteen years old. When Léon got closer, he realized the young man was older, just very small. He was noticeably shorter than Léon, who offered him a job on the spot. The youth gasped, "Yes!" But his father would have to give his blessing. Luckily, his father worked at the White House as well.[298]

Nineteen-year-old Isaac Willis had been a White House messenger since age fourteen, during the term of President Grover Cleveland. His father, John, had been a cart driver before becoming a White House doorman. Isaac was his only son. Letting him go was painful, but Isaac's income would enable fifty-five-year-old John to slow down. When Léon Herrmann presented his offer, John Willis solemnly extended his arm and shook hands with the magician.[299] Léon turned to Isaac and said, "Come with me! You begin tonight." Just like that, Isaac Willis left behind the only world he had ever known. Except for tour performances and brief visits, he would never return home again.

Isaac William Willis had grown up a city boy. Like most African Americans, his family was poor and relegated to manual labor. Yet they were much better off than most Southern sharecroppers and field hands. Isaac was born on Christmas Eve, 1878, in Alexandria, Virginia. His family soon moved to Washington, DC, where Isaac lived with his parents, John and Isabel, his older sister, Bessie, and maternal aunt Mary Ellis. Their tenement flat in Jackson Hall Alley was located right off the

National Mall, practically in the shadow of the US Capitol.[300] Isaac's parents were from Virginia. John had been a child during the Civil War and had most likely been enslaved. Isabel, a decade younger than her husband, was born two years after the Emancipation Proclamation.[301] In the 1880 US Census, John Willis's race was listed as Black, but the

Isaac Willis as a White House messenger at age fourteen.

rest of his family—Isabel, Isaac, Bessie, and Mary—were all listed as "Mulatto."

In the 1890s in America, the majority of Black adults remained uneducated. But in Washington, DC, Black children attended primary school. In Jackson Hall Alley, where the Willis family lived, the husbands' incomes as laborers, waiters, messengers, and drivers were sufficient to support their families. Their wives kept house and took care of the children, just like the white wives in nearby Boyle Alley whose breadwinners, mainly recent immigrants from Italy and Prussia, included a watchman, a blacksmith, and a fruit store owner. Both Black and Caucasian families supplemented their incomes with boarders, often unmarried female relatives, who worked as chambermaids, laundresses, and seamstresses.

BOOMSKY DUSTUP IN DC

That evening, when M. H. Everett arrived backstage at the Columbia Theater, he was shocked to see a young Black man dressed in Boomsky's brass-buttoned uniform and jaunty cap. This Boomsky was very small, just a kid, thought M. H., until he got closer and saw that Isaac Willis was not so young after all. Léon Herrmann approached, gestured toward the new Boomsky, and said to M. H., "Teach him your role."

M. H. saw what was happening. He was being replaced. It was true that he and Léon had never quite connected. But the real reason was obvious. Léon, exquisitely sensitive about his height, had hired an assistant shorter than himself. M. H. wondered what Madame would have to say about this, if she even knew. Will Robinson would likely have choice words too. M. H. fumed. He had just been profiled in *Mahatma!* That very week Washington's *Evening Star* had noted "the ever-popular Boomsky." Yet Léon was about to fire him.

M. H. Everett had nothing against Isaac Willis, but he was angry and upset. The mature action would have been to stand aside. Adelaide would have stood up for Alexander's favorite assistant. But M. H. Everett's emotions overshadowed his judgment. Unwisely, he took matters into his own hands.

Onstage that night, instead of helping the novice, M. H. did everything he could to trip him up. M. H. blocked Isaac's path and bumped into him, causing the new assistant to drop props. It was so bad that even the audience noticed—an egregious theater faux pas. The *Evening Times* critic noted the "awkwardness of the assistants," writing that, at one point, Léon had to intervene to prevent an assistant from injuring himself.[302]

Afterwards, the Herrmanns were furious. The theater has always been a sanctuary for alternative behaviors and lifestyles. Offstage, much is forgiven, but the stage itself is sacred ground. Deliberately sabotaging a performance was unforgiveable. Abruptly and harshly, Adelaide delivered her pronouncement. "You are fired!" Stunned and devastated, M. H. Everett packed his bag and departed. As the stage door closed behind him, M. H. felt his long career with the Herrmanns slip away. He had been the first to carry the name Boomsky. Now it was someone else's. Deeply depressed, Everett headed to a nearby bar to drown his sorrows.

LÉON AND ISAAC

The Herrmann the Great Company continued with Isaac Willis as Boomsky. From the beginning, Léon Herrmann and Isaac Willis got on famously. In the fractious company, the good-natured newcomer was a breath of fresh air. Léon delighted in training his own assistant from scratch, without constant cajoling and correcting from Madame Herrmann and Will Robinson. They had pushed Léon to adapt to M. H. Everett, Alexander's assistant, to learn the master's style and timing. But Léon was tired of adapting. *He* was the magician, not his assistant. Everett's loyalty had clearly been to Madame, not him. By contrast, Isaac Willis was a blank canvas. Léon could mold his ideal assistant without outside interference. As they began, Herrmann discovered with pleasure that Isaac was quick and adept, with a knack for being in exactly the right spot at the right time. Isaac was also the only male in the company who literally looked up to Léon. For his part, Isaac enjoyed helping Léon

Léon Herrmann and Isaac Willis.

along. He genuinely liked the young Frenchman and was awed by Herrmann's skill. The starstruck teen followed his boss around, catering to Herrmann's every need with a worshipful devotion. In Léon's two years in America, nobody had treated him with such deference and respect. In a dysfunctional company full of infighting and backstabbing, Léon's new Boomsky brought a welcome boost. Léon Herrmann would not forget this.

EVERETT JOINS THE NAVY

After being fired, Milton Hudson Everett was despondent. He made his way to New York, where he continued drinking at a series of seedy portside taverns. Three weeks after leaving the Herrmann the Great Company, M. H. woke up queasy and groggy. He felt himself swinging and swaying in a hammock, which made him feel sicker. The rhythmic sounds of creaking wood and sloshing water told him he was on a ship. A man in uniform leaned into the tiny compartment, shook Everett out of the hammock, and delivered shocking news. In a drunken stupor, M. H. Everett had enlisted in the US Navy. His rank was "mess attendant," the Navy's servant rank, reserved for African Americans. His term of enlistment was three years. He was aboard the receiving ship, USS *Vermont*. [303] Everett had fallen for a shady military recruitment scheme. Recruiters lurked at seaport saloons, targeting drunk young men. After buying them more drinks and coercing them into signing enlistment papers, the staggering men were ushered aboard a prison-like Navy receiving ship docked nearby. Like M. H., the new sailors woke nursing miserable hangovers and monumental regrets. M. H. immediately began plotting his escape.

M. H. was transferred from the *Vermont* to the USS *Indiana*, the Navy's premier battleship. Endlessly, day after day, week after week, Mess Attendant Everett served food, washed dishes, mopped floors, slopped garbage, emptied chamber pots, and cleaned the officers' cabins. In 1898, the year before Everett enlisted, the *Indiana* had been a significant force in the Spanish-American War. Although the war was already over and Everett never saw combat, the Navy categorized him a veteran of the Spanish-American War, albeit a sailor whose weapons were a paring knife and a mop.

7-9-23-5000 (40-78)			
UNITED STATES NAVY			

NAME	RANK OR RATE	DATE OF APPOINTMENT OR ENLISTMENT	
EVERETT MILTON HUDSON	MESS ATT.	JAN. 30 1899	

ENLISTED AT OR APPOINTED FROM	TERM	SERVICE NO.
NEW YORK N.Y.	3 YEARS	1956517

TRADE	RESIDENCE AT APPOINTMENT OR ENLISTMENT
NONE	NEW YORK N.Y.

BIRTHPLACE	DATE	HEIGHT	EYES	HAIR	COMPLEXION
GEORGIA	JAN. 6TH 1878	5F 5"	NEGRO	NEGRO	NEGRO

VESSELS OR STATIONS (DO NOT GIVE DATES)
VERMONT INDIANA

ENGAGEMENTS
NONE SERVED IN THE SPANISH AMERICAN WAR

FINAL DISPOSITION	DATE	CAUSE	RATE
DESERTED	MAY 3 1899	UNKNOWN	M.ATT.

OTHER NAVAL SERVICE
NONE

(STATE OF NEW YORK FORM)

Milton Hudson Everett's US Navy enlistment card.

M. H. Everett made the best of it, but regret consumed him. Here he was, the same man who had starred onstage with Herrmann and Bancroft, who had been given his own write-up in *Mahatma*, now the lowest, most abused, least respected man on the ship. For twenty-year-old Everett, a three-year enlistment seemed like a lifetime. He vowed to jump ship at the next port of call. In the meantime, like so many sailors serving in the subtropics, he came down with a case of malaria.

EMPTY HOUSES, EMPTY PURSES: THE BIG SPLIT

By spring 1899, the Herrmann the Great Company was in trouble. Audiences fell off and the tour was losing money. The arguments carried on nonstop. Finally, Will and Dot Robinson couldn't take it anymore and quit midseason.

For Adelaide, this was one disaster too many. She was sick of working with Léon, but she could not run the show without him. Still, her own reputation as a magician was rising. The *Boston Globe* reported that "Madame Herrmann is now considered one of the world's foremost magicians, as well as the only woman magician on the American stage."[304]

Madame's next move was a breathtaking betrayal. In May 1899, Adelaide secretly signed a vaudeville contract for just herself to headline her own solo magic act. Without telling Léon, she canceled the upcoming season of the Herrmann the Great Company, erasing all Léon's future bookings.

Léon discovered her plan to undermine him and was livid. He recovered the tour dates and took charge of Herrmann's company. Adelaide in turn was enraged. But the die was cast. After three seasons together, the Herrmanns, widow and nephew, were now rivals.

Adelaide, Léon, and Marie Herrmann had all been living at Herrmann Manor at Whitestone. In an act of symbolic finality, the lease was terminated, and the home's contents were sold at auction. Except for some of Alexander Herrmann's treasured items, all the Professor's collectibles were gone overnight. The bulky Herrmann illusions, performed across Europe and the Americas for twenty-five years, went into a warehouse. Both Adelaide and Léon would seasonally raid this treasure trove of magic, making old warhorse illusions seem novel again with fresh paint, new costumes, and different stories. As widow and nephew prepared to begin their separate seasons, the knives initially stayed sheathed. But everyone knew that would just be temporary.

≈

CHAPTER EIGHT

Rival Herrmanns, Rival Boomskys (1899–1903)

Adelaide Herrmann and M. H. Everett in Vaudeville

In May, after six months in the Navy, M. H. Everett saw his chance and jumped ship. A month later, he was standing onstage next to Adelaide Herrmann. He had apologized and she had hired him back.

Now Adelaide was on her own, playing vaudeville with her own five-person traveling company. Adele Dewey and M. H. Everett assisted Madame onstage, while two unseen stagehands handled the equipment.

As the Queen of Magic, Adelaide Herrmann performed her

Adelaide Herrmann Tea Chest illusion circa 1899, with M. H. Everett and unidentified assistant.

act A Night in Japan. Everett and Dewey continued their biracial illusion, The Asiatic Trunk Mystery, which still raised eyebrows. African Americans were rarely seen on vaudeville stages, and M. H. was almost always the only Black performer in the lineup. Behind the scenes it was

Adelaide Herrmann and Adele Dewey circa 1899.

different. A legion of Black stagehands, curtain pullers, and assorted crew members kept the show running.

Playing in vaudeville was very different than performing in the Herrmann show. Now Adelaide was an employee, responsible for her "turn" in a program featuring seven to ten other variety acts. Performers worked two shows a day, staying in each city for a week. Then the entire cast moved to the next city on a proscribed vaudeville route, working in theaters owned by the producers. It took over a year to play the entire route through the US and Canada.

Already an established star, Madame started out as a headliner. Her name was at the top of the bill, and at thirty minutes, her act was longer than the others. Adelaide no longer had autonomy. She shared the bill with strangers and had no control over the other acts. Most were human—singers, dancers, musicians, actors, comedians, acrobats, and other variety performers. In her vaudeville career, Madame's company also shared the bill with trained dogs, monkeys, parrots, ponies, bears, roosters, and seals.

Finally, Madame's arduous serpentine dances were gone. Instead, she performed graceful, feminine magic tricks. Dewey floated in the air in an illusion called Sleeping Beauty, which was simply the renamed Herrmann classic aerial suspension, The Slave Girl's Dream. Adelaide presented an act with billiard balls that magically appeared, multiplied, then evaporated at her fingertips. She was the first woman ever to perform this trick. The *New York Times* gave Adelaide a new title, "Prestidigitatrice."[305] Harry Kellar saw her act in Columbus, Ohio, and sent a warm congratulatory letter, which Adelaide deeply appreciated. It marked the beginning of a supportive friendship between the former foes.

Nov 30, 1900

My dear Mrs. Herrmann: Allow me to congratulate you on your grand success. . . . Your manifestation of the billiard balls was the finest piece of handiwork I ever saw. Your dresses were superb and

your personal appearance imposing and grand. . . . May every suc-
cess attend you in your profession, for you deserve it. You certainly
are a plucky, hardworking little woman, and the big world must be
kind to you. . . .

Truly your friend Harry Kellar.[306]

The Herrmann Company's leisurely summer vacations were a thing of the past. The sixty-week vaudeville circuit worked straight through. Performers could take their vacations at the end of it, although many just jumped back in and immediately started the route all over again. Unusual for vaudeville, Adelaide Herrmann carried her own elaborate stage set, with gorgeous painted backdrops and scenery pieces. When the curtain went up, the audience gazed in awe at the sight of a beautiful Japanese garden.

ADELAIDE HERRMANN, QUEEN OF MAGIC

Vaudeville was not very welcoming to African Americans. However, it provided tremendous new opportunities to America's largest underclass—women. Many vaudeville acts starred female singers, dancers, musicians, comedians, and variety artists. Still, a female *magician* was new and startling. There were plenty of male magicians, but as a female magician in vaudeville, Adelaide Herrmann was unique. Adelaide Herrmann's presentation was distinctive beyond her gender. She was the only magician in vaudeville to perform without speaking. Dispensing with the usual "patter," she conjured with slow, deliberate movements set to music. She was spellbinding. Rochester's *Democrat and Chronicle* marveled that Madame Herrmann "holds the audience entirely by pantomime."[307] Confetti in cups turned to steaming coffee. An empty paper cone suddenly erupted with hundreds of paper flowers. Every night, audiences marveled at the full-sized billiard balls somehow appearing from her tiny hands. Remarkably, she performed in a sleeveless gown, making her magic even more mystifying.[308]

Adelaide was an instant hit. The *Buffalo Review* reported that hundreds were turned away. "Standing room was hard to get, and men and women stood on tables in the foyer to get a look at the stage."[309] Madame Herrmann continually garnered praise in the press, quickly becoming one of vaudeville's most admired acts. The New Orleans *Times-Democrat* raved, "Vaudeville possesses no more popular act than that given by Adelaide Herrmann, widow of Herrmann the Great. No less than 60,000 people saw her duplicate Herrmann's greatest feats at Keith's, Philadelphia, during a recent fortnight. Throughout the act she does not speak, and her arms are bare; yet no male magician has presented such a mystifying entertainment."[310] In Chicago, Adelaide Herrmann was the headliner. An act lower on the bill would soon become an international star—the sharpshooter Annie Oakley.[311]

As far as competition went, Adelaide Herrmann had none. Variety acts that could be easily copied were ruthlessly purloined. Loie Fuller's serpentine dances had spun off dozens of imitators. Magic was different. No ordinary woman could possibly hope to gain access to its secrets. Only a family connection could open the door, and even then, many magicians resisted teaching a girl.[312] Adelaide's only real female rival at sleight-of-hand was a brilliant coin manipulator named Mercedes Talma, who debuted her act in England in 1899, the same year as Adelaide's vaudeville debut. However, Talma, whose real name was Mary Ann Ford, would never tour a solo act. Instead, she would spend her career touring with her husband, magician Servais LeRoy, as one third of the troupe, LeRoy, Talma, and Bosco. For this reason, Madame Herrmann would remain largely free of competition her entire vaudeville career.

Adelaide missed Alexander with all her heart but not his profligate spending and seesawing bank balances. When the dust of Alexander's financial mess had finally settled, and she had paid off Herrmann's debts, Adelaide received a significant payout from his life insurance. Madame was a good money manager and naturally frugal. Now with her vaudeville work, her nest egg began to grow. To a reporter from the New Orleans *Times-Picayune*, Adelaide asserted that "if Mr. Herrmann had listened to me about his investments, I should have kept him out of buying theaters and mines and other things in which he lost. Women are better money managers than men are. They think longer about spending their money. We had made fortunes, but like so many men to whom money comes easily, he threw it away."[313]

As M. H. Everett knew all too well, Adelaide Herrmann was an unusual woman. Even when not performing, Madame frequently provoked gasps of shock, even screams, with a tiny mouse named Magic that rode on her shoulder, secured by a gold chain and a tiny, jewel-encrusted collar.[314] Magic liked to hide in Madame's luxurious curly hair, only to emerge and startle the unsuspecting. One night in Chicago, Magic fell ill. Adelaide summoned a Dr. Mulvey, who diagnosed Magic with appendicitis. Assisted by two nurses, Dr. Mulvey operated on the tiny patient. The operation was a success, and Magic lived to ride again.[315]

In September, the *New York Times* announced that Adelaide's manager, George Lederer, had arranged for Adelaide to play engagements in Paris and London for "the largest terms ever paid an American artist."[316] When asked about the trouble between herself and her husband's nephew, Léon, she didn't hold back. "I brought him over to this country, taught him most of what he knows, and started to lift him into the place held by my late husband. He got jealous of me, and—but why dwell on the subject? You know Léon and can imagine what I had to stand from him."[317]

BETRAYED BY BOOMSKY

For over a year, Adelaide Herrmann, Adele Dewey, M. H. Everett, and two backstage assistants plied the Burke and Chase vaudeville circuit. All was going smoothly until August 1900, when they opened in Detroit. After Monday's show, Adelaide could not find a precious ring valued at $1,000. Normally Dewey hid the ring in a secret compartment in Adelaide's powder box, but it was not there. The ring consisted of two 7-carat diamonds set in a cross bar. Its sentimental value exceeded its monetary worth; it was the last gift given to Adelaide by Alexander.

Adelaide reported the theft to the theater manager, who accused her of making up the story for publicity. Madame was furious at the inference. The manager suggested that perhaps the goose ate it. No performer was ever more attached to her animals than Adelaide Herrmann. Her trained white goose was a highlight of her act. But Madame was desperate to find her ring. The goose was killed and cut open—and proven innocent. No ring was found. Adelaide was beside herself with anger and grief.[318]

Adelaide reported the theft to the police. By the end of the week, no progress was made on the case. However, two detectives assigned to the theater believed they had narrowed down a suspect. They wired their report to the authorities at the company's next stop. In Chicago, Police Captain Colleran had his detectives secretly follow the suspect as he made his way to a pawn shop. There they caught M. H. Everett attempting to pawn the setting for Madame Herrmann's ring. Everett immediately confessed to the theft. A search of Chicago's other pawn shops recovered the two 7-carat diamonds. Everett was arrested and sent back to Detroit to stand trial.

When told that M. H. was the thief, Adelaide was doubly furious and heartbroken. No motive was given for M. H.'s betrayal. Gambling debts were suggested.[319] Friendly backstage craps games could turn ugly and dangerous when losers failed to pay up. At his trial, Madame stared coldly at Everett, who hung his head in shame. Adelaide's newest "mascot," a tiny chameleon, sat on her shoulder in the courtroom. She fed it some grape juice, and it seemed content. But when the attorney for the defense began to speak, the chameleon fell dead onto Madame's lap. Adelaide took it as a sign and announced that she was done with mascots because "oh, well, they die too easy."[320] M. H. Everett was convicted. He was sent to the county jail in Detroit to await sentencing.

Miserable and terrified, M. H. found someone to help him write a letter. The *Omaha World Herald* reported that "Madame Adelaide Herrmann is in receipt of a pathetic letter from Hudson Everett, the colored youth who stole her diamond ring at Detroit a short while ago, and who is now under arrest for the crime in the Michigan metropolis. The prisoner begs Madame Herrmann to intercede for him and declares that he will take his life rather than go to the penitentiary. Madame Herrmann is inclined to help the young man but has been prevented from doing so by friends who assert that the negro ought to pay the penalty for his theft."[321]

When Adelaide did not intervene on his behalf, M. H. was devastated. In the meantime, at the Detroit County Jail, Everett was a celebrity. Everyone had grown up seeing Herrmann the Great and Boomsky. His jailers often let him out of his cell to regale the sheriff and deputies with stories of the Herrmanns. One afternoon they were joined by a reporter from the *Detroit Journal*. With nothing left to lose, and feeling "vengeful towards the Madame," M. H. exacted his payback. For two hours, in a twist on the term captive audience, he revealed secret after secret of the tricks that were Adelaide Herrmann's bread and butter.[322] The *Detroit Journal* reporter took copious notes and began writing his sensational story.

M. H. Everett was sentenced to eighteen months in the state prison in Ionia, Michigan, the same town where, years before, M. H. and the rest of the Herrmann company had pitched in to rescue trapped train passengers. Madame Herrmann continued her tour, fuming to a reporter that she would not replace Boomsky. She also speculated that unsolved thefts over the years could be attributed to him.

Angry remarks aside, Madame still needed an onstage assistant. She hired a teen named Roland Travers. The son of a Chicago attorney, Travers, whose real name was McKitrick, had just finished high school and was working as a photographer. Handsome and effeminate, Travers was the first and only white assistant to wear Boomsky's crisp brass-buttoned uniform, although he did not retain the name. Adelaide adored her new assistant, who soon began calling his boss "Aunt Addie," just like Dewey. Meanwhile, Adelaide had no idea of the time bomb that was ticking on another front.

Roland Travers became Adelaide's assistant during M. H. Everett's prison term. A successful magician himself, Travers remained Madame Herrmann's friend and helpmate for the rest of her life.

BOOMSKY'S REVENGE

It hit the *Detroit Journal* first, a long article, rich with details of Adelaide's cherished magic secrets. M. H. Everett was called "cunning," "clever," and "bright." The tone of the article implied that audiences were fools to fall for such simple tricks.

The first illusion M. H. exposed was Strobeika.

"That's easy," chuckled Everett last night. "The man who does the act is paid in advance. He is laid out on the platform and shackled by the committee. Before the trick is set Mme. Herrmann takes her place on the platform. There is a post in each corner, from which the curtains are strung. When the trick is to be played, Mme. Herrmann steps into a stirrup on the left hand post. The curtains when opened fold around her and hide her. The minute the curtains are drawn, she hops down and releases the man with a key which opens all the locks at once. The man takes her place, and she lies down, and draws the locks over her arms and neck. The curtains are opened and hide the man.

"The best trick Mme. Herrmann does is the billiard ball trick, and that's pure sleight o' hand. The trick as the audience sees it, consists of producing five billiard balls at different times from the air and holding them between the fingers of one hand. It's a hard trick for a woman because her fingers are smaller than a man's.

"Three of the balls are genuine solid balls. Besides that, she has a half shell, which from the audience, looks like a genuine ball. She holds the shell between the thumb and first finger of the left hand. Every time she waves her left hand around and produces another ball she is getting the next one out of a pocket at her side with her other hand. Then she apparently makes a pass at her left hand with the right, while in reality she conceals another genuine ball in the half shell. Then when she waves her left hand around again she drops the ball out of the shell between her other fingers and shows an extra ball.

"The trick in which she produces a cup of boiling coffee and a cup of boiling milk from a box of paper is dead easy. She has four cups instead of two. She dips the empty cups into the boxes of paper and pours out the cut paper, showing the empty cups to the audience. The third time she dips each cup in she changes it for the cup of coffee or milk, which has been prepared in advance. It has a paper top glued on to hold the hot coffee in. When she raises it up and shows it to the audience it looks as if it was full of paper. Then she passes her handkerchief over it and takes the paper lid off. The steam comes up from the hot coffee as the audience goes 'nutty.'

"Her duck trick is one with a trick table. She pulls a lot of paper ribbons out of a paper hoop and throws them on the table. Then she does some 'flumididdles' and grabs up the bunch of paper ribbons. She jerks out a live duck and runs down to the footlights for applause. The duck is previously put in a cloth bag, with a stick run through some rings at the top, closing the bag. The duck and bag are hidden in the top of the table and when she picks up the paper she picks up the duck, too. Then she pulls the stick and the bag opens and lets the duck out.

"One of the prettiest tricks that 'the old man' (Everett used the term lovingly) . . . used to do with the madame is easy, too. Mrs. Herrmann, you know, was put on a chair and raised up on a swing into the air. Herrmann fired a pistol, and the madame disappeared, the chair dropping to the floor. That's done with a black background. You can do anything with a black back, you know.

"Mrs. Herrmann is dressed in white and shows very plainly against the black back. When she sits in the chair she is sitting on a false bottom. The ropes that raise her pass under the false bottom, but they are not fastened to the chair. When they commence to raise her she holds the chair with her feet, and when the shot is fired drops it. She is not lifted into the flies as some people think, because her light dress would show where she is going. Instead, when the shot is fired it holds the attention of the audience for an instant, and in that brief space of time a couple of black curtains are pulled over the madame's light dress. The audience thinks she has dissolved, and cheers when the professor runs down to the footlights with the empty chair.

"The 'Trilby' trick done by Herrmann, Jr., shows a woman mesmerized and laid out on an ordinary plank. The plank is placed on two chairs. Herrmann, Jr., waves his wand and one end of the plank raises and rests on thin air. He waves it again and the other end raises. He takes the chairs away and walks around the plank, showing that there is nothing supporting it. With a stick he strikes through the air above, below and at all sides. The audience is tickled half to death. You know it is easier to fool an audience of cultured people who have studied spiritualism and mesmerism, and all that, than a lot of ignorant persons.

"As a matter of fact, when the plank is placed on the chairs, an iron bar about an inch thick is run out from the background and slipped into a slot in the center of the plank. Machinery in back of the background raises the plank and the woman. The illusion is done by the professor. When the audience thinks he walks clear around in back of the plank, he only goes up to the iron bar, which is covered with red, and doesn't show against the red background, and leans against it. Then he goes around to the other side and does the same, and the audience has a brain fag trying to figure it out."[323]

Everett went on to expose Escape from Sing Sing in detail, finishing the interview with the claim that he would serve his term, then go on the road and duplicate any trick the other magicians do.

The above are good likenesses of Mr. and Mrs. W. E. Robinson, who have just closed another season with Herrmann the Great Co., making their twelfth season.

The man that invented and owned all the Big Delusions with Herrmann The Great Show

THE MAN THAT MADE mlle Herrmann Diamonds dissapear at Detroit. 1901. 1 YEAR at Jackson mich to think it over

M. H. Everett, known professionally as "Boomskie," is a well known and clever assistant to Herrmann the III. Mr. Everett has all the qualifications that go to make up the quick witted assistant who at all times is able to cover up and help out in case of an accident in the workings of the professor's problems. He was an assistant to the late Bancroft, and was with him until his death last winter, he then joined Herrmann II. and was given the name of "Boomskie," and Herrmann's entertainment was not complete without seeing Boomskie, who is a clever comedian in the part he plays upon the stage. His mimicry is perfect and his actions were all so natural that he became a great favorite with the "Herrmann the Great Co." Mr. Everett fills in his idle time in the summer in giving magical entertainments at which he is exceedingly clever.

for Revenge He exposed all of mr. Herrmanns Tricks in the Cincinnati Enquirer.

Houdini saved articles on M. H. Everett and the Robinsons and added his own hand-written notes.

When the *Detroit Journal* article hit the newsstands in December, Adelaide was embarrassed and furious at the public exposure of so many professional secrets. It jolted her and scandalized the theatrical community. Like a bandage slowly ripped off a wound, the humiliating article popped up in newspapers all over the US for an entire year. A young Harry Houdini took note, writing in his scrapbook next to the clipping of Everett's *Mahatma* profile, "The man that made Mlle [*sic*] Herrmann's diamonds dissapear [*sic*] at Detroit. 1 year at Jackson Mich to think it over. For revenge he exposed all of Mrs. Herrmann's tricks in the 'Cincinnati Enquirer.'"[324]

There was much speculation in theatrical circles as to how much lasting harm the exposures would cause Madame Herrmann. It certainly brought her stress and annoyance. But Adelaide simply charged back into her career, now with Dewey and Everett's replacement, Roland Travers, as her assistants. She plied the Burke and Chase vaudeville circuit, as reviewers continued to shower praise. In August 1901, as M. H. Everett served his term, Adelaide and company sailed to Berlin to begin a two-month engagement at the Wintergarten Theater. Upon their return, Adelaide's company jumped back into vaudeville.

The following year, Everett's prison term was ending. In one way, he had benefited greatly from his incarceration. At Ionia Prison's school for inmates, M. H. Everett had finally learned to read and write. Just after his release, the same *Detroit Journal* reporter who had written the scandalous exposure article interviewed him again. "I worked hard out at Ionia, went to night school and studied a lot and now I think I can make another start. You know the old man, Herrmann, I mean, taught me all his tricks. I can give a better show than his widow ever knew how to. I guess I'll go and see her and wish her luck, though. Then I'll go back to New York and get a job."[325]

Time had softened Adelaide's anger toward Everett. Before his release from prison she had spoken of him to a reporter. "He was exceedingly bright and useful, but, alas! was only human. In fact, he erred when there

223

was no occasion for it." Just after M. H.'s release, Adelaide was playing in Detroit. One night after the show he was waiting for her at the stage door. His boastfulness gone, he apologized profusely and begged for his job back. Adelaide always had a soft spot for her husband's favorite assistant. By coincidence Roland Travers, Everett's replacement, had just left Adelaide's company to launch his own solo magic act. For the third time, Madame forgave M. H. and took him back.[326]

Léon Herrmann and Isaac Willis on the Road

After splitting with Adelaide, Léon Herrmann continued touring the full-evening show with Isaac Willis playing Boomsky.

When M. H. Everett's criminal conviction and subsequent exposure article scandalized the Boomsky character, Léon Herrmann did not change his own assistant's name, creating, according to *The Sphinx*, a "jumble of identity by calling his colored assistant 'Boumski,' though the original and simon-pure Boumski languishes in a durance vile for a disappearance trick."[327] Years later Isaac Willis expressed his own ideas about how M. H. Everett had stolen Adelaide's ring. Willis said that Everett had threaded the stolen ring onto a long string, rolled it into a piece of dough and fed it to the goose. The ring was later retrieved with the string. Whether this is truth or lore is unknown.

Léon Herrmann and Isaac Willis were very well matched. While some judged Léon as fussy and aloof, Isaac admired his boss's precision, discipline, and no-nonsense personality. Léon appreciated how his young assistant anticipated his every move. In the Boomsky tradition, Isaac also served as Léon's valet and personal attendant. Wherever the magician went, Isaac was at his side.

Isaac Willis's small physique was a bonus for Léon, whose figure was constantly noted in the press as "short and stocky." Léon was frequently referred to as "the little magician."[328] According to his future manager, Jesse L. Lasky, Léon wore high heels "to add three inches of prestige to his small stature."[329] In group photographs, Léon Herrmann disguised his height by standing on a staircase above the others, or by sitting in a chair while everyone else around him stood. But onstage he looked tall

Poster of Léon Herrmann and Isaac Willis, circa 1903.

and imposing next to his tiny wife and the pint-sized Boomsky. After three seasons sidelined, Marie Herrmann was finally back on stage. The bejeweled Marie Herrmann proved to be a capable illusionist, to the chagrin of the original Madame Herrmann.

While Adelaide now toured in vaudeville with a pared-down company of five, Léon Herrmann's full-evening show carried thirteen people. Léon's show varied little from his Uncle Alexander's. The format was the same, as were most of the tricks and illusions. To Adelaide's annoyance, her nephew John Kretschmann chose to stay with Léon. Later, John's younger brother, Felix, joined Léon's company as well.

Two views of Léon and Marie Herrmann.

Isaac Willis performed Boomsky's signature tricks, falling on hats and regurgitating eggs. The watch trick was also a staple. A Savannah

Morning News reporter noticed that this was a different assistant. "The saffron-hued attendant who assists him is called 'Boomsky,' but he is not the same 'Boomsky' who waited on the famous wizard, for all that."[330]

While Léon Herrmann's show was eerily similar to Alexander's, it lacked the same draw. Reviews were warm but audiences, while enthusiastic, weren't large. The *Morning News* reported that "Léon Herrmann gave a pleasing performance to a small audience."[331] Their runs were also shorter. In cities where the Herrmanns had always played a week or longer, Léon was lucky to book more than one night.

Léon disliked street publicity stunts. Introverted and somewhat shy—the opposite of his uncle Alexander—Léon's performance ended when he stepped off the stage. But Léon understood the value of marketing. The *Kansas City Journal* told of Léon and his company sitting in the crowded waiting room of a train depot. Presently, Léon spotted a tattered pocketbook on the floor and picked it up. All eyes turned to Herrmann as he opened the pocketbook and pulled out old newspapers. A bystander snickered at seeing the magician pranked. But then Léon reached into the pocketbook and pulled out a large roll of greenbacks. He flipped the bag upside down and silver dollars rained into his palm. Across the waiting room, jaws dropped. "He placed the money in his pocket and threw the pocketbook away just as his train was pulling out, and, accompanied by his dusky attendant, the celebrated 'Boomski,' carrying his gripsack, the magician boarded the train and disappeared."[332]

As Adelaide adjusted to vaudeville and Léon struggled with one-night stands and low attendance, the rivals' resentments toward each other gathered steam. Two months into the season, Léon was the first to explode with a vicious attack published in the *Topeka State Journal*.

"'I now know what is meant when they said 'love is blind,' said the little magician last night. 'My dear uncle was surely blind or he could never have married my aunt. She was only a ballet dancer. . . . He met her and poor man he went blind. He married her. She is English and I am French. She is cold and I am warm: two extremes that could not

227

meet. She would see a man murdered on the street and never tremble. That is her nature.'"[333]

After unloading his pent-up anger, Léon focused on his tour. A reporter from the *Sioux City Journal* noted the younger Herrmann's astonishing sleight-of-hand skills: "In some things he is better than his predecessor, Alexander Herrmann, particularly in the art of palming." Léon challenged the audience to catch him by performing with a strong spotlight focused on his hands. Adelaide's absence was noted, but her presence "is not missed to such an extent that the show cannot be enjoyed without her."[334]

For months Léon Herrmann's company plied the Midwest with one-night stands through Kansas, Nebraska, Iowa, Missouri, Indiana, and Kentucky. Reviewers consistently praised the show. In Louisville, the *Courier Journal* stated that "with the exception of the beautiful electrical dances given by Adelaide Herrmann last year, [the performance] is far superior to that given when Mr. Herrmann was last here."[335] Yet, they continued to be plagued by small houses. The *St. Joseph-Gazette Herald* noted that "the audience was not large."[336] The *South Bend Tribune* reported that "there were more at the matinee than in the evening" and that, even after touring in the US for over two years, Léon Herrmann was "handicapped by his inability to speak English fluently."[337]

A few months into the season, Léon added an astonishing new trick called The Mysterious Tub of Neptune. Boomsky rolled onto the stage a wooden tub filled to the brim with water. Léon tossed in four eggs, one by one. He fired his pistol, and four live ducks appeared, swimming in the tub. In America's farmlands, the trick appeared especially miraculous. According to the Louisville *Courier-Journal*, "Herrmann's method of producing live ducks from hen's eggs would be of interest to poultry fanciers."[338]

Isaac Willis was well treated, yet, as was standard for the times, he had to endure boorish and racist behavior from his employer. Léon continued the Herrmann tradition of using Black porters and waiters as

Poster of Léon Herrmann and Boomsky. Racial caricatures of African Americans were typical of the era.

unsuspecting objects of impromptu entertainment and ridicule. Such a story about Léon was printed in the Elmira *Star-Gazette*.

Léon's target that night was a Pullman porter. What began as a simple magician's stunt quickly went wrong. The sleeper train had stopped in Denver, and the porter was about to exit the car for a cup of coffee. Léon saw a chance to have some fun with the man. First, he pulled a watch, then some jewelry, and finally a wad of cash from the astonished man's pockets. Instead of grasping that it was a joke, the porter was horrified and humiliated at the inference that he was a thief. He left the train and didn't come back. Everyone had a good laugh. When the train reached the next stop, Léon had the conductor wire back to Denver to apologize and make sure the man was all right. But he had disappeared. The Elmira *Star-Gazette* reported that some months later, in San Francisco, Léon was served with a lawsuit by the man for defamation of character and an inability to provide "services to his wife." Léon's stunt, which destroyed the porter's career, was presented as a lighthearted yarn.[339]

Blatant racism was a fact of life for Boomsky. Despite his years of experience and his highly specialized skills, he was paid much less than anyone else in the company. Even after years with Herrmann, Isaac Willis's name was not printed in the program. On Léon Herrmann's personnel page that listed each person's name and role, Boomsky was played by "Himself."[340] But even this was a step up in recognition from Alexander Herrmann's days, when Boomsky was not acknowledged in the program at all.

Léon continued his winter tour into New York State, where he attracted fair-sized audiences. Reviews were positive but not gushing. The Elmira *Star-Gazette* described Léon as a "short, graceful dark-haired man. . . . He is a good talker and possesses personal magnetism to a degree."[341]

In the interest of drawing more crowds, Léon, now thirty-two years of age, proclaimed himself the new "Herrmann the Great." All of Léon's advertising now displayed Alexander's old moniker. When she found out, Adelaide was apoplectic with rage. Her own advertising used the phrase, "Widow of Herrmann the Great." She viewed Léon's appropriation of her late husband's title as an outrageous infringement on her own claim to the title. She would strike back.

The endless series of small towns and one-night stands began wearing on Léon. In Raleigh, he complained that the previous night, in Greensboro, they had played in a church hall advertised as an academy of music.[342] Léon was painfully aware that he lacked his uncle's drawing power, but he set his jaw and persisted.

That winter, the company got a welcome reprieve when they sailed to Cuba for a ten-show run in Havana. For Isaac Willis, it was his first time on a ship. For Léon Herrmann, it was a tremendous relief not to have to speak English for a while. Fluent in Spanish, Léon finally relaxed and enjoyed himself onstage. He charmed his Cuban audiences, who laughed, applauded, and feted him like a star. Léon's surprised crew felt newfound respect for their boss. The break was short-lived. They ground through four more US states before finally finishing up the season.

Léon and Marie Herrmann summered in Europe. Isaac Willis spent the summer working his fallback job, waiting tables, before rejoining the Herrmanns in late August 1900.

Léon launched his second solo season in North Carolina. As Herrmann the Great Jr. persisted, audiences continued warming to him. In New Orleans, the company played a full week, with the "startling" Cremation illusion attracting a large audience.[343] While in New Orleans, Léon, assisted by Boomsky, gave a free entertainment at the Jewish Orphans Home, delighting more than a hundred children.[344]

Léon's elegant sleight-of-hand dazzled. "He is a most wonderful man with a most wonderful pair of hands," gushed the *Montgomery Advertiser*.[345] Léon himself said, "My hands are my fortune."[346] Theater lobbies displayed a poster with pictures of an exposed view of Léon's hands demonstrating "The Art of Palming." Magicians objected, asserting that the photos revealed secrets. But in truth, audiences were still fooled by Léon's work, whether they had studied the poster or not.

Isaac became Léon's devoted student. By the hour, Isaac practiced finger-twisting manipulations of coins, cards, and billiard balls until every move was smooth and clean. Eventually, Isaac's hands would become his fortune as well. For Isaac, card tricks were valuable currency in gaining favors from Pullman porters while "en route." Most porters were fanatical players of the card game Whist, and someone always had a deck of cards in his pocket.[347] Isaac Willis needed these favors from porters, since the company now lived on trains, sleeping in Pullman berths nearly every night.

Boomsky was ever-present. Léon Herrmann was never seen in public without him. Although Boomsky was a crucial part of every show, both performing onstage and as part of the backstage crew, he rarely received much press coverage. But one night in Indianapolis, two critics from different newspapers singled out Boomsky. Their impressions of the same show were poles apart. One was positive, the other negative, but neither quite understood Boomsky's role.

The *Indianapolis News* reporter cooed,

> Léon Herrmann . . . has improved wonderfully since he was last seen in this city, and in some respects the performance he gave at English's last night exceeded even the shows given by the elder Herrmann. . . . The redoubtable "Bumpski," Herrmann's faithful colored servant, is still with him, his uniform creased so that it looks as if it must hurt him. "Bumpski" materially assists Herrmann in his tricks, now falling down and breaking a lady's gold watch or else burning up, through sheer carelessness, some lace handkerchief intrusted [*sic*] to his care. It is fortunate he is in the service of so clever a master for no matter what the damage may be, even to the entire destruction of an immaculate silk hat, Professor Herrmann makes it go. It is evident, too, that

"Bumpski" has been well-trained, for last night Herrmann got at least a dozen new laid eggs from the colored servitor's mouth without "Bumpski" suffering any inconvenience.[348]

The *Indianapolis Journal* ran a sour review. Apparently, the humorless critic failed to grasp that Boomsky's "accidents" were intentional.

> Herrmann the Third, undeservedly called "Herrmann the Great," made his second appearance in two years at English's Opera House last night [performing] illusions known to theatergoers of many seasons back. . . . Mr. Herrmann had the assistance of a young colored man whom he called by the euphonious title of "Boomsky," and the entertainment had not progressed very far until it became apparent that "Boomsky" and the magician did not have their minds very well adjusted to each other. This caused a number of unfortunate displays of awkwardness which required all of the performer's mastery of the "gift of gab" in an effort to conceal them from the audience. In the disappearing cage and bird act the cage was handed to Mr. Herrmann by "Boomsky" in such a condition that the feathered occupant made its escape, necessitating a tedious wait until it could be recaptured. Another time the dusky assistant had not properly loaded a pistol which was required in one of the feats of magic.[349]

As the company worked their way through Iowa, Nebraska, Missouri, and on into Texas, Léon vacillated between failure and success. He attracted "a meager audience" in Des Moines. "Local interest in legerdemain seems to have died with the late Alexander Herrmann," noted the *Des Moines Register.* "It is in palming, however, that Herrmann reaches the summit of his skill."[350] In El Paso a few weeks later, "The Myar Opera house was taxed almost to its utmost last night by the audience that turned out to see the wonderful magician, Léon Herrmann, better known as Herrmann the Great. In his line, Herrmann is truly great."[351] The review in the *El Paso Herald* mentioned Herrmann's "negro assistant."

The Tub of Neptune was a hit, and Herrmann's ducks were multiplying. In Kentucky, four ducks appeared. In El Paso, "Herrmann then throws five eggs into the water, fires a pistol into it and out climb five grown ducks, which waddle across the stage and disappear behind the wings."[352] In San Francisco, "A highly amusing feat is the throwing of six eggs into a tub, which is filled with water, and six ducks coming out and swimming about."[353]

Like their predecessors, Léon and Marie Herrmann were animal lovers. They had a well-fed Chihuahua they took everywhere with them.[354] In places where dogs were not allowed, including Pullman cars, restaurants, and hotels, Léon would hide the little dog under his coat. In Scranton, Pennsylvania, Léon and Marie boarded a streetcar, but the conductor spotted the dog and told them they would have to get off. The magician flung open his coat. The dog had disappeared! The conductor stood firm, declaring that he had seen the dog. Léon tried to charm him by removing the dog from the conductor's pocket. It didn't work. The Herrmann contingent had to exit the streetcar.[355]

By April 1901, the company had already played thirty-seven states. They began the month in Wisconsin and finished it with a full week in Montreal, where Léon, performing in French, pleased "a big audience at the Academy."[356] Léon Herrmann worked his way through Vermont and ended his second solo season on a high note, attracting a large audience at New York's Grand Opera House.[357] The exhausted company members parted ways for the summer. Léon and Marie sailed off to Europe. Isaac Willis visited his parents and worked as a waiter while nursing his own magical ambitions. He hatched a plan to increase his public profile.

In August, the *Indianapolis Freeman* printed that "'Boomski' has left New York for Chicago to join Herrmann's show."[358] The widely distributed African American weekly was a main news source for many Black Americans, and Isaac's notice generated much curiosity. Isaac Willis's eleven-word announcement was the first time most readers of the *Freeman* had ever heard of Boomsky, or of Léon Herrmann for that matter. The *Freeman*'s next issue noted Herrmann's tour stops, where Boomsky could receive his fan mail.

Isaac Willis faced a challenging season. He had been greeted at the first rehearsal by a huge backstage barnyard of assorted creatures. The usual doves, bunnies, guinea pigs, and ducks were now joined by chickens, geese, several dogs (big and small), and a piglet. Isaac estimated about thirty animals in total. Alexander Herrmann's old Noah's Ark illusion sat in the wings, spruced up with new paint and trim after nine years in storage. For Isaac, setting up each performance of Noah's Ark required much quick, careful work. Right before the act, dozens of creatures had to be lifted gently into their secret compartments. Upon emerging from the ark, after a brief moment of onstage freedom, each had to be recaptured and placed in its cage. With all the extra feeding, watering, and cage cleaning—in addition to his regular tasks—Isaac's work never ended. During rehearsals, he wondered if one illusion was

Illustration of Léon Herrmann performing the Noah's Ark illusion.

worth all the extra time and effort, but at their first matinee performance, the squeals and screams of hundreds of delighted children convinced him that it was.

ᴀNOTHER ᴃOOMSKY Iꜱ ᴀRRESTED

In October 1901, after a week in San Francisco, Léon Herrmann's company headed for the Pacific Northwest. Just ten months had elapsed since their last visit, which had been profitable, despite cool audiences. Isaac Willis fondly recalled the area's spectacular natural beauty, the towering forests, snow-capped peaks, seaside cliffs, and sparkling rivers, bays, and inlets. This time, however, all they saw was fog.

Their itinerary included a quick two-night dash into British Columbia, Canada. When the Herrmann company arrived at the Seattle ferry terminal on Wednesday morning, October 15, everybody around them was in a bad mood. The thick fog that had descended four days earlier refused to lift. Foghorns sounded day and night. Out in the Puget Sound, several ships had collided; thankfully, none had sunk. At least the returning sealing fleet had docked safely, albeit with a disappointing harvest of pelts in their holds. The Herrmann company's train had arrived late to Seattle, and their ferry to Victoria, British Columbia, the *Rosalie*, had to be held for three hours. When the Herrmann company's fifteen members finally boarded, the inconvenienced passengers and crew glared at them.

When the *Rosalie* finally docked in Victoria, Isaac Willis noticed a female passenger looking all around, visibly upset. She spoke sharply to several crew members then rushed off the ship, disappearing into the fog. As Isaac was unloading Herrmann's cases from the baggage area, he found an unfamiliar purse. Just as he opened it, a hand gripped his shoulder. Isaac turned and found himself facing two police officers.

The newspapers carried only the officers' version of the story, which kept shifting. One newspaper reported that Isaac Willis had heard the passenger, Mrs. Wilkinson, describing her lost purse but thought she had said it contained no money.[359] Another article said that Isaac had refused to turn over the purse to the officers, saying he intended to take it to the police station himself.[360] Whatever Isaac's defense, Constables O'Leary and Carlew did not believe him and placed him under arrest. Despite furious protests from Léon Herrmann and Manager Edward Thurnaer, the constables led a stunned Isaac Willis off to jail.

That night was the darkest of Isaac Willis's life. As he sat in that Canadian jail cell, he thought of Milton Hudson Everett, then in prison in Michigan, and feared that his own career was about to end the same way. As evening descended, Isaac wondered how Léon was managing without him.

Herrmann's show that night at the Victoria Theater was a disaster. The *Victoria Daily Times* review led with, "It was a poor show. The Herrmann company extinguished themselves last evening." Declaring the performance "the worse ever seen in Victoria," the critic continued, "It is extremely doubtful if Herrmann received even a mental invitation to call again."[361]

The next morning, local citizens crowded into the police magistrate's hearing room, spurred by the newspaper story about Mrs. Wilkinson's purse. As he was led in, Isaac Willis scanned the crowd. His heart sank. Nobody from the Herrmann company was there. They had left for Vancouver, where they were playing that night. In that packed hearing room, Isaac Willis had never felt so alone. Abandoned and devastated, he steadied himself, said a prayer, and tried to breathe. The roomful of white people stared at him and commented to each other on the defendant's well-tailored suit and crisp appearance. Not your common thief, they noted.

The hearing opened with the two constables' testimony. It was an open-and-shut case. Willis had been caught with the missing purse. The magistrate agreed that there was no doubt that the defendant was guilty. The penalty for the crime of theft was either twenty dollars or a month in jail. The previous night, Isaac's jailers had told him that the magistrate always chose imprisonment over the fine. Isaac steeled himself for the verdict.

Then the chief of police stood, waving some papers. He had received testimonials from the defendant's employers. The chief read aloud the two letters, one from Léon Herrmann and another from Edward Thurnaer. Isaac's employers apologized to the court for any misunderstandings and begged for forgiveness and leniency for their employee. Both praised Isaac Willis's good character, long employment, dedication, and work ethic. He was an essential member of the Herrmann company, and his return was urgently requested.

Up to that point, Isaac had held his head high and remained emotionless. But as the chief read the letters, Isaac openly wept. The mood in the room shifted. The magistrate, noting the defendant's professional appearance and his employer's fondness for him, decided not to impose jail time after all. Instead, Isaac Willis would be fined twenty dollars and released.

It was over. Isaac had escaped the abyss. It felt like a miracle. Isaac Willis hoped his first night in jail would also be his last. But he had no delusions. His wonderful life with Herrmann hung by a fragile thread, subject to the whims of local authorities.

Isaac did not make it to Vancouver for that night's performance. Again, Herrmann's show was panned. The review in *The Province* bore the headline, "A Tenth Rate Show." The same critic twisted the knife: "The first part of the program opened with Thirty Minutes with Herrmann, and it seemed like thirty years."[362] Another review was kinder but still noted that an assistant had exposed the animals hiding inside the Noah's Ark illusion by opening the wrong door during the trick.[363]

In Vancouver, Isaac Willis's absence was not Léon Herrmann's only problem. A few months earlier another magician had stolen the city's heart. Dressed in buckskins and sporting Buffalo Bill-style, shoulder-length hair, Del Adelphia, the Cowboy Magician, had romanced the frontier audience. Normally, Léon's superior sleight-of-hand feats overcame his bad English and European stuffiness, but the Cowboy Magician had been highly skilled, easy to understand, and lots of fun to boot.

Isaac rejoined the company in Vancouver on Friday, two days after his arrest. The Herrmann company had always enjoyed British Columbia, but this time they could not wait to leave this place of overzealous police, nasty critics, and unrelenting fog. Everyone breathed a sigh of relief when they crossed back into the US for dates in Seattle and Tacoma, Washington. Isaac Willis declared himself done with Canada. Four years later he would change his mind.

The Herrmann Feud Gets Ugly

Early in February 1902, it finally happened. After three years of managing to avoid each other, Léon and Adelaide found themselves scheduled to play Newark, New Jersey, at different venues on the same night. Two Boomskys would play head-to-head as well. Isaac Willis now supported Léon throughout his entire show. M. H. Everett, recently released from Ionia Prison, had rejoined Adelaide for her vaudeville act.

Madame was not at all happy. She continued to rage over Léon using the name Herrmann the Great. In Newark, Adelaide sued Léon for copyright violation, insisting that she had copyrighted the name, Widow of Herrmann the Great. But Vice Chancellor Emery decided in favor of Léon, stating that Adelaide should not have waited three years to bring proceedings. The court held that there was no copyright on the title Herrmann the Great. Léon was free to use it, as was Madame.[364] Adelaide was furious.

After their respective performances, a reporter for the *Newark Daily Advertiser* sought out each of them. When asked what he thought of his aunt Adelaide, Léon took the high ground. "She is a fine lady and a wonderful illusionist." When asked what she thought of Léon, Adelaide replied, "He's a bum."[365]

Two months later, Adelaide and Léon crossed paths again. This time they would play opposite each other for a full week in Boston—Adelaide at the Music Hall and Léon at the Grand Opera House. On April 8, Léon's and Adelaide's opening night performances were reviewed on the same page of the *Boston Globe*. Both reviewers were dazzled. Clearly, nephew and widow had tried to outdo each other with their tricks.

Of Léon, the *Boston Globe* reporter raved, "The first part of the program lasted about a half an hour, and during that time Mr. Herrmann held the audience spellbound with his wonderful dexterity. All the time the powerful electric lights were playing on his hands."[366] Léon was lauded for the crowd-pleasing illusions Escape from Sing Sing and Noah's Ark.

Adelaide rose to the challenge. She had recently added one of her husband's most colorful and surprising routines. The *Globe* reporter who reviewed Adelaide loved her entire act, but "best of all, 'The Trooping of the Nations' a pretty patriotic novelty in which Mme. Herrmann produces out of the paper which she had burned score on score of flags from various nations, beginning with tiny ones and ending with a grand flourish of two huge ones 12 feet long, American and British, respectively. Mme. Herrmann can be credited with creating a furor."[367] The reviewer was so enchanted by Adelaide that he barely remembered to mention the eleven other acts on the same vaudeville bill. Their names were jammed into the final paragraph of the review—comedians, singers, dancers, acrobats, hand balancers, and a dog act, completely unmemorable in comparison to the Queen of Magic.

The next day, the *Globe* noted that on the morning of her first show, Madame Herrmann had staged a publicity stunt. As Boston's fashionable Back Bay women did their daily marketing, "a superbly dressed woman of attractive face and figure might have been seen wending her way along the wholesome stalls of Faneuil Hall Market. She was accompanied by a dusky negro youth." At a farm stand, Madame purchased an egg, which she held high in the air at her fingertips. Around the market, heads turned as she cracked the egg on a table edge and removed from the yolk a twenty-dollar gold piece. She picked up and displayed a live rabbit. She appeared ready to toss the bunny in the air, but instead she rapidly separated her hands, and suddenly she held two bunnies! Madame handed the bunnies to M. H. Everett, then displayed two pigeons. One pigeon was all white, and the other was all black. Briefly turning away, she spun to face the audience and the pigeons had exchanged heads! The white pigeon now had a black head and the black pigeon had a white head. By that point a large crowd had gathered, and someone asked Everett who this lady was. He smiled broadly and announced, "That is Madame Adelaide Herrmann."[368]

Adelaide's efforts paid off. The next day the *Boston Globe* reported, "Adelaide Herrmann, widow of Herrmann the Great, is attracting exceptionally large audiences to the Music Hall this week, and it is noticeable that hundreds of these visitors are ladies and children."[369] A few days later, the *Globe* condemned Adelaide's publicity stunt as a "low trick" on Léon. Her press agent had gotten wind that Léon was preparing to do his own marketplace sojourn, so she did it herself, a day ahead of Léon's planned performance.[370]

That week in Boston playing against Léon touched a raw nerve in Adelaide. Her anger toward him festered. A few weeks later, M. H. Everett provoked her rage as well. For the fourth time, he failed her. Madame had given him train fare from Chicago to New York, with instructions to meet her there. Instead, M. H. simply vanished.

In June 1902, Adelaide and Dewey departed for London without Everett. Madame would tour England's top music halls, culminating with performances marking the coronation of King Edward VII, for whom Alexander Herrmann and the Black teen William Adams had performed when Edward was Prince of Wales. Madame Herrmann toured in England for nearly four months. Her enormously successful trip concluded with a performance attended by England's royal family.

After her triumph in her home country, Adelaide's return to America was a letdown. In her first vaudeville show back in the

States, she shared the bill with a bear and monkey act. Her anger toward both Léon Herrmann and M. H. Everett seethed. Arriving in San Francisco a month after Léon's run there, Madame disgorged her bitterness in a disparaging interview with a reporter from the *San Francisco Examiner.*

As the *Examiner* reporter tried to steer her toward other topics, Adelaide unloaded on both her targets. Regarding Everett's most recent betrayal—taking money for a train ticket and disappearing—she said, "I never want to see him again." But most of her venom was directed toward Léon. In a tirade highly offensive by today's standards, she attacked Léon for calling his own Black assistant Boomsky. "Yes, and didn't that nephew steal the very name? . . . He's not satisfied with using my husband's name, calling himself Herrmann the Great, but he must even plagiarize my husband's nigger. After I taught his ignorant tongue to speak English. Don't ask me about him. I wouldn't have anyone think I knew he's alive."[371]

When the reporter asked about Léon calling himself Herrmann the Great, Adelaide reacted violently. "'Bah!' exclaimed Madame Herrmann, the muscles tightening in her plump, good-natured face, the blood rushing to it until her cheeks flamed in harmony with her deep red hair. 'Bah! You mean Léon, that worthless nephew of Herrmann the Great that I brought over here and tried to teach the business to. I don't want to advertise the ingrate, but you might just say for me that I brought him to this country from France, and as he has proved unsuccessful, I have taken up the career myself. That's all I want to say about him; not a word more."[372]

Yet she could not stop herself. She continued. "It's ridiculous and absolutely humiliating" that "through ill luck [we] were billed simultaneously in the same town. The manager said, 'This will never do. Herrmann the Great at one theater and the Widow of Herrmann the Great at another.' It was awful. But I wouldn't be that clod's widow even for the satisfaction of knowing he is no more."[373]

Adelaide's anger at Léon reflected no small amount of jealousy. Here he was, at the helm of what had been her show, while she was stuck in vaudeville playing against monkeys and seals. But Léon's worst sin of all was using the name Herrmann the Great. Léon responded to her attacks with barbs of his own. But in truth, his life was not so rosy. His career had turned into a grind of one-night stands across small-town America.[374] It wore on him. He didn't much like being an illusionist, either. He would have been happier just performing in smaller theaters and cabarets, as he had done back in France.

Léon Herrmann Soldiers On

When Léon Herrmann began his 1902–03 season, Isaac Willis returned as Boomsky.[375] Léon's company worked harder than ever, playing the same cities across America for the fourth year in a row. Boomsky was ever-present yet rarely mentioned in the press. Reviews and houses were generally good, but Léon's heavy French accent still plagued him, as noted in the *Sioux City Journal*: "At present it is possible to catch about one out of every ten words."[376]

The grind of one-night stands was relentless. Over nine days in November they played Missoula, Butte, Anaconda, Great Falls, Helena, Bozeman, and Livingston, Montana. In December, they played Jamestown, Fargo, and Grand Forks, North Dakota; Winnipeg, Manitoba; Crookston, Brainard, Duluth, Minneapolis, Saint Paul, New Ulm, and Mankato, Minnesota; West Superior, Ashland, Eau Claire, and Redwing, Wisconsin; Sioux Falls, Norfolk, and Lincoln, Nebraska.

January began in Iowa in Des Moines, Ottumwa, Cedar Rapids, Dubuque, Sterling, and Iowa City. With no days off they played Aurora, Grand Rapids, South Bend, Toledo, Fort Wayne, Dayton, Indianapolis, Muncie, Louisville, Nashville, Chattanooga, Knoxville, and Asheville, finishing the month with three days in Atlanta.

In February, they played Savannah, Jacksonville, Macon, Augusta, Columbia, Charlotte, Danville, Lynchburg, Petersburg, Norfolk, Charlottesville, Staunton, Winchester, and Chester. The last week of February they crossed into Pennsylvania, playing Easton, Pottsville, Harrisburg, Allentown, and Reading, then Trenton, New Jersey.

March began with a full week in Providence, then through Massachusetts, Maine, New Hampshire, and Vermont, culminating with a full week in Montreal, where Léon always received a warm welcome.

By April, Léon, now thirty-four years old, was tired of hauling around the big show. He told a reporter from the *Sioux City Journal*, "I would prefer to give an exhibition of sleight-of-hand only, leaving out the illusions and mystery tricks."[377] Yet the season continued with more dates in New York State, Indiana, Iowa, Missouri, Kansas, Kentucky, and Ohio.

After so many months of sleeping on rocking Pullman cars, on the rare nights the company stayed in hotels, they all complained that they had trouble sleeping.[378] Léon's exhaustion made him irritable, which started spilling over into his performances. One night when a trick didn't work, he crept to the backdrop and muttered angrily to his assistant backstage, loud enough for the audience to hear. Another night, Boomsky forgot to fold down a servante, a secret shelf behind a chair. When Léon tried to vanish a bunny, its secret hiding place was not there. Léon stamped offstage with the rabbit. Then he returned, walked directly to Boomsky and gave a sharp yank on his hair.[379]

Worse yet, Léon's supporting act was dragging him down. The Musical Goolmans played a plethora of xylophones, drums, and weird-looking homemade instruments, including one made with alarm clocks and another consisting of long metal tubes played by stroking them with resin-covered cotton gloves.[380] The Goolmans always walked on to enthusiastic applause then squandered that good will with clumsy, off-key playing.

Suddenly, the cavalry appeared. In the early spring, Léon and Marie attended a variety performance at Keith's Union Square in New York.

The opening act snapped everyone to attention. Two caped Russian Hussars marched briskly onto the stage, turned to the audience, and raised trumpets to their lips. They exchanged rousing military bugle calls, then marched into the wings and returned immediately, dressed as Spanish-American War soldiers. The shorter of the two, a young woman, played a dizzyingly impressive cornet solo. The two marched offstage once more and instantly returned as Teddy Roosevelt's Rough Riders, playing a quickstep march as a large American flag was lowered to the stage to fervent applause.[381] Léon loved the act. He immediately fired the Musical Goolmans and hired The Laskeys, Military Trumpeters.

The Laskeys (they added an *e* for their stage name) were a brother-sister act managed by their mother. At twenty-two, Jesse L. Lasky was the same age as Isaac Willis. His sister, Blanche, was just eighteen.

Léon Herrmann and company, circa 1903. Left to right: Sarah Lasky, Isaac Willis, Marie Herrmann, unidentified standing man, Léon Herrmann, Jesse Lasky (directly behind Léon), unidentified man, Blanche Lasky (holding dog), unidentified man, manager Edward Thurnaer.

Sarah, their mother, sewed their costumes and chaperoned. Originally from San Francisco, the Laskys had finally found success after falling victim to several scams following the failure of the family business. Jesse had gone to find gold in Alaska, where his trumpet playing saved him from starving. When young Blanche showed surprising talent for the trumpet, mother and son had designed their current act, honing it at low-paying summer park gigs.

The energetic Lasky family quickly bonded with Léon and Marie, whose French accents enchanted the Americans. To the Herrmanns, unmoored from their Jewish family and practices, the observant Laskys were a delightful port in a storm. The Herrmanns nicknamed the fastidious Blanche, "Lady Lasky."[382] With The Laskeys aboard, Isaac Willis felt the tension lift. On the train, backstage, at meals, Léon and Marie smiled and laughed with their new friends. Isaac realized with a pang that in all these years, he had never seen the Herrmanns this happy.

Jesse Lasky was unlike other musicians, who did their jobs and kept to themselves. He had arrived with few skills beyond playing the trumpet, but he watched everything, always learning and ready to help. Jesse and Blanche Lasky had never toured, but their education was quick.

In Coffeyville, Kansas, a Saturday night crowd of drunk, rowdy cowboys filled the theater. For the hat trick, Léon unwisely borrowed a ten-gallon Stetson from a drunk man in the front row. When Boomsky fell on the duplicate hat, the cowboy flew into a rage. Léon tried to rapidly finish the trick. But when he tore the hat to pieces and stuffed it in the cannon, the man unholstered his pistol and leapt toward the stage. Léon rapidly fired *his* revolver, the signal for the restored hat to drop from the proscenium. Except it did not drop. It was stuck. Léon helplessly fired shot after shot into the air. The whole audience turned on Herrmann, shouting and cursing. The quick-thinking theater manager dropped the curtain and yelled at the company, "Run for your lives!" The entire Herrmann company ran out the stage door. Some ran for the train station and some for the hotel. A melee of audience members, joined by townspeople, swarmed the hotel, blocking their exit. Sympathetic hotel workers quickly rushed the company members out the kitchen door. They hurried to the train, relieved to leave Coffeyville behind.[383]

As Isaac Willis ran for his life, he wondered if it was time to leave Léon Herrmann behind as well.

∾

Act Three

Black Magic: Boomsky Takes Center Stage

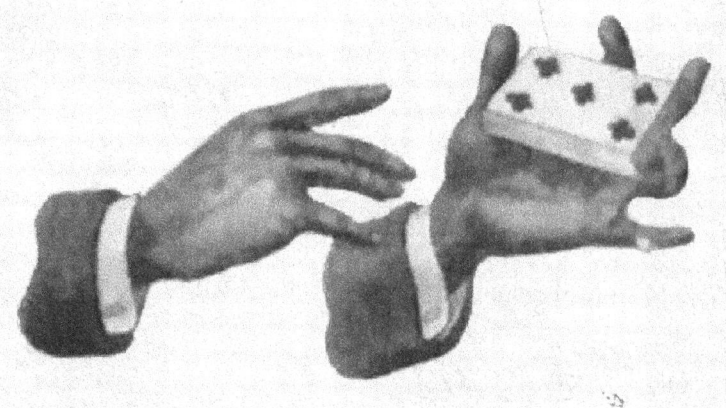

Richards & Pringle's Famous Georgia Minstrels poster featuring The Great Boomsky, Isaac Willis.

CHAPTER NINE

Isaac Willis, The Great Boomsky

From Boomsky to The Great Boomsky

After five years with Herrmann the Great, Isaac Willis was now a remarkable magician himself. His manipulations of cards, coins, and billiard balls rivaled any professional conjuror's. Léon was proud of his student's fine work and enjoyed showing him off to backstage guests. Isaac wedged his sleight-of-hand practice into the free moments between his valet chores and magic assistant duties, while imagining that *he* was standing in the spotlight performing magic every night.

It was no idle fantasy. The Great Black Carl—the first Boomsky, Edward Johnson—had been a mainstay of Black minstrelsy for nearly two decades. At age thirty-six, the Great Black Carl was heading his own forty-five-member touring show called "The Hottest Coon in Dixie." The title referred to Black Carl himself, who served as both lead actor and magician in a hilarious musical farce that was a hit with both Black and white audiences. When he was a child, Isaac Willis had probably seen Black Carl when Isaac's family, and most everyone they knew, packed into theater balconies for the Black minstrel extravaganzas that roared through town. While other magicians had called themselves the Black Herrmann, Black Carl personified it. His old-style European court dress had been antiquated even in Herrmann's time, but it signified classic elegance—the brocade tailcoat, waistcoat, and flouncy white shirt, topping knee breeches, hose, and pointed buckled shoes, signaled "magic" to audiences.

One day, Isaac read a theatrical notice in the *Freeman* that made his heart jump. Richards and Pringle's Famous Georgia Minstrels Company was auditioning variety acts for their spectacular new production. Here was Isaac's chance. But it was a long shot. The popular Black company featured renowned stars, and Isaac Willis had never even performed a solo show. He would need help to stand a chance. Unsure of how his boss would react, Isaac told Léon Herrmann that he would like to audition. Léon looked Isaac up and down then said, "We must get to work."

Isaac Willis would need a stage name. "Professor Willis" was already taken. James A. Willis, Alexander Herrmann's former assistant, was touring the minstrel circuit as magician and music director with the Alabama Warblers.

Most likely it was cornetist Jesse Lasky who came up with "The Great Boomsky." In his future career, Lasky would demonstrate a genius for inventing brilliant screen names for soon-to-be movie stars. As they traveled from city to city, the Herrmann company helped Isaac prepare for his audition. Léon coached Isaac's rehearsals, and seamstress Sarah Lasky constructed The Great Boomsky's new costume, with all its secret pockets. Manager Edward Thurnaer wrote a reference letter for Isaac on Herrmann the Great's stationery.

Finally, the big day arrived. Isaac Willis marched into his audition wearing white tie and tails. The company's producers, middle-aged white men, straightened in their chairs. First-rate Black magicians were rare and always in demand. This young man's finely tailored suit and exquisitely carved tables signaled fine taste and attention to detail, as well as a significant monetary investment. With a bow, Isaac Willis introduced himself as The Great Boomsky. Isaac bowed again as he handed to the producers his reference letter. They passed the letter around, whispering to each other, "Protégé of Herrmann the Great!" The magician began his act with palming tricks, his hands performing a graceful dance as white billiard balls appeared and disappeared. As large silver rings melted through each other, mysteriously linking and unlinking, the producers

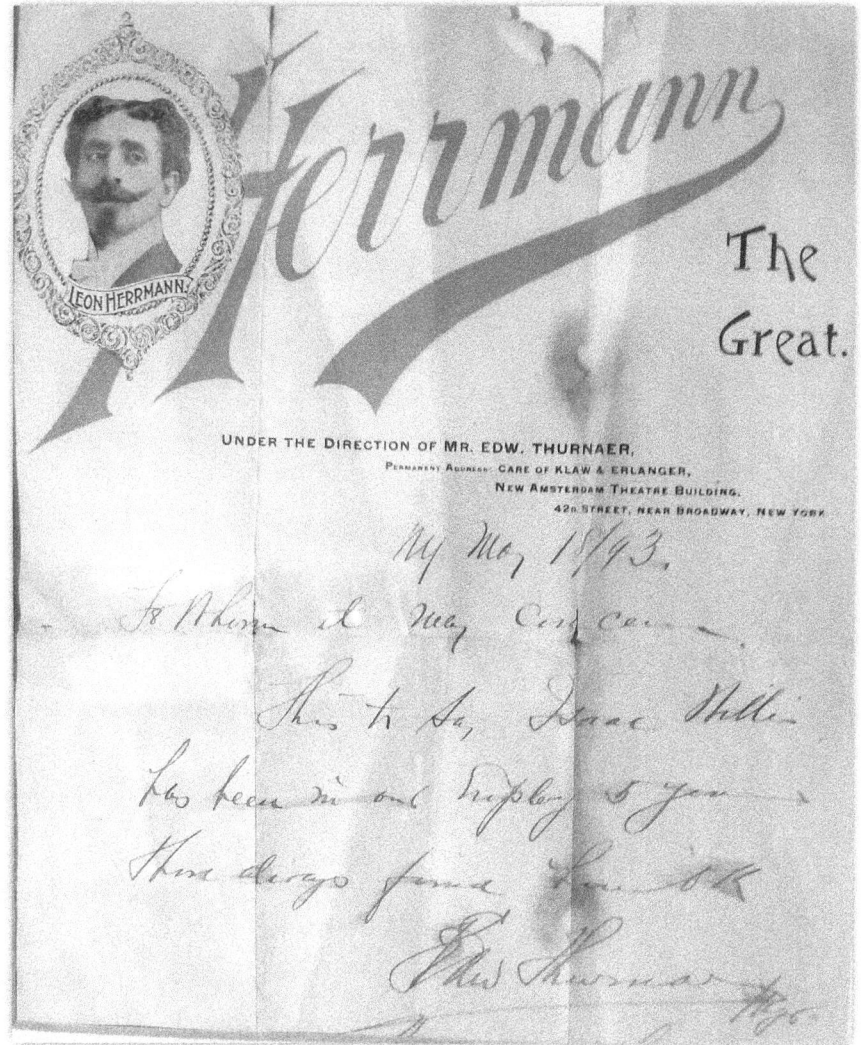

Reference letter for Isaac Willis, written by manager Edward Thurnaer on Léon Herrmann's letterhead.

sitting just a few feet away stared, bewildered. Isaac finished by rolling out a large tub of water. The Great Boomsky tossed in four eggs, fired a pistol into the air, and suddenly four live ducks appeared, swimming around the tub. The producers applauded enthusiastically and offered The Great Boomsky a contract, starting in July.

Léon Herrmann hailed Isaac's good fortune, even though it meant losing his favorite assistant. As the season wound down, Léon helped Isaac fill up his new touring trunk with props and illusions. After their final show together, Herrmann the Great presented Isaac Willis with the Tub of Neptune and the ducks. Touched by his boss's kindness, The Great Boomsky promised to stay in touch.

MINSTRELSY

In the twenty-first century, just the mention of America's tradition of minstrel shows—most of which were performed by whites wearing blackface—evokes understandable revulsion, pain, and anger. Minstrelsy's slavery-era caricatures of African American stereotypes, in which even Black entertainers often wore freakish blackface, would repulse and shock today's audiences. In the post–civil rights era, minstrelsy is anathema, nearly impossible to process, and, for many, too abhorrent even to examine closely.

Yet for over fifty years, minstrel shows were the most popular type of entertainment in America. Blackface minstrel shows began before the Civil War and remained popular for decades following emancipation. Originated as a form of propaganda by pro-slavery factions, minstrelsy evoked nostalgia for a time that never actually existed—happy slaves on the plantation singing, dancing, and joking around.[384] Even at the time, many people found these portrayals odious, but many others bought into the myth, not understanding that smiling and acting happy was demanded by slave owners and bought better treatment. The earliest minstrel shows featured whites in blackface. As the genre's popularity exploded, all-Black minstrel shows soon followed.

Many modern readers are surprised to learn that both Blacks and whites considered minstrelsy an art form. Performers took great pride in their work. While decidedly racist, the shows were also wildly entertaining and provided hundreds of Black comedians, singers, musicians, dancers, magicians, and variety artists with performing careers and a steady income that could provide a path to the middle class. At their pinnacle, giant all-Black minstrel extravaganzas traveled the country, playing to packed houses in grand theaters and opera houses every night. It was the one genre in which a Black magician could become a star.

All minstrel shows followed a similar basic format—stylized comedy skits, a variety show (the olio), music and dance numbers, and a full-company finale of rousing songs, usually written by white composers, most famously Stephen Foster. Early musical arrangements heavily featured the banjo, an instrument of African origin.

There always were far fewer Black companies. In any given year, between three and five large-scale Black entertainment companies toured the US and Canada, while at least a dozen whites-in-blackface minstrel shows plied the same routes. Black companies and white companies were managed by the same white producers, and all performers were expected to play the same Black stereotyped characters. All the white touring minstrel companies were all-male, with men playing any female roles. By contrast, some of the Black minstrel companies included women. Although their formats were virtually the same, companies were never racially integrated. Yet their audiences included everyone. Black people sat in the balcony and white people downstairs, on the main floor.[385]

As a relic of American slavery, whites-in-blackface minstrel shows retained the same content over time, changing little through the decades. But Black minstrel companies were constantly evolving, playing new, popular music. As Black companies moved away from self-deprecating "coon" stereotypes, the white companies continued to wholeheartedly embrace them. At the dawn of the twentieth century, whites-in-blackface, nappy-wigged choruses a hundred strong still crooned Stephen Foster songs to strumming banjos. At the same time, Black minstrel bands were tearing off theater roofs with sizzling hot ragtime renditions featuring horns and saxophones.

Black minstrel shows were universally popular, but it was almost as if Black and white audiences were seeing two different shows. White patrons in the orchestra seats would tap their feet and applaud vigorously after an upbeat song, while above them the balcony throbbed with so much screaming, cheering, whistling, and stomping that whites often refused to sit directly under the balcony for fear it would collapse.[386] Black performers slid in countless in-jokes, barbs, and coded cultural references that flew over the white audiences' heads straight to the balcony. White people sitting below were oblivious to being skewered from the stage. Sometimes white reviewers who judged comic scenes as boring or too long would also note that screams of laughter continued nonstop in the gallery.

Black Americans attended Black minstrel shows in droves. Performances were often "top heavy." That meant that the balcony was packed, while the spacious whites-only section was populated more sparsely. Sometimes heavy Black turnout turned a performance "upside down"—white patrons were moved to the balcony, and the overflowing Black crowd rushed down to fill the orchestra and mezzanine seats.

Minstrelsy created employment for African American performers of all specialties. In the beginning, wages were comparatively low, but they were still among the best-paying jobs for African Americans. The shows themselves were so profitable that when Black performers rebelled against wage exploitation and started managing themselves, white producers sued them for theft of property. Minstrelsy was big business, and the few Black stars who controlled their own companies were among the world's highest-earning people of color. As minstrel companies competed for top talent, performers' pay increased, until minstrelsy became the one area of employment in which Blacks were paid significantly more than whites.

THE MINSTREL MAGICIANS: FORMER BOOMSKYS & FORMIDABLE RIVALS

In 1903, as The Great Boomsky prepared to set off on his new career, he faced some serious competition. Minstrelsy was at its apex. Five Black companies were touring America, and three rival troupes already featured world-class magicians. All of them—Black Carl, Alonzo Moore, and James A. Willis—were former Herrmann assistants. As he sized up his colleagues, Isaac Willis realized that they had set a very high bar. All three personified Herrmann, copying the master magician's elegant court dress, wickedly clever comedy, and spectacular sleight-of-hand. The Great Boomsky braced himself for the challenge.

The Great Black Carl, headlining in "The Hottest Coon in Dixie," was Isaac's most daunting rival. More than twenty years earlier, Edward Johnson had been nabbed on the runaround as a young teen in Herrmann's show. Now, at thirty-six, Black Carl was the oldest former Boomsky playing the minstrel circuit. A veteran showman, Black Carl's adventures were legendary. He had taken over as company manager when a previous manager had left his company stranded in Australia. Later he successfully sued a steamship company for discrimination. He co-wrote and directed an earlier all-Black extravaganza, "Senegambia Carnival." When working as a manager, he used the name Carl Dante.

Black Carl was known as a wonderful magician. He played the dandy—a wise-cracking, irreverent fancy dresser who called himself the "Hoodoo Magician." Never modest, he was billing himself as the "Greatest Magician on Earth" in 1894, two years before Alexander Herrmann's death.[387] Black Carl was popular with both Black and white audiences. The *Buffalo Courier* reported that audiences were surprised and delighted by "the first colored magician ever seen here."[388] Black Carl performed with two midget assistants, Little Chick and Little Price, the latter also being his wife.[389]

Magician Black Carl emulated Alexander Herrmann's look and performance style.

Black Carl's signature trick was like Herrmann's famous watch trick but was done with finger rings. The magician borrowed rings from five audience members. He smashed the rings with a hammer. He magically restored four of them and then went on with the show, seemingly forgetting the fifth. Sometimes this didn't go well. The *Brooklyn Daily Eagle* reported that the stunt "almost caused a woman to burst into tears" at the sight of her pulverized ring.[390] But Black Carl saved the day by smashing a bottle to reveal that inside was a guinea pig with the missing ring tied on a ribbon around its neck.

Alonzo Moore, another former Boomsky and rival, was touring with Black minstrelsy's greatest star, Billy Kersands. At age twenty-seven, Alonzo Moore, Prince of Magic, was nearly a decade younger than Black Carl but was quickly becoming every bit as popular. Like several other former Boomskys, Alonzo Moore sometimes called himself the Black Herrmann. After Edward Maro had snatched him away from Herrmann around 1893, Moore had assisted his new boss for many years before setting out on his own. Like Léon Herrmann, Maro, whose real name was Walter Best, had boosted his protégé, providing him with stylish tables, props, and some of his own signature oriental magic tricks, including flowing productions of colorful silks and ribbons that unfurled into stunning streamers when tossed over spectators' heads. Moore's sleight-of-hand work was dazzling, his huge hands manipulating cards and billiard balls with an incongruous delicacy. And he was hilarious. How he presented himself depended on his audience. With Chicago's white society patrons, Moore was refined and relatively restrained. In front of Black and minstrel show crowds, Moore's outrageous antics kept audiences screaming.

Moore had worked with Maro on the Chautauqua circuit. "Chautauquas," named after the small New York town where they originated, were weeklong summer gatherings consisting of Christian-themed education lectures, concerts, and entertainment. People often traveled long distances to attend and would camp nearby for the week.

Alonzo Moore performed on the Chautauqua circuit with an act modeled after his mentor, Edward Maro.

Liberal in nature, Chautauquas featured America's only integrated rosters. Black musicians, entertainers, and lecturers appeared alongside whites.

Alonzo Moore's success on the Chautauqua circuit is reflected in his high-quality promotional materials.

Chautauquas were the only venue where African American performers could drop the racial caricatures expected of them everywhere else and, to their tremendous relief, just be themselves. As the circuit's only Black magician, Alonzo Moore amazed his mostly white Chautauqua audiences with his beautiful sleight-of-hand and colorful oriental magic while keeping them in stitches with his gentle ribbing of audience volunteers. The mainstream press compared Moore favorably to top white magicians. According to a *Fort Worth Telegram* review in September 1905, "Alonzo Moore (the Black Herrmann) is now rated as one of the foremost magicians of the day. This season he is carrying an entirely new and up-to-date act, not only being one of the most expensive acts of its kind, but the most amazing and wonderful illusion before the American public this season."[391]

Upon entering Black minstrelsy, Alonzo Moore stepped into an opposite world. The head of his company, Billy Kersands, was a brilliant comedian who had become a huge star by capitalizing on minstrelsy's most extreme racial caricatures. As reported by the Annapolis *Evening*

Capital, the Billy Kersands Minstrels show opened with the company of comedians and singers sitting inside a piece of scenery that looked like a giant watermelon, "an extravagant setting emblematic of the race." Then "they cut up with all the abandon and idiosyncrasies of their race."[392] Kersands played a lazy Sambo character. His mouth was so large that it fit a whole cup and saucer or several billiard balls, which Kersands would insert before performing a raucous dance. Although he was nearly two hundred pounds, he was a nimble acrobat.

In the large company, one performer stood out. The *Evening Capital* raved, "The olio was clever and amusing, the honors easily falling to the lot of Alonzo Moore, an ebonized magician."[393] In the Billy Kersands show, Alonzo Moore presented a hilarious caricature of a northern dandy, speaking in what was called "broad Negro dialect," full of malaprops and mispronounced words. When magic happened, he appeared as surprised as anyone else. The *Voice Republican* noted that "Alonzo Moore performed some wonderful feats in magic and kept the crowd in a continual uproar with his laughable tricks played on different ones of the audience."[394]

According to the *Evening Capital*, the appeal was nearly universal. "Minstrelsy of the genuine type was presented at the Colonial last night by 'Billy Kersands' Famous Troupe.' As a result, Annapolis' white, black and tan chuckled in glee, since there was a fairly good house downstairs, while the gallery was full to overflowing, where a host of admirers of Kersands' own color shouted themselves hoarse."[395]

Thirty-four-year-old magician and pianist James A. Willis (no known relation to Isaac) was touring with a smaller minstrel company, the Alabama Warblers. Professor Willis had assisted Alexander Herrmann in the late 1880s before venturing out on his own. He was the first to call himself the "Black Herrmann," although others would soon follow.

James Willis liked calling his own shots. In 1894, he had formed his own touring troupe consisting of singers and musicians, all of them white. Willis performed magic and piano solos, then accompanied the singers in classical and popular songs. The small troupe performed at lodges, benefits, concert series, and community events, mostly across the Midwest, always to excellent reviews.

In 1899, James Willis signed on with a minstrel troupe, the Georgia Up-To-Date Company. His magic act closed the olio, the spot reserved for the company's strongest variety act.[396] In 1903, he was lured away by the Alabama Warblers, who hired him as magician and music director. According to the *Napa Journal*, at seventeen members, the Alabama Warblers troupe was "small and hasn't a very prosperous appearance, but it gave a performance which, save in spectacular features, is not excelled by any company on the road."[397]

RICHARDS & PRINGLE'S FAMOUS GEORGIA MINSTRELS

On July 8, 1903, Isaac Willis arrived in Benton, Michigan, for rehearsals.[398] As musicians and specialty performers warmed up all around him, Isaac could not believe his good fortune. Richards and Pringle's Famous Georgia Minstrels represented the highest echelon of mainstream entertainment. Over the course of twenty-eight seasons, the all-male company had toured America and the world. In England, they had performed for Queen Victoria.

However, the previous season everything had fallen apart. Minstrelsy's biggest star, Billy Kersands, had been Richards and Pringle's headliner for several years. When management refused his demands for more money, Kersands had quit to form his own company, taking many of the Georgia Minstrels cast with him. Now Richards and Pringle's was bouncing back with a spectacular new show to compete with, and hopefully crush, their traitorous former star.

When band auditions had been announced the previous spring, scores of eager African American men carrying instruments boarded Chicago-bound Jim Crow cars. Many returned home disappointed as the Georgia Minstrels required a high level of musicianship, including the ability to read music on sight. Forty-eight musicians were hired for the two bands, orchestra, and precision drum corps. They played violin, viola, cello, double bass, cornet, trombone, baritone horn, tuba, "clarionet," saxophone, and drums.[399] Advertised positions for piccolo and oboe players went unfilled.[400] Pointedly, the advertisement did not list any positions for banjo players.

The company's new talent lineup featured a dizzying array of popular stars and intriguing newcomers. Newspaper ads promised twelve comedians, sixteen dancers, twenty-four solo singers, and ten "Big Olio Acts." They would travel with a carload of scenery and special company Pullman cars. To save space, only the specialty acts, including The Great Boomsky, were allowed to bring their own trunks.[401]

After two weeks of rehearsals, the Famous Georgia Minstrels opened at Chicago's Alhambra Theater to standing-room-only crowds, selling out every show. Isaac Willis was pleased and proud when The Great Boomsky's first write-up appeared in the *Indianapolis Freeman*, despite the misspelling of his name. "The great Boomsby, a pupil of Herman [*sic*], is mystifying the people with his tricks in closing his act by making four live ducks appear swimming around in a tub of water at the report of a revolver. He leaves the audience screaming. Boomsby has the finest stage settings of any similar act, and as this is his first season as principal and being a young and ambitious gentleman, much is in store for him."[402] Isaac clipped the notice and sent it to Léon Herrmann.

After Chicago they played a week in Kansas City, which Isaac had visited every year with Herrmann. It was very different being with the minstrels, where fans at the stage door, after saying hello and asking for autographs, then took the visiting showmen out on the town. Kansas City's Black citizens threw open their doors and invited them into their homes. This hospitality would be repeated in town after town.

From early on it was apparent which minstrels would still have money at the end of the tour. For all the performers, the job was a rare and colossal opportunity to support their families and accumulate a nice nest egg. But temptations to spend were everywhere. Delectable food, drink, fancy clothes, shoes, watches, and jewelry all beckoned—enticements they could never afford before, but now they had money in their pockets. Gambling kept a couple of the men perpetually broke, their hard work and futures thrown away on rolls of the dice. And many a randy showman deposited his pay at the colored brothels to be found in every town with a Black population. Isaac Willis resisted all these lures, squirreling away every penny and adding to his sizeable savings from his five years with Herrmann.

The Great Boomsky shared the olio—the variety part of the minstrel show—with nine other acts, including a ventriloquist, acrobats, a hoop controller, comedians, musicians, and the show's biggest star, Clarence Powell, with his collection of funny sayings. Ventriloquist John W. Cooper, with his five talking figures, was a whole company in himself. His act was set in a barbershop, where his "wooden-headed family"[403] sang a trio. Isaac Willis noticed that Cooper's little characters got away with controversial statements that no Black man ever could.[404]

The hoop controller, twenty-year-old Harry Kraton, brought down the house nightly.[405] Kraton juggled the hoops, rolled them over his body, and rapidly formed them into pleasing patterns. Audiences went wild for the quick-moving act.

Because of the crowded bill, Boomsky's turn was brief, consisting of just three tricks. First, he changed a pitcher of water into red wine. He continued with the classic trick, the linking rings, then finished with the Tub of Neptune.[406] Minstrel audiences did not get to see Willis's superior sleight-of-hand work. The raucous, fast-paced show had no time for elegant billiard ball and card manipulations. Magicians who knew Isaac's work said that the show was poorer for it.

Usually only established stars were displayed on the minstrel company's posters, but for The Great Boomsky, the tremendous cachet of Herrmann the Great justified the significant expense of creating a stone lithograph featuring the newcomer. Isaac Willis posed for a photographer while presenting his rising cards trick, and an artist created the poster based on the photo. On the poster's wide red border, the artist created detailed drawings of twenty-eight pairs of Black hands performing classic sleight-of-hand tricks.

Richards and Pringle's Pullman sleeper cars were advertised as an extravagant feature, but they were in truth a touring necessity. Since trains and hotels were segregated, private sleeper cars were the only way a company of African American performers could travel. By day, just like public Pullman sleepers, the upper berths tucked up into the ceiling and the lower berths were folded back up to form coach seating.

Even so, it was not safe, especially in the South. Their unmarked Pullman cars often had secret hiding places that doubled as stores for food, because, according to Black Carl, "though white folks always want to see our show, they don't want to house us or feed us."[407] Sometimes guns were fired at minstrel companies' cars.

In 1903, mob violence and lynchings were escalating in the Deep South. For ease of doing business as well as safety concerns, a white manager always traveled with the company. Sundown towns, where Blacks had to leave before dark, and known trouble spots in deepest Dixie were avoided. During The Great Boomsky's tenure, Richards and Pringle's Famous Georgia Minstrels never played in Georgia.

From Kansas City, the company hit the road in earnest, playing their way south through Arkansas toward Texas. At each stop, the fifty-man company paraded from the train to the theater. Strutting in their snappy, brass-buttoned uniforms, the drum corps beat the rhythm while horns and saxophones blared ragtime marches. Spectators pointed and laughed as The Great Boomsky's four ducks marched alongside him. Less than a month into the tour, the minstrels' parade sparked a tragedy. In Dallas, the horns and drums startled some carriage horses, causing them to stampede. One carriage overturned and fatally crushed a white man.[408] Fortunately, the sorrowful minstrels were allowed to leave Dallas without further incident.

A week later severe illness hit the company. Some felt they were cursed after the tragedy in Dallas. Many of the men were struck down by fever, vomiting, and diarrhea, their misery compounded by the close quarters. Several became so sick they had to temporarily leave the tour, including the show's star, S. H. Dudley, and Harry Kraton, the hoop controller. In the Indianapolis *Freeman*, the company scribe, Napoleon Johnson, though himself sick, singled out Isaac Willis's work in carrying on with the show. "The Great Boomsky is still mystifying the people with his tricks and so artistic is he in his work that after the show, it is quite amusing to hear the people trying to explain how this and that trick is done. Boomsky in closing his turn uses the duck trick which is the hit of his act, and any one after the show in speaking of him asks for 'the man with the ducks.'"[409]

As the company members recovered, Isaac Willis continued to hold his own. Even in the large cast, The Great Boomsky stood out both in the group's publicity and in reviews. The *Commercial Dispatch* of Columbia, Mississippi, noted, "Boomsky, who has appeared here many times as the assistant of Herrmann the Great, this season is appearing as a full-fledged magician."[410] The *Montgomery Advertiser* observed that The Great Boomsky, playing to two "top-heavy" audiences in Alabama, "did some legerdemain work which can only be done by a pupil of the great magician."[411]

Overall, Isaac's responsibilities were lighter than with the Herrmann show. Like the other specialty performers, Isaac sang and danced in the full-company production numbers. For anyone else, transporting and caring for four ducks on tour might have seemed daunting. But after tending Léon Herrmann's menagerie, touring with a few ducks was practically a vacation. There were no actual vacations. Like vaudeville performers, Richards and Pringle's minstrels worked through the summer. The heat didn't keep audiences away. As the *Fort Worth Star* reported in August, the "gallery was packed with colored humanity." The theater proudly promoted its new electric fans, which, with open windows, kept a pleasant breeze flowing through the show.[412]

As with Léon Herrmann's show, the minstrels performed mainly one-night stands at opera houses, crawling from one town to the next. When possible, they did two shows, matinee and evening. As they toured North Carolina, the company's new magician kept garnering good reviews. The *Durham Sun* remarked, "The Great Boomsky, pupil of Herrmann the Great, as a magician was fine."[413] In South Carolina, the *Gaffney Ledger* noted, a "small but enthusiastic audience" saw the "best colored magical show ever witnessed."[414] Isaac continued to impress his colleagues. In his weekly report in the *Indianapolis Freeman*, the company scribe, Napoleon Johnson, reported that "Boomsky, formerly assistant to Hermann the Great, has the necessaries to put on a two hour show, but now, owing to time, he is only using a few of his tricks."[415] By April 1904, The Great Boomsky's act had expanded to include his billiard ball manipulations. In Grand Junction, Colorado, the *Daily Sentinel* reviewer described a "sleight-of-hand performance equal to Herrmann."[416]

The entertainment industry's major trade journals, the *New York Clipper* and the *New York Dramatic Mirror*, published the Black minstrel companies' touring routes, but they almost never included African Americans in their feature stories. The *Indianapolis Freeman* filled the gap, devoting an entire section of the African American newspaper to theatrical news for Black readers. "The Stage" featured a full page, sometimes two, of chatty updates from all of the Black road companies, as well as classified postings of messages for friends and colleagues in the field. In exchange for this free service, a note at the bottom of the page reminded performers to buy their own copies of the *Freeman* and not to share them with each other.

Isaac Willis enjoyed his new job. After so many years with Léon Herrmann's company, being in an all-Black troupe brought surprising pleasures. Seeing each theater's dressing rooms occupied by Black performers felt deliciously satisfying. Local Black communities continued to fete the Famous Georgia Minstrels, sometimes with parties or dances organized for them. Since the minstrels hailed from all over America, they frequently played in or near one of their hometowns, where the hospitality would be ramped up. In New Orleans, a band member's family cooked a Creole dinner for the entire company.[417] Over just one week in Texas, they were treated to family barbeques in Galveston, Houston, and Beaumont.[418] As the tour progressed, friendships and groups organized around similar interests. The company's baseball team began playing local teams between shows. The fishing club often returned with strings of fish for the company's dinner. The Bible study group huddled together on long train rides.

A town's affluence and racial makeup were reflected in the ticket price. In Jennings, Louisiana, and Idaho Springs, Idaho, tickets were seventy-five cents and one dollar—unaffordable for most Black folks, especially those with families. Most places, the tickets ranged from twenty-five to seventy-five cents for adults and ten cents for children. The balcony was almost always full.

Managing a fifty-man company on the road was an intense challenge. Some of the men were show business veterans, and others were young and away from home for the first time. All of them lived and worked together in close quarters month after month. In an era when all show people were considered disreputable, and many whites feared Black people, managers Rusco and Holland were eager to reassure the public in advance. They ran the same newspaper announcement in every town just prior to the minstrel company's arrival: "The excellent deportment of the entire company on the streets, in the theater, and in fact everywhere, is one of the noticeable things with Richards & Pringle's Famous Georgia Minstrels. People remark daily on the way the boys carry and behave themselves. They are never seen hanging about saloons and tough negro dives, or associating with loose characters. It is this discipline that makes it possible for them to give such a really excellent performance as they do. The reputation of the organization is world wide."[419]

In an interview in Montana's *The Missoulian* in June, the company's business manager, J. J. Holland, took credit, explaining how this exemplary behavior was maintained.

> Speaking of discipline, why, . . . we have strict rules laid down to each one, and attach a penalty for the breaking of each rule. We deduct all the way from 10 cents to $25 from their salary. The highest is for drunkenness. We find that this is the only way to keep them under control. We have our own cars and the members eat and sleep there. . . . If [a member] is late at parade it costs him . . . $2; . . . using profanity, $2 to $5; speaking disrespectfully to manager, $10, and so on for every offense. You see we hold back $30 on each member's salary, which is given him at the end of the season, and should he object to the fine and quit, why, we take the entire $30. This is part of the written contract we make with each one.[420]

In addition to characterizing the troupe's skilled professionals as incapable of self-discipline, the company's fine system was primed for potential abuse. Thirty dollars in 1905 was the equivalent of nearly $900 in today's currency. When a performer began his contract, he received no pay until he had banked his thirty-dollar escrow with the company. If he left the company before his contract's end, or was fired, he forfeited that money. Some of the offenses, such as "speaking disrespectfully to manager," were arbitrary, and a man who objected and spoke up, even for valid reasons, risked piling on additional fines.

J. J. Holland was in a revelatory mood that month, as he plied the route in advance of his company. The company's business manager revealed much in an interview in the *Great Falls Tribune* that was not only informative, but also racist and patronizing, as was normal for the time.

> Speaking about the salaries of negro talent . . . , I wish to explode the idea that negro talent is cheap. . . . The truth

of the matter is we pay higher salaries than the average white show, for the simple reason colored talent is scarce. Take the musicians, for instance; you know that every white person who has a [son who] . . . wants to travel and see the world, and as "pa" will look after his future, the question of money is not so much an object as it is to get away from the home and travel. Not so with the negro musicians; they are, as a rule, self-educated, and are scarce, they have got to make their living and save enough to live on when not traveling, and, as I say, are a scarce article, especially those that are capable of reading music at sight, which we demand of them. Then come the singers. . . . We can get hundreds of "barbershop" tenors, but pardon me from asking any one to come and hear them sing. Well, it is so with all lines of negro talent, they are scarce, and come high, especially those capable of entertaining an intelligent audience.[421]

The Georgia Minstrels worked through the summer of 1904, suffering through a July heat wave in Iowa. Despite the sizzling temperatures, theaters were packed. In Marshallton, the *Evening-Times-Republican* noted that "fans kept the audience cool."[422] The *Kansas City Star* reported that they began an eight-day run on a "hot night for an indoor performance." The reviewer noted that "everybody used fans."[423] In Arkansas, the *Jonesboro Weekly* observed that the "temperature was a little high for theater going and the ice-water boy was not present."[424]

In October 1904, Napoleon Johnson reported to the *Indianapolis Freeman* that after many months on the road, the minstrels were happy to hear that new parade suits would soon arrive. Boomsky was "still mystifying."[425] He elaborated, "Boomsky and his tricks like good liquors become better with age, and the success he is having this season puts him on the top shelf with the best in the business, regardless of color."[426] As always, Isaac sent the clipping to Léon.

Time passed quickly as they ranged across America. In the fall of 1904, Napoleon Johnson continued to send his weekly road reports to the *Indianapolis Freeman*. By the time they reached Kansas, where "we leave them screaming nightly," the weather had changed. "Coats are in order, and we're wishing for the warm days of summer."[427] A few weeks later they were in New Mexico, "the land of high wind and sands."[428] A week after that they serenaded a wedding in Bisbee, Arizona, before crossing into Mexico to take in a bullfight. Some of the men rushed about buying expensive gifts for their families because, after working eighteen months straight, they were getting a week off for Christmas.[429]

After their much-needed Christmas break, the Georgia Minstrels met up again in Oklahoma. When Isaac Willis arrived, it was clear he had not spent his break relaxing. He had with him a bevy of new crates and animal cages.[430] Willis announced that The Great Boomsky would soon be presenting an entirely new act featuring the sensational Noah's Ark illusion.[431] A week later the *Indianapolis Freeman* announced the date. "On the 9th, in Gainesville Texas, Boomsky will discard all of his old tricks and put on new ones, dealing with illusions and the higher class of art."[432]

As The Great Boomsky worked the new tricks into his act, a *Nashville American* reviewer thought he spoke strangely. "Isaac Willis gave some creditable expositions of magic which he said he learned while an assistant to 'the Great Herrmann.' Willis, like all the members of the company, is a negro, but speaks with a German accent, which seems out of place."[433] It is possible that Willis imitated Léon Herrmann's French accent, which the reviewer mistook for German.

After months of grinding out one-night stands, the Famous Georgia Minstrels played a week in Chicago, where the specialty acts, including Boomsky, were all fitted with new double trunks. As they loaded in and out of theaters, the fine new luggage boosted road-weary spirits. Directly after their Sunday matinee in Saginaw, Michigan, on May 7, the entire company boarded a trolley to Bridgeport for dinner at the summer home of their manager, W. A. Rusco. According to Napoleon Johnson in the *Indianapolis Freeman*, "Neither time nor money was spared in making this the grandest spread we have enjoyed since the organization of the company over thirty years ago. Every one satisfied the inner man immensely."

Boomsky Tours Canada and Finds Love

Napoleon Johnson continued sending his weekly road reports to the *Indianapolis Freeman* as Richards & Pringle's Minstrels crossed into Canada for a three-month tour of Ontario, Quebec, New Brunswick, and Nova Scotia. They had made brief dashes into Canada before, but this was their first extended tour. They were a sensation. "In this country the company is even more successful than it was in the States, and we are getting the money and pleasing the people. In St. Thomas, Ont., May 12, we played against a circus, yet that night we turned them away and standing room could not be had."[434]

From St. Catharines, Ontario, some of the performers made a "flying trip"—a one-day excursion—to visit Niagara Falls, "one of the most wonderful sights of a lifetime."[435] In Brantford, they had dinner at the home of a retired minstrel performer named Jim Wilson. His beautiful home and surroundings were "an object lesson to all. They show what saving will do for you in after life."[436] Their week's stand in Montreal "was the most pleasant week ever spent in show business . . . the unsolicited press notices we received would do honor to a king."[437] As always, The Great Boomsky stood out. In Quebec City, "Mr. Willis performed clever feats of legerdemain and jugglery."[438]

Boomsky's new act was playing well. "Although it is true as a rule that you can't fool all the people all the time, yet so successful is Boomsky with his tricks in magic he is proving an exception to the rule and is nightly keeping the audience wondering. He is now featuring the 'obedient ball' and Noah's Ark after the flood, in which, at his command, the ball will move and stop on an incline plain at his bidding and producing from a seemingly empty ark pigeons, chickens, ducks, rabbits, pigs, and finishes this trick by calling forth a big Newfoundland dog."[439]

As summer blossomed and they began six weeks of mostly one-night stands through Quebec, New Brunswick, and Nova Scotia, the American showmen fell in love with Canada, where they received more respectful and deferential treatment than in America. Napoleon Johnson proclaimed, "I know not what course others may take but as for me I will take Canada for my future home for what mine eyes hath seen, my heart is bound to believe where a man's a man for a' that."[440]

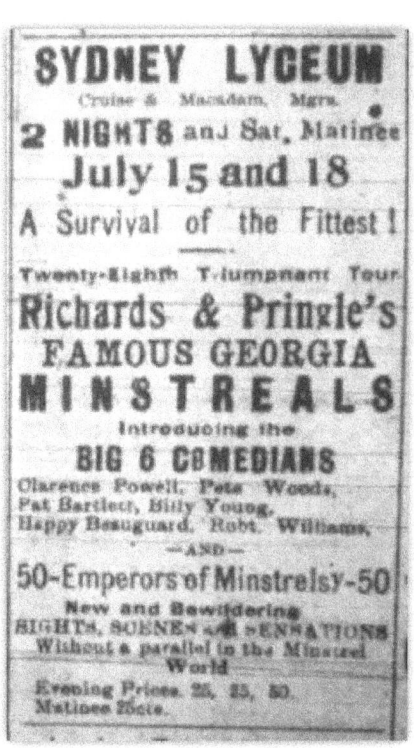

The company's hyperbolic ads promised "A Gleeful Comingling of Joviality" and "A Coalition of Mirth, Vivacity and Gaity."[441] Their show in Windsor, Nova Scotia, which was also a firemen's benefit, foretold "An Ornate Blaze of Glory."[442] Ads listed the performers, including The Great Boomsky.[443] *Amherst News & Sentinel* readers learned that "A special train of Pullman cars, models of convenience, comfort and elegance, has been constructed to transport the mammoth production."[444]

The Famous Georgia Minstrels played in eighteen locations throughout Nova Scotia in July and August, 1905.

That summer, Richards and Pringle's Minstrels played to big houses. In Nova Scotia, Black Canadians turned out in large numbers. The small Atlantic coastal province was home to a third of Canada's Black citizens. Many were descended from Black Loyalists, escaped American slaves who had sided with the British in the American Revolution in exchange for their freedom, safe passage to Canada, and the promise of a plot of land. In 1796, nearly six hundred Maroons, a group of freed slaves, had arrived in Nova Scotia after being deported from Jamaica. During the War of 1812, another two thousand Black refugees had settled in New Brunswick and Nova Scotia.[445]

The Georgia Minstrels were scheduled to play eighteen Nova Scotia towns in three weeks. On Sunday morning, July 23, 1905, the troupe woke aboard their train in the Halifax rail yard. They would play three nights at the Academy of Music starting the next night, on Monday. In Canada, there were no shows on Sundays, and that July day, the men had the whole day off. All the performers had been raised as churchgoing Christians. When traveling, they held their own Sunday services, as Black performing troupes had no shortage of charismatic preachers. If a town along their route had a Black church, they would attend services. That morning some of the troupe walked along the dirt road to the Seaview Baptist Church in Africville.

First settled by Black Loyalists in the late 1700s, Africville was one of North America's oldest free Black communities. The community occupied a stunningly beautiful location on the Bedford Basin section of Halifax Harbor. Dozens of colorful houses were staggered on the sloping hillside. Nearly every home had a view of the lovely harbor. Heavenly cooking aromas tantalized the visitors.

Seaview Baptist Church rose up over a community of homes and businesses. That summer day, the performers hoped to see one of the church's famous mass baptisms, where a hundred or more people would line up to receive the holy sacraments and be dipped in the harbor by a robed preacher standing in waist-deep water. As the men tacked up flyers for their upcoming shows, residents gathered around. They welcomed the showmen, and most everyone said they planned to attend the performance. Elsewhere in Canada, the performers had felt the familiar cold shoulder of racial prejudice, though not as blatantly as in

America. But in Africville, children ran free and adults warmly greeted the visitors, offering them food, beverages, and friendly conversation. The showmen were surprised to learn that the residents owned their own homes, part of the Black Loyalists' early deal with the British. Like minority communities everywhere, Africville's location also had its unpalatable features. Africville was next to Halifax's town dump. On the whim of shifting winds, the community smelled of either sea-fresh air or putrid burning garbage smoke. Nevertheless, to the minstrel

The Academy of Music in Halifax, Nova Scotia, hosted Alexander and Adelaide Herrmann in 1896, The Famous Georgia Minstrels in 1905, and Léon Herrmann in 1906.

performers, who had visited every corner of North America, Africville in 1905 was the most magical place they had ever been.[446]

The next day, as the Famous Georgia Minstrels paraded from the Halifax rail yard to the Academy of Music, Isaac Willis spotted a beautiful, brown-skinned girl watching from the steps of stately Government House, the Lieutenant-Governor's residence. She held a broom, and her hair was tied up with a scarf. Isaac gazed at her, and when she smiled back, something in him melted. As soon as he could, Isaac circled back to find her still there, sweeping the Government House steps. As Isaac approached, he saw that she was very young and quite tall. When they stood face to face, she loomed over him. Her clothes and shoes were old and worn, but she held her head high. The Great Boomsky introduced himself and held out two passes to that night's performance. Seventeen-year-old Blanche Stoutley introduced herself and smiled as she took the passes from the handsome and confident showman. It was an exciting treat for her. As head of her seven-person household, Blanche could never afford such an extravagance. The handsome stranger invited her to meet him at the stage door after the show. Blanche smiled and nodded and went back to sweeping the steps.

Isaac's performance had a little extra zest that night. The Halifax audience was wonderful. Downstairs a sea of white faces smiled, laughed, and bobbed to the music. As he performed, Isaac scanned the balcony for Blanche, but it was no use. Just like in the States, the balcony was one big mass of pulsing Black energy, with people clapping and cheering for every part of the show. The Great Boomsky held them spellbound with billiard ball manipulations, the obedient ball, and Noah's Ark. The finale, the appearance of the Newfoundland dog, brought huge applause and cries of "Bravo!"

After the performance, Isaac wondered if Blanche would be at the stage door. He had given her two tickets as a courtesy, and of course she might bring a fiancé or husband. A girl like her must have many suitors. When Isaac emerged from the stage entrance, there she was, in a nice dress, her hair styled. Blanche did indeed have another male with her—her sixteen-year-old brother, Will Stoutley.

The Stoutley siblings had been dazzled by the show. They bubbled with energy and questions as they walked Isaac back to his train. The two were fun and easygoing and seemed older than their years. Will was clearly protective of his beautiful older sister. When they reached the minstrels' railcar, Isaac asked if they would like passes for the following night as well. "Yes!" exclaimed Blanche and Will in unison.

The Famous Georgia Minstrels drew big crowds during their three days in Halifax and were declared to be "the best minstrel show in years." The *Acadian Recorder* mentioned The Great Boomsky but misspelled his name: "Isaac Millis performed some feats of modern magic."[447]

For the next two nights in Halifax, Blanche and Will met Isaac at the stage door. Isaac felt himself falling for this tall Canadian girl. After the final night's show, Isaac promised Blanche that he would return. Then as abruptly as they had arrived, The Great Boomsky and the Famous Georgia Minstrels were back on the road. Blanche was sorry to see him go but breathed a sigh of relief. For now, the truth about her family, which had rendered them pariahs in Halifax, remained unknown to her new suitor. If Isaac returned, he would learn soon enough. If he stuck around after that, he was special indeed.

Richards and Pringle's Minstrels played through Maine and Vermont before heading to the American Northwest. Crossing into Saskatchewan, their love affair with Canada continued. Napoleon Johnson wrote in the *Freeman*, "It is very gratifying indeed to see so many of our own color owning their own homes and competing with all other races."[448] In late October, after playing Vancouver, all the specialty acts were abruptly released from their contracts. A revamped Richards and Pringle's company continued the tour with just one member held over, the star Clarence Powell.

Suddenly out of work, Isaac Willis made a beeline back to Halifax and Miss Blanche Stoutley. As he knocked at the ramshackle house at 74

Albemarle Street, the address she had given him, he surveyed the tough, run-down neighborhood. The door cracked, and a disheveled woman looked him up and down before swinging the door open. As his eyes adjusted to the dimness, Isaac saw that he was inside a seedy tavern, just the sort of place that he had been forbidden to patronize as a minstrel. Isaac said he was a friend of Blanche and Will Stoutley. The woman shouted up the stairs behind her, "Blanche! Will!" Suddenly they were there, followed down the stairs by their younger siblings: Eula, Ralph, Clarence, and five-year-old Muriel. Blanche was delighted to see Isaac, but she fidgeted as she introduced him to the unkempt innkeeper, her mother, Rachel Stoutley.

Blanche took Isaac's hand and led him outside. As the two of them walked, Blanche took a big breath and told Isaac the truth.

Blanche was the oldest child of Edward and Rachel Stoutley. Blanche was born at Mount Uniacke, Nova Scotia, in 1887 but had spent her early childhood in Truro. Three years prior to meeting Isaac, her family had been stable. Blanche's father was working as a house painter to support his wife and their six children.[449] In early 1903, after the drowning death of their four-year-old son, Edward Stoutley began to unravel. He moved his family from Truro to the dilapidated house on Albemarle Street. There, in Halifax's notorious "upper streets," the squalid district of derelicts and the desperately poor, Edward opened an unlicensed tavern. Halifax's busy seaport provided a constant clientele of seafaring men.

Things quickly spun out of control. Within a year, both parents, Edward and Rachel, had descended into heavy alcohol abuse. Police were regularly summoned to break up loud fights and drunken brawls. Finally, to evade jail time, Edward ran off with the family's young housekeeper, never to be seen again.[450]

Rachel Stoutley continued to run the illegal tavern until May 1904, when complaints from neighbors of disturbances and drinking rows brought the police to her door. Rachel and three other women were arrested. Rachel Stoutley was convicted of being the mistress of a brothel.

She was sentenced to six months in jail, leaving sixteen-year-old Blanche and thirteen-year-old Will to care for their four younger siblings, ages ten, seven, six, and four.[451] Somehow the two teens kept their family afloat. After Rachel's release, her drinking got worse. In March 1905, just six months prior to the minstrels' visit, Rachel had been arrested for drunk and disorderly conduct and sentenced to a fine of two dollars or ten days in jail.[452]

Blanche finished her story and looked at Isaac. He smiled and squeezed her hand. For the next two months, Isaac waited tables in Halifax and helped support the Stoutley family. But The Great Boomsky was not ready to settle down. In November, Isaac Willis gave notice of his availability in the *Indianapolis Freeman*. Touting his "four successful seasons" with the Georgia Minstrels, he announced that he would sail for New York on December 20.[453] "Regards to all members of the Georgia Minstrels, Billy Kersands Minstrels and Black Patti Troubadors. Address: The Great Boomsky, 74 Albemarle Street, Halifax, N.S."[454] Ever prudent, Isaac Willis also sent notice to his old boss, Herrmann the Great.

LÉON HERRMANN CONTINUES

When Herrmann the Great set out in September 1903—his first season without Isaac Willis—The Laskeys, the cornet-playing siblings, had joined him once again. Léon had hired a new Boomsky, a very young and very small teenager.[455] This Boomsky may have been J. Edward Clarke, who debuted the following year with the Maryland Jubilee Company as a "young magician" who had apprenticed with Herrmann the Great.[456] Alternatively, he may have been fourteen-year-old William Keeling Smith from Washington, DC, who would later change his name and have a long, successful career as magician Eugene Hellman.[457]

The season got off to a bumpy start. On opening night in New Orleans, the new Boomsky fell on the hat on cue. But when Léon fired his gun, the restored hat did not fall from the ceiling. Twice more he fired, to the annoyance of the audience, yet the hat still did not fall.[458] Two weeks later in Arkansas, for the ending of the hat trick, Léon added a racist touch: The restored hat floating above the stage had a "black baby" hanging from it.[459] The intention behind the little black doll hanging from that hat, added by Frederick Bancroft as well, remains unclear.

When they played the Columbia Theater in Washington, DC, Boomsky rushed backstage and breathlessly delivered incredible news. The President of the United States, Theodore Roosevelt, and the First Lady were in the audience! Jesse Lasky was so overcome with nerves that he marched on stage in his Rough Rider costume only to realize his cornet was not in his hands.[460] After the show President and Mrs. Roosevelt congratulated the entire company. It was the first and only time Léon Herrmann met a US president, and he was immensely proud.[461]

After five seasons of dragging his full company all over America, Léon was ready for a change. He remarked to a *Sioux City Journal* reporter that months of one-night stands "is a pretty tiresome sort of life."[462] According to *The Sphinx*, by March he "had traveled 25,000 miles, visited the principal cities in 27 states, and had had enough excitement in railroad wrecks, floods, fires and steamboat disasters to last a man a lifetime."[463] In several flooded cities in the Ohio valley, they'd been obliged to get to the theaters using boats.

His company manager, Edward Thurnaer, wasn't helping things. Thurnaer had been with the Herrmanns for many years, starting out as a young assistant manager for Alexander Herrmann. But his vice was alcohol, and he was gradually slipping in his duties. His most crucial job was collecting box office receipts, making sure they weren't being cheated. When Thurnaer could no longer function, Jesse Lasky asked Léon if he could be promoted to company manager. Léon was surprised, since the twenty-three-year-old cornet player possessed no business experience. But Léon gave him a chance, and Jesse immediately showed a knack for the job. In fact, Lasky discovered he liked managing much better than performing. After their second season with Herrmann, Jesse and his sister, Blanche, sold their act to another pair of sibling cornetists. Then Jesse turned around and managed them as well. Blanche was thrilled. She did not love performing and was happy to retire at age nineteen.

Jesse Lasky set about arranging a less tiresome sort of life for Léon. To the delight of the Herrmanns, Lasky got Léon booked for eight weeks at the Palace Theater in London, then at the Alhambra in Paris. Lasky then convinced Léon to cut his unwieldy two-hour show down to a thirty-minute vaudeville act. In 1904, Léon was quickly booked on the Orpheum circuit for $900 a week, making more money for less work and far less grueling travel. It was a success all around. Manager Lasky joked that he wished he had four Herrmann the Greats.[464] In his vaudeville act Léon was assisted by Marie "and his faithful Boomsky."[465]

Jesse L. Lasky would become a top theatrical manager before leaping into a brand-new industry—motion pictures—and founding Paramount Pictures. His sister, Blanche, married a man named Sam Goldfish who later changed his name to Goldwyn. With Louis B. Mayer, Samuel L. Goldwyn founded Metro Goldwyn Mayer studios.

Boomsky Returns to Canada

Herrmann the Great's 1905 fall season got off to a rough start. Léon's mother had died in Paris the previous spring. The Herrmanns had just returned from Europe and were heading to Scranton, Pennsylvania, to begin their vaudeville season. In the bustle of transferring from the Hudson River ferry to catch the train in Hoboken, Marie left her purse on the ferry. Inside were several hundred dollars and some jewelry, including her wedding ring. Eventually the purse was found, minus the valuables.[466]

After a year in vaudeville, Léon had changed his act. It now had a mystical, East Indian theme. While in England, Léon had hired the mind reader Madame Sa-Hera and her husband. In Léon's show, the couple performed Second Sight, during which Mme. Sa-Hera discerned the thoughts of audience members. Other mentalists professed psychic powers or, at the very least, did not discount them. But Mme. Sa-Hera frankly disclosed that she had no supernatural abilities and that everything she did was a trick.[467]

In April, Léon was playing Omaha when he received news of the death of his father, Benjamin Herrmann, in Paris. Léon learned of his father's passing on the anniversary of his mother's death, the day he was to remove the badge of mourning from his coat sleeve. Devastated, Léon sought a change of scenery. Herrmann the Great decided to combine work and vacation into a tour of Eastern Canada. After two years in vaudeville, it would require temporarily resurrecting his big, full-evening show. For that, he would need more assistants.

After his stint as The Great Boomsky with Richards and Pringle's Famous Georgia Minstrels, Isaac Willis was hired to assist Léon Herrmann for his 1906 Canadian tour. Willis would play dual roles, portraying both Boomsky and a "Hindu" assistant to the robed and turbaned magician Mohammed Khan, who was actually the white, English husband of Mme. Sa-Hera.[468]

Cultural appropriation by magicians was not new. Nearly twenty years earlier, William Robinson had appeared in the Herrmann show as Abdul Khan, presenting his Black Art act. Now, as Léon plied his American vaudeville route, Will and Dot Robinson were selling out theaters in England, performing as Chinese magician Chung Ling Soo and his assistant, Suee Seen. Robinson's act was a near-perfect imitation of the Chinese magician Ching Ling Foo, who had inspired many copycats since taking America by storm eight years earlier. Around magic circles, Robinson's true identity was an open secret, but the British public was thoroughly fooled. It was uncommon to see actual Asian people, and Robinson went to great lengths to conceal his true identity. In public, he traveled in character and with a "translator," with whom he conversed in vaguely Asian-sounding gibberish. He carried on this charade successfully for years, with the complicity and support of London's Chinese community, who felt that Chung Ling Soo elevated their image.

In the summer of 1906, the *New York Clipper* published Léon Herrmann's dispatch from Canada.

> For the first time in ten years have I missed my annual vacation in Europe and am making a short tour through Nova Scotia, Cape Breton, New Brunswick, and Newfoundland, combining pleasure with business, magic and mystery, with fishing and shooting on the side. The season which opened in Sydney July 3, Dominion Day, will end at Montreal on Aug. 13. During my travels I will visit towns where no wizard has even ventured. I will carry my company through these remote parts by train when possible, but as some towns are only accessible by water, I have chartered a small steamer, which will be freighted with illusions, rabbits, guinea pigs, mind readers and Hindus, to spread my fame in territories yet unconquered. I will display my marvels in theaters in the largest towns, but in one town at least I will use a tent. This has been made specially for me and goes along with the other paraphernalia. From sure indications the tour will be a huge success.[469]

Léon Herrmann was hopeful. His six-week Canadian tour was a foray back into touring with a large company of ten people, which included Isaac Willis, as well as Mme. Sa-Hera and her husband. Herrmann took his "fishing and shooting" vacation in June, boating between villages on the coast of Newfoundland, giving performances for locals and vacationers under a tent. Although Léon portrayed the entire route as somewhat isolated, once they reached Sydney, Nova Scotia, in July, all of the towns he visited were rail stops regularly visited by touring performers. Just one year earlier, The Great Boomsky had played all the same theaters with the Famous Georgia Minstrels. Now Isaac Willis was touring the route once again as Léon Herrmann's assistant.

Their three nights in Sydney drew good houses and strong reviews. But as they continued, Léon's prediction of a huge success faltered. Normally, a visit to Nova Scotia by Herrmann the Great would generate much excitement. Unfortunately, Léon discovered too late that he was booked opposite overwhelming competition, namely, Barnum and Bailey's Circus—the Greatest Show on Earth. Every town they arrived in was papered to the brim with circus posters. At each destination, Barnum and Bailey's was coming soon, had just been there, or, worst of all, was playing that night. The newspapers ran enormous circus ads and delirious reviews. Herrmann the Great's ads, though large and expensive, were dwarfed by circus press.

In Amherst, Nova Scotia, Léon Herrmann drew a small crowd. A *News and Sentinel* reviewer wrote, "The exhibition was of a highly sensational nature and deserved a much larger house."[470] But the town was so covered with circus posters that Léon went virtually unnoticed. Amherst was hit-or-miss anyway. Just the previous summer Richards and Pringle's Minstrels, featuring The Great Boomsky, had packed the house. But ten years earlier, at the same theater, Houdini also had failed to draw a crowd.

Moncton, New Brunswick, was also plastered with circus posters. At the Opera House, Marie Herrmann made her first solo appearance. Billing herself as the "Queen of Illusions and the Marvelous Prophetess," Marie appeared alongside Sa-Hera, "The Enigma of the Century." To publicize the show, Sa-Hera drove a cart with "spirited horses" through Moncton while she was blindfolded.[471] The Herrmanns appeared at the Opera House in Saint John from July 16 to 21.[472] Mme. Sa-Hera gave a performance just for women where no men were allowed in the theater. The week started strong, opening to "good business" with solid advance sales and an audience that was "pleased." But on Friday, July 20, Barnum and Bailey's Circus played in Saint John, and few attended Herrmann's show.

It got worse. Herrmann the Great was booked to play a whole week in Halifax, Nova Scotia, but on his opening night at the Academy of Music on July 23, Léon again played against the circus, which drew twenty-five thousand people in one day. The newspapers the next morning were all about the circus and told of eye-popping spectacles. The Dip of Death, in which a Mrs. Butler drove a motorcar down and around a curved ramp, flying upside down in the air before landing on another curved ramp, was the season's biggest sensation. Despite the competition, Herrmann the Great's opening night drew a good crowd and, according to the *Herald*, "well sustained his reputation of being a master magician."[473] Reviewers noted that it was ten years, almost to the day, since Alexander and Adelaide Herrmann dazzled audiences at the same theater. While audiences were warm and reviews kind, Léon couldn't live up to expectations. At just under three hours, Léon's show was too long and not exciting enough. People remembered Alexander's hilarity and Adelaide's spectacular dances.

For Isaac Willis, it was an exciting time. Exactly one year since playing the Academy of Music with Richards and Pringle's Famous Georgia Minstrels, he was performing there once again. It was the anniversary of his meeting Blanche, who celebrated by bringing her family to Herrmann's show. Over the previous year, Isaac had made many friends in Halifax. Now he gave them free tickets. They cheered and applauded every time Herrmann's assistant took the stage, to the puzzlement of the rest of the audience.

Léon Herrmann was happy to see the circus leave Halifax on Tuesday. But Barnum and Bailey still dominated the news. That morning, an open switch diverted the speeding circus train to a siding, causing many cars to derail. The Barnum and Bailey company missed their afternoon show in New Glasgow. There were railroad problems the next day as well, and the circus missed their afternoon show in Amherst. The two canceled shows resulted in a forty-thousand-dollar revenue loss for Barnum and Bailey. As the story unfolded, Herrmann the Great's advertisements were buried in a mountain of circus coverage. As Léon moved into Quebec, so did the circus. Herrmann ended his circus-dampened tour on August 13 after a week in Montreal. With money in his pocket, Isaac Willis hightailed it to Halifax—and Blanche.

Blanche's family was in chaos. Two weeks after Isaac's arrival, Rachel Stoutley was arrested for public drunkenness and profanity.[474] Three months later, while Isaac was again touring with Léon Herrmann, a drunken assailant broke down the door of the Stoutley home and violently assaulted Rachel. The screams of her children had alerted the police.[475]

When Isaac returned to Halifax the following spring, he got drawn into the spiral. In May 1907, Isaac "Boonstky" and William Stoutley were arrested and fined four dollars or twenty days in jail for causing a disturbance.[476] But nothing could dampen the family's joy that summer. On July 14, 1907, twenty-eight-year-old Isaac Willis and Blanche Stoutley, age twenty, were married in Halifax by Reverend Arthur Challenger of the African Methodist Episcopal Church. In October, Isaac Willis was off again to join Léon Herrmann for his new vaudeville season.

In December 1907, Léon and Marie played a week in Chicago, sharing the bill with Harry and Bess Houdini. Léon's stunning sleight-of-hand work dazzled the Houdinis, as did Marie's gorgeous costumes and several impressive new illusions. Houdini in turn performed a new trick, escaping from a galvanized iron liquid air can.[477]

The two magicians bonded during their shared week. Like Léon and Marie Herrmann, Harry Houdini was Jewish. No doubt the five-foot-five, height-sensitive Houdini was pleased that next to "the little magician" and his diminutive Boomsky, he appeared tall.

The Chicago Tribune, *December 15, 1907. Léon Herrmann (assisted by Isaac Willis) shared the vaudeville bill with Houdini.*

Walking to dinner with their tiny wives, Houdini practically towered above the rest. After that week together, Houdini always expressed admiration for Léon Herrmann.

Léon Herrmann's Fateful Russian Tour

Just a year after playing opposite Houdini, Léon and Marie Herrmann began a tour of Russia. Eager to return to his new wife in Canada, Isaac Willis did not join them. This time, their farewell was bittersweet. Boomsky's long collaboration with Herrmann was officially over. Lucién Herrmann, Léon's thirteen-year-old nephew, was scheduled to begin training as Léon's assistant the following summer. The boy assistant role had come full circle.[478]

Léon had not visited Russia since his teens, and his grasp of the language was quite rusty. Still, his initial week in Moscow was a success. But as they traveled, the Herrmanns were dismayed at the steep escalation in anti-Jewish sentiment since Léon's last visit many years earlier. Unlike his uncle Alexander, Léon had not thought to take extra precautions. Although he had lived and performed in America for twelve years, Léon remained proudly French. As a result, his French passport identified him as Jewish. Léon never learned his uncle Alexander's trick of establishing back-slapping friendships with local police and military, especially in unfriendly locales. Most importantly, Léon lacked his uncle's famous ability to charm his way out of sticky situations.

Not long after leaving Moscow, Léon and Marie's sleeper car was invaded by thieves. All the couple's valuables were stolen, and they were left terribly shaken. Although the family kept it quiet, rumors circulated that Léon and Marie had been roughed up in the incident. Deeply traumatized, the Herrmanns pushed on with the tour, but Léon became increasingly depressed and demoralized. He came down with a respiratory infection that he could not shake, and when his Russian winter cold progressed to pneumonia, Marie canceled the rest of the tour and rushed her ailing husband home to Paris. She took Léon to the south of France, where he sat in the sea air and warm sun and began to improve. By April he felt well enough to return to Paris, but soon his pneumonia relapsed. He lingered for nearly a month, Marie constantly at his side.

On May 16, 1909, Léon Herrmann, the last of the Herrmann dynasty, died in Paris at the age of forty-two. He was buried at Cimetiére de Pantin in Paris.

As soon as she could get away, Adelaide Herrmann sailed to France to see Léon's devastated widow. Their bitter feud forgotten, Adelaide never again said an unkind word about Léon Herrmann. In her memoir, written twenty years later, Madame had only praise for her husband's nephew. Marie owned the couple's Paris home, but she desperately needed money. She advertised for boarders and sold Léon's magic props and stage settings to a young female magician. Clementine de Vere, whose stage name was Ionia, would have a brilliant but brief career.[479]

Léon's untimely death was a shock to the magic world and especially to Isaac Willis, who had worked with the magician longer and more closely than any other assistant. Though deeply pained by Léon's passing, Isaac carried a paralyzing fear of death and never spoke of his mentor's demise.

FELIX HERRMANN
AND ASSISTANT

Upon Léon Herrmann's death, Adelaide's nephew, Felix Kretschmann (younger brother of John) changed his name to Felix Herrmann and began billing himself as "Nephew of Herrmann the Great." Seen here with an unnamed assistant, Felix enraged his aunt, sparking a bitter feud. Adelaide omitted any mention of Felix in both her memoir and her will.

MINSTRELSY WINDS DOWN: BOOMSKY'S REINVENTION

By around 1910, America's fifty-year infatuation with minstrel shows was fading. Jazz was all the rage now, and minstrelsy felt stale and dated. Magicians on the minstrel circuit now faced a new kind of competition in the form of an audacious young entertainer called Black Herman. There had been previous Black Herrmanns, but this Black Herman was altogether different.[480] His real name was Benjamin Rucker. Born in Virginia in 1890, he likely assisted Harry Kellar. Although Black Herman was never a Boomsky and had no connection with any of the Herrmanns, he happily capitalized on the famous name.

The flamboyant Rucker dropped the minstrel show caricatures and instead celebrated his African roots, stirring the waters of the nascent Civil Rights Movement. Black Herman's traveling tent show blurred the line between magic show and religious revival. Claiming that his miracles had been taught to him by Zulu witch doctors, Black Herman grew rich hawking various wares, including his "Secret African Remedy," which contained mostly alcohol, and a self-published book: *Black Herman's Secrets of Magic-Mystery and Legerdemain*. A showman like no other, Black Herman finished the first half of his act by being buried alive in an outdoor area marked as "Black Herman's Private Graveyard." Three days later, after doing shows in other towns, he would return to his temporary grave to be dug up, revived, and escorted to the stage where he would finish his performance. His act was so convincing that when Black Herman died in 1934 at age forty-four, many of his fans refused to believe he was really dead. His assistant sold admission to view Black Herman's body at the mortuary for ten cents per person.

After Minstrelsy

As minstrelsy declined, a new generation of Black magicians took different paths. In the 1920s, the Theatrical Owners Booking Associating (TOBA) managed a Black vaudeville circuit of forty-five theaters, most white-owned, in the South and Midwest. Working "Toby Time," performers endured harsh conditions and low pay and jibed that TOBA stood for "Tough on Black Actors." Smaller circuits operated in the Northeast and mid-Atlantic, while tent shows toured the South. Collectively referred to as the Chitlin Circuit, the system employed magicians and variety artists but greatly favored singers, dancers, and comedians. The Chitlin Circuit produced dozens of future stars, including Ma Rainey, Stepin Fetchit, "Moms" Mably, the Nicholas Brothers, and Sammy Davis Jr.

Alternatively, some African American magicians donned turbans and robes and presented themselves as East Indian wizards, notably Maharajah (William A. Barclay) and Jovedah De Raja (true name unknown). Since high-caste East Indians were not subject to segregation laws, these "Hindu magicians" patronized white restaurants and hotels, their identities unchallenged over successful careers.

Other magicians carved out niche careers with self-contained, full-length shows. They performed at theaters, schools, churches, and social gatherings. Among the most successful were W. B. Maxwell, Leon Long, Eugene Hellman, and the Armstrongs, a family of magicians from South Carolina led by patriarch J. Hartford Armstrong. His daughter Ellen Armstrong (1914–1979) would become the era's sole female, African American, professional magician. While some Black magicians employed female assistants, Ellen Armstrong was the only Black woman to headline in her own magic show.

Herrmann's protégés responded in varying ways to the rise of Black Herman and the corresponding decline in minstrelsy.

Early Boomsky James A. Willis (no relation to Isaac), had toured his own act for nearly twenty years. In 1909, at age forty, the magician and pianist married a twenty-nine-year-old white actress named Lottie Austin. They settled in Cleveland, Ohio, where James taught music lessons and supplemented his income by writing greeting cards for a local department store. After twelve years of marriage, when James was fifty-two years old, Lottie divorced him and married a widowed piano tuner seven years her junior. After his divorce in 1921, James A. Willis vanished from the public record. The date and place of his death are unknown.

Minstrelsy star Black Carl had remained popular for twenty years. The Salt Lake City *Broad Ax* noted that "Black Carl, the magician, like the wine he served, improves with age."[481] When, in his late thirties, he felt the winds shift, he abruptly quit performing, stating he was tired of touring. In truth, performing opportunities were becoming scarce. Black Carl continued managing other companies but would revive his magic act only during family visits back to Topeka, presenting fundraisers at his mother's church. In New York City, he began a second career, which would bring him even more fame than the first.

For the last twenty-five years of his life, former Boomsky Black Carl (as he was still called) was the head carriage man at the Metropolitan Opera House. As patrons arrived, he opened carriage and automobile doors and helped guests emerge. At the end of the performance, he called for carriages and cars and sent guests off with a cheery goodnight. He wielded much power in the second capacity, unabashedly playing favorites among New York's glitterati, all of them eager to have their own conveyances arrive next. His clever banter and ostentatious manners delighted opera patrons. As the first and last person that patrons saw, Black Carl became as iconic to the Met as the singers onstage. He knew and remembered the names of every regular opera patron and personally greeted three US presidents: Theodore Roosevelt, William Howard Taft, and Woodrow Wilson. Black Carl was the last Met employee to shake hands with Enrico Caruso before the great tenor's death.

Black Carl died in 1930 at age sixty-three, after complications from a series of strokes. He was eulogized in newspapers across the country. The beloved carriage man's long-ago career as a famous magician was noted only as an afterthought.[482]

When Black Carl retired, the younger Alonzo Moore stuck it out, seizing every opportunity in a shrinking marketplace. More than any other magician of color, Alonzo Moore remained an enduring favorite of both Black and white audiences. When his old boss Edward Maro (Walter Best) died of typhoid in 1908 at the age of thirty-nine, Moore inherited many of his props, as well as some of Maro's high-society clients, as noted in the *Chicago Tribune*: "Alonzo Moore, the club magician, entertained the children of the Evanston Country club with oriental magic at its Christmas party."[483]

Moore continued garnering good reviews on the Redpath Chautauqua circuit. The *Lincoln Sentinal* reported that "Alonzo Moore, a colored magician put on a very entertaining performance. His tricks are all good and clean. The platform manager claimed that he was considered one of the best in his line in the business and before he was through with his evening's entertainment there was not a single person in the audience who doubted the assertion."[484]

Moore remained close to his late boss Maro's wife. Two years after Walter Best's death, Moore was living in the same house with Best's widow, Allie, in rural Michigan.[485] He moved out a year later when Allie remarried but came back into her life after she divorced.

In 1916, the *Indianapolis Freeman* reported that Alonzo Moore had been killed in a carriage accident in McBane, Missouri. While crossing a stream, the horse balked, throwing Moore into the icy water. The account said that Moore's heavy case fell on top of him, crushing him.[486] Twelve days later, the paper issued a retraction after receiving a letter from Alonzo Moore himself explaining that he was very much alive. He had escaped and "walked a mile or more . . . with his clothes froze stiff."[487] Passersby had seen Moore's smashed case and assumed the worst.

For over twenty years, Moore alternated between the Chautauqua circuit and minstrel shows, traveling from Europe to Australia and every corner of North America. Then, with the advent of motion pictures and the decline of both minstrel shows and Chautauquas, his performance engagements dropped off steeply. In 1926, at the age of fifty, Moore retired to Leland, Michigan, where he worked as a waiter and cook at Allie Best's tea room, the Blue Lantern, until 1928.[488] A famously heavy drinker, his health declined.

Alonzo Moore, the most celebrated African American magician of his generation, died in an indigents' home in Chicago in 1930 at age fifty-four. He was buried in an unmarked pauper's grave.[489]

In 1908, Isaac Willis had finished his final tour with Léon Herrmann and returned to another big mess in Halifax. While he was away, his mother-in-law, Rachel Stoutley, had been arrested three times, first for obstructing police from searching her premises for liquor,[490] then for public drunkenness,[491] and finally, for selling liquor without a license.[492] Seventeen-year-old William Stoutley had been arrested for drunkenness as well.[493] It was time to leave Halifax and Albemarle Street.

Isaac Willis moved the entire family to Truro, Nova Scotia. Located on the tidal Salmon River on Cobequid Bay at the easternmost corner of the Bay of Fundy, the resource-rich area had been fished, hunted, and farmed first by the indigenous Mi'kmaq, followed by the Acadian French, and, ultimately, the English. The railroad had come through in 1858, bringing Black laborers, some of whom stayed. Isaac rented a flat for the family on Monroe Street, an area of hotels and rooming houses near the Truro train station.[494] Rachel Stoutley told the census taker that she was widowed, which was far less complicated than the truth. When asked about her husband, Rachel would simply say that one day Edward Stoutley had gone out to the store and never returned.[495]

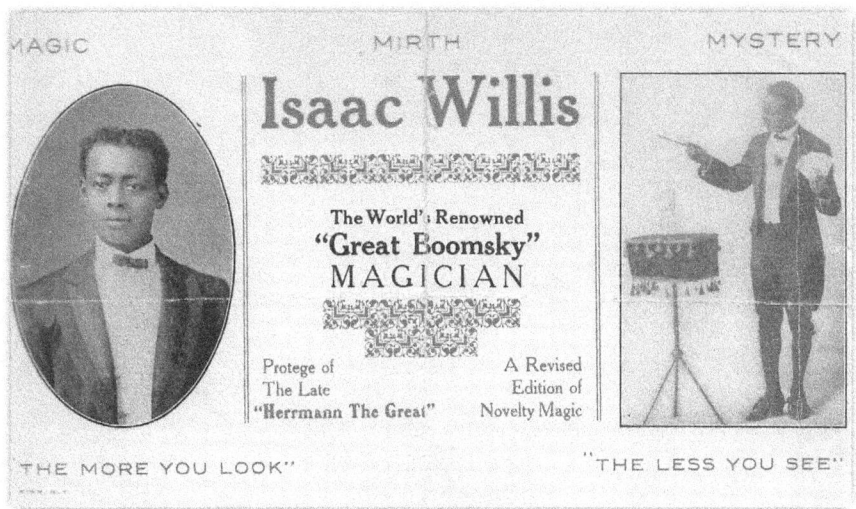

MAGIC   MIRTH   MYSTERY

Isaac Willis

The World's Renowned
"Great Boomsky"
MAGICIAN

Protege of   A Revised
The Late   Edition of
"Herrmann The Great"   Novelty Magic

"THE MORE YOU LOOK"   "THE LESS YOU SEE"

Isaac Willis promotional card, circa 1911.

In Truro, Isaac Willis took charge as man of the house. He opened a shoeshine business on Inglis Street near Truro's train station, employing his twelve-year-old brother-in-law, Clarence Stoutley, as assistant. With Clarence overseeing his shoeshine business, Isaac was able to accept performance opportunities when they arose. In 1911 The Great Boomsky embarked on a solo comeback tour though parts of Canada and the US, culminating with three nights in November at the Crescent Theater in New York.[496]

The newly renovated Crescent Theater on 135th Street was Harlem's most lavish movie house and the only one offering reserved seating in its plush auditorium. The silent film industry was taking off, but most movies were still only a few minutes long. In this elegant movie palace, Black vaudeville's top stars performed between the film showings.[497] As always, The Great Boomsky's appearing ducks brought gasps and happy applause.

For Isaac Willis, The Great Boomsky's New York run was a career highlight. It also marked the end of his touring life. After playing the Crescent Theater, the thirty-one-year-old showman returned to Truro and never toured again. After years spent in a different city every night, now he went home to his wife and his own bed. His shoeshine business prospered, and Isaac and Blanche opened a restaurant in downtown Truro, where Blanche did the cooking.

Isaac Willis, the Great Boomsky.

The Great Boomsky continued to entertain at local and regional events. However, Isaac and Blanche shared a private sorrow; their five-year marriage had produced no children. In July 1912, the couple adopted a newborn, Elizabeth (Bessie), the child of a niece.

Isaac was a hard worker and had always been good with money. Over his years of touring he had saved a significant nest egg, which he invested in a beautiful parcel of land on Young Street on Foundry Hill, a predominantly Black neighborhood well above Truro's flood zone. Like Africville, the scenic neighborhood was located near the town dump. Although classified as farmland, it was only a short walk downhill into downtown Truro. Isaac built a small home for Blanche and baby Bessie and another, much larger home for his mother-in-law, Rachel and her children. Within a year, to the Willis's delight, Blanche became pregnant. Over the next years, Blanche would give birth to eight Willis children: Isaac Jr., Eula, Blanche, Ralph, Merle, Helen, John, and James.

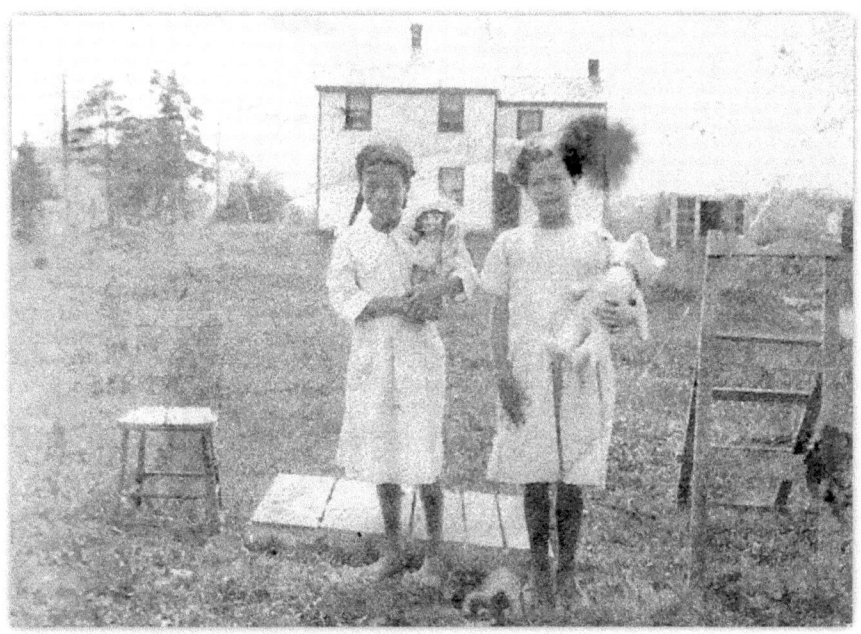

Bessie Willis (daughter of Isaac and Blanche) and a Stoutley cousin in front of Rachel Stoutley's house in Truro, Nova Scotia, circa 1918.

The Truro houses and property were a paradise for the Willis children and eventual grandchildren, with its orchards, berry patches, and farm animals—chickens, pigs, a horse, and a cow. When a neighbor's house burned down, the ever-frugal Isaac acquired the still-intact front porch and attached it to his own house. While they encountered significant levels of racial prejudice in the greater community, inside the compound, the family felt free and safe.

Around 1921, in his early forties, Isaac Willis took a job as a Red Cap with the Canadian National Railway. At the Truro train station, as he handled passengers' luggage, Isaac's career in magic remained part of his identity. People addressed Isaac and Blanche as Professor Boomsky and Mrs. Boomsky. Their sons were known as the Boomsky Boys. Isaac was a good provider. As was standard for the era, his children were required to reply "yes, sir" and "no, sir" to their father. Isaac Willis and his family prospered. Even though he didn't know how to drive, he owned the first car on Young Street. He hired his neighbor, Mr. Green, as a chauffeur. When Blanche was overwhelmed with five small children, Isaac hired a live-in servant.

Isaac Willis in his forties.

Isaac Willis enjoyed being a Red Cap. Chatty and effusive, he loved entertaining magicians who passed through his station. One magician wrote in the *Linking Ring*: "Would it interest any of my readers to know that Boomsky is alive and working as Station Porter in Truro? He still has some of Hermann's old apparatus and a wonderful scrap book of photos, etc., that I couldn't buy, beg or steal. Boomsky was the colored assistant to Hermann."[498]

In 1925, Isaac Willis spotted a Black man with a magician's trunk traveling through the Truro train station. Rhadolph Marcelliee was touring with a show called "Three Mysterious Knights" and happily accepted Isaac's invitation to visit his house on Young Street. Marcelliee, who described the forty-five-year-old Willis as an "old man," was impressed by the "collection of Herrmann lithos and handbills and some of the old apparatus they used."[499] Marcelliee regretted that he only had a short time to visit.

Truro train station in the 1920s, at the time Isaac Willis was employed as a Red Cap by the Canadian National Railway.

One thing Isaac never spoke about was the death of Léon Herrmann. Isaac Willis was superstitious, refusing to even touch the doorknob of a room where someone had passed away. Isaac Willis chose to display his cheerful sunny nature, keeping his personal troubles to himself.

In August 1932, just before midnight on a hot Tuesday, Blanche Willis shook her husband awake. Outside their bedroom window, the sky was glowing bright orange. They ran outside and saw, to their horror, an enormous cross burning on Foundry Hill. The Ku Klux Klan had come to Truro. Earlier that evening, between two and three hundred people had attended an introductory rally presented by several Klansmen from other areas. Now, a hundred white citizens of Truro stood around the burning cross as Black Foundry Hill residents scurried to stamp out cinders on their lawns.[500] To Truro's Black residents, who had coexisted in the town for many decades, the cross-burning was a knife to the heart. Isaac had thought that Canada was safe from racial violence. His confidence in his adopted country was deeply shaken. The cross-burning was widely condemned, earning Truro the moniker, "the Alabama of the North." The KKK did not gain wide traction in Canada, and American-style lynchings and racial violence did not spread north of the border. But Isaac Willis did not live long enough to be reassured.

A few months after the cross-burning, Isaac Willis became afflicted with cancer. He suffered for several months before passing away at his Young Street home on March 1, 1933, at the age of fifty-three. His death certificate reads "Isaac William Willis (Prof Boomsky)."

Isaac Willis's funeral was held at his house, led by the ministers of St. John's Anglican Church and Zion Baptist Church. Despite bad weather, many people attended, and the family was inundated with flowers and hundreds of cards. His obituary was printed in the *New York Times*. It did not mention his affiliation with Léon Herrmann. "Isaac Willis, well known in the theatrical circles under the name of Professor Boomsky, died in his home here yesterday at the age of 53. At one time he was a messenger in the White House at Washington."[501] The entertainment magazine *The Billboard* ran a brief obituary, but it, too, failed to note Isaac Willis's association with Herrmann.[502]

Sympathies were extended by the Canadian National Railway. "One of the most colorful figures in the local railway service passed away

Wednesday of this week, in the person of Isaac Willis, or better known to the railway employees, and the public as 'Professor Boomsky.' As a Red Cap at the local passenger station for a number of years, 'Boomsky' was popular and well-received."[503] Isaac Willis was buried at Terrace Hill Cemetery in Truro.

Sometime after his death, some magicians appeared at Isaac Willis's house, hoping to purchase the valuable magic props he had inherited from Herrmann the Great. But it was too late. At the height of the Great Depression, money for toys was scarce. The Great Boomsky's children and grandchildren had played with and broken all his props. But they remembered those very special toys even many years later, fondly recalling a fake knife that retracted into its handle. One of Isaac's sons liked to spread ketchup on himself, position the knife, and have one of his sisters scream for help.

Nine grandchildren of Isaac and Blanche Willis gathered on the site of Isaac's home on Young Street in Truro in 2017. From left to right: A. T. McCready, Sheila Ryan, Donna Willis, Charles Willis, Isaac Willis III (seated), Glenn Willis, Phyllis Marsman, Yvonne Glover, Agnes Lattie.

After Isaac's death in 1933, Blanche lived on for another thirty-eight years, all the while sharing rich stories of her husband with her children and grandchildren. Blanche Willis died in 1971 and was buried next to her husband.

Their oldest daughter, Bessie, raised seven children and lived to age one hundred, outliving all but one sibling. The other Willis children raised their own families. Isaac and Blanche Willis now have over three hundred living descendants.

The house Isaac built for Blanche was demolished in 2016 after being seized by the town of Truro for unpaid taxes. However, years earlier, several individual parcels of Isaac Willis's land had been divided up and given to his children. As of 2024, several of Isaac's grandchildren still live in houses built on the original Willis property on Young Street.

～

Act Four

The Last Boomsky

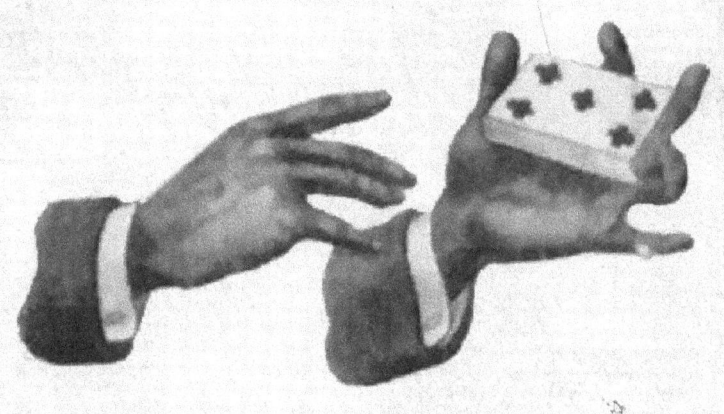

Adelaide Herrmann as Cagliostro, with Milton Hudson Everett.

CHAPTER TEN

M. H. Everett and Adelaide Herrmann

(1904–1932)

Madame Herrmann's Ambitious Gamble

Adelaide Herrmann held a grudge until it suited her not to. When M. H. Everett skipped out on her after she had rehired him post-prison, she had ravaged him in the press. But nobody possessed Everett's vast skills, experience, and memories of Alexander. When he resurfaced in 1903 and begged for his job back, she quietly hired him again. But she warned him that this chance would be his last.

After five years in vaudeville, Adelaide had replaced the over-exposed Night in Japan act. In her new Egyptian-themed act called Cleopatra, Queen of the Nile, M. H. Everett assisted Madame as a "stalwart Ethiopian in Moorish garb."[504] M. H. and Adele Dewey resumed performing their biracial illusion, the trunk now decorated with Egyptian hieroglyphics.

In May 1904, at the Chicago Opera house, Madame Herrmann was surprised and delighted to find herself sharing the bill with Irving Jones and his wife, Sadie. Adelaide called M. H. over to introduce them. Though twenty years had passed, Adelaide remembered well the hilarious little boy who could keep neither magic secrets nor a straight face. Irving and Sadie Jones convulsed the audience with laughter with their fast-paced, comedic song-and-dance act. M. H. Everett and Irving Jones spent the week sharing stories about working with Herrmann at age thirteen.[505]

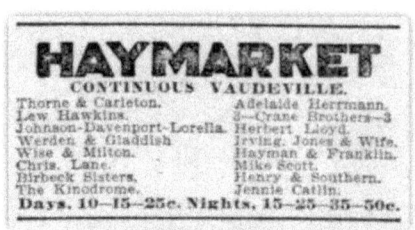

Chicago Tribune, April 23, 1904. Adelaide Herrmann shared the vaudeville bill with former Boomsky Irving Jones.

Adelaide was tired of vaudeville. Usually it was bearable, but some weeks were awful. She was headlining at Chase's in Washington, DC. Also booked that week was Brannan and Martini, whose comedy act consisted of exposures of magic tricks. The theater manager put them on directly after Adelaide, and they proceeded to show the audience how her tricks were done. According to *The Sphinx*, "To say that Madame Herrmann was deeply hurt and incensed is putting the case mildly." She protested, but the manager, amused, kept the act. A magic spokesman, Henry Ridgely Evans, declared in *The Sphinx*, "It is a dirty business."[506] To Adelaide, it was simply humiliating.

Adelaide desperately missed heading the Herrmanns' full-evening show. She plotted and schemed, designed and rehearsed. In August 1905, at the age of fifty-two, after six years in vaudeville and at great personal expense, she launched her own touring production—Adelaide Herrmann and Company. Her two-hour show consisted of three acts in which she starred. M. H. Everett played dual roles as onstage assistant and as chief electrician.[507]

As always, Adele Dewey ably assisted her aunt. Two specialty acts filled out Madame Herrmann's show. Adelaide hired Edward Thurnaer as manager, unaware that Léon had fired him due to his spiraling alcoholism. This choice would soon come back to haunt her. Late in August, Adelaide Herrmann and her sixteen-person company set sail for Savannah on the steamer *Memphis* for a forty-week tour of America. The reviews were good. Madame Herrmann was universally praised. But from the very beginning the tour faced challenges.

A pattern quickly emerged. The matinees were always packed, yet the evening shows were often sparsely attended. Reviewers noted that the audiences filling the theaters in the daytime consisted almost entirely of women. On weekends and holiday matinees, there were also many children. Yet in the evening, when women were home with their families, houses were thin. As they traveled through Colorado to the Pacific Northwest, the tour struggled to stay profitable, and Adelaide took cuts to her own salary to keep the company afloat.

Adelaide relied on twenty-seven-year-old M. H. Everett more than ever. As both star and company leader, her responsibilities were all-encompassing. Ed Thurnaer was drinking heavily, so she became the de facto company manager, too. Everett was a strong link. Adelaide knew that at every show, her props and sets would be perfectly in place. The lights would be placed just right so as to never reveal the secrets of her tricks.[508]

They continued through Virginia, North Carolina, Alabama, and Mississippi, finally arriving in New Orleans for a weeklong run. The deeper into the South they got, the more the female-headed company encountered ill treatment. The company members complained of deplorable conditions—disgusting hotels and horrible food. Thurnaer, the manager, was useless. The tour was losing money. Adelaide became exhausted. After just ten whirlwind weeks, Madame Herrmann was forced to abandon the tour and return to New York. It was a great disappointment to her.[509] Utterly dejected, Madame returned to vaudeville and began building back her savings.

The Merry Widow Company: Fiasco in Cuba

Two years later, on February 4, 1908, Adelaide Herrmann, M. H. Everett, and Adele Dewey were performing at Poli's Vaudeville Theater in Scranton, Pennsylvania. That same night, less than two blocks away, the world's grandest illusion show was playing at the Lyceum. Harry Kellar, Alexander Herrmann's former rival, was on his farewell tour. Starring with him was his successor, Howard Thurston.[510] Over the years, Harry Kellar had become a supportive friend to Adelaide.

That night, as Madame Herrmann took the stage for her vaudeville turn, she badly missed heading her own show. After her performance, she, Adele, and M. H. stepped around the corner to the Lyceum stage door to say hello. Glimpsing the star magicians' bustling backstage made Madame long for her old life even more.

Adelaide's visit with Kellar and Thurston inspired and energized her. When Harry Clark, former manager of The Great Raymond, offered to manage a tour of Cuba for her, proceeding from there to Central and South America, Adelaide jumped at the chance to escape vaudeville for good. Digging deeply into her savings, she commissioned new scenery and hired new specialty acts. Madame also advanced the money for the company's passage to Cuba. She derived her new company's name from a popular operetta by Franz Lehár, *The Merry Widow*. In September 1908, three years after the early demise of her first big touring show and twelve years after her husband's death, Adelaide's Herrmann's Merry Widow Company arrived in Havana.

For this tour, M. H. Everett again served as both performer and chief electrician. It was his second trip to Cuba; the first, fourteen years earlier, had been cut short by Alexander Herrmann's illness and hasty return to New York. Adelaide's route promised to rival the grand tours of the old Herrmann company. Her cast included a comic acrobatic troupe from Australia called the Four Stagpoles, as well as an operatic soprano, Johanna Christoffy. For the first time, Adelaide also brought

Inspired by Herrmann, Howard Thurston hired his own Black assistant, George White, from Virgina. White joined Thurston in 1899 at age twelve and remained Thurston's chief assistant for the magician's entire career.

along another magician, her old assistant Roland Travers, who performed a Chinese magic act in imitation of Ching Ling Foo.[511] Six years after leaving Madame's employ, twenty-five-year-old Travers had recently impressed Houdini with his "quick and snappy way of presenting his tricks."[512] Adelaide's nephew John Kretschmann headed the crew, but his cousin Adele Dewey Owles was not with them. Twenty-nine-year-old Adele had just married Charles Wellesley Smith, a distinguished architect who had recently designed Newark, New Jersey's expansive new train station. For once, unlike so many holidays and family events that conflicted with her touring schedule, Adelaide had been able to attend her favorite niece's wedding.

The Merry Widow Company opened to a crowded house at Havana's Payret Theater on September 25. Havana's high society turned out in force on opening night, and Adelaide was gratified by the enthusiastic response. Yet despite good reviews, the theater was just one-third full the next night. Each night, fewer people came. On Thursday when they finished their week, only a hundred people sat scattered in the large theater.[513] Adelaide's confusion and disappointment turned to fury when she discovered that Manager Clark had not promoted the show. Adelaide had advanced over eight hundred dollars to Clark for tour expenses. Instead of buying newspaper ads and securing travel arrangements, Clark pocketed the money and disappeared. Adelaide was suddenly totally broke, stranded in Cuba, with no funds to continue the tour and no way to get home. Over the years, Alexander Herrmann had regularly rescued stranded theater companies. But in her thirty years performing, Adelaide had never become stranded herself. This time, no angel appeared to bail them out. As their situation became desperate, the public back home followed the story through press updates.[514]

Someone suggested that they raffle their jewelry. The idea caught on in Havana's theatrical community. Madame Herrmann treasured her jewels. Acquired in a lifetime of travels, each piece carried sentimental value. Always adorned with necklaces, bracelets, earrings, and brooches, Adelaide often wore rings on every finger and toe. Although it tore at her, Adelaide and the other performers contributed whatever they had, and raffle tickets were sold for one dollar each. The raffle raised $700, enough for the company's passage back to New York. But jewelry-loving Madame Herrmann was forced to part with some of her most treasured pieces.[515]

M. H. Everett sailed with the company to New York from Havana on the *Saratoga*, barely two weeks after arriving.[516] With no solid touring plans, Everett began looking for an apartment to rent in Harlem.

Adelaide, angry and bitterly disappointed, stayed behind in Cuba to pursue a legal case against Manager Clark, who was eventually arrested. But it was too late. At age fifty-five, Adelaide Herrmann's last hope for heading her own company had been dashed. Battered emotionally and financially, she sailed back to New York and planned her return to vaudeville.

ADELAIDE AND HUTCHIN TWO DECADES ON

Twenty years after joining the Herrmann company, M. H. Everett remained in Madame Herrmann's employ. As Adelaide turned sixty, she faced the realities of being an older performer, especially an older female performer. She was no longer a headliner in vaudeville. Now a supporting act, she gradually dropped lower and lower in the lineup. Newspaper stories and reviews dwindled. Movies were fast replacing vaudeville. Gradually, Adelaide's goal shifted from maintaining her stardom to simply working. Once again, she redesigned her act, surprising everyone by portraying a male character—Cagliostro, Master of Mysteries. She still carried ornate backdrops, which made her four-person act seem much grander. M. H. Everett assisted her in this act as well, not as the crisply uniformed Boomsky, nor as a stalwart Ethiopian, but dressed as a harlequin.

Adelaide Herrmann's stage set for her Cagliostro act, circa 1917. Only three people appear onstage. The rest are painted images. From left to right: Adelaide Herrmann, unidentified female assistant, M. H. Everett. The act was filmed on the day this photo was taken, but the reels have never surfaced and were likely lost.

Now in his thirties, with lessons learned from jail time and Madame's absolution, M. H. avoided getting into trouble again. He continued to work for Madame Herrmann off and on for the rest of her life. M. H. also performed on his own as Everett the Magician as he put down roots in Harlem, New York's fastest-growing neighborhood.

Black Americans were moving north in droves. Between 1910 and 1920, factory jobs attracted millions of Southern Blacks to Northern industrial cities. In Harlem, real estate speculation had sparked a building boom, creating an entire neighborhood of grand, upscale apartment buildings. But the speculators had miscalculated. Although Harlem was traversed by new rail and subway lines, middle-class Manhattanites proved unwilling to move five miles north. Thousands of spacious new apartments sat empty. At the same time, predominantly Black neighborhoods downtown were being razed for massive projects such as Pennsylvania Station. Black New Yorkers moved uptown, while Pullman porters spread real estate fliers throughout the South. By 1920, three hundred thousand Southern Blacks had moved to Harlem.

In 1910, nearly two decades after leaving Americus, Georgia, Milton Hudson Everett was once again living with family. His beloved older brother, Sidney E. Everett, had moved up to Harlem from Americus, bringing their widowed mother, Leitha. Within a year, Sidney met and married Amanda ("Mandy") Jones, who had come from Tennessee. When not performing on the road, M. H., now thirty-one, lived with them at their apartment on West 134th Street.[517]

The extended Everett family moved six blocks uptown to 140th Street. The Everett brothers were devastated when their mother, Leitha, passed away at about age sixty. Unschooled, she had learned to read in adulthood.[518] She was born into slavery in Georgia and had grown up destitute. Only six of her fourteen children had survived to adulthood, and she and her late husband had struggled to feed and clothe them. Hutchin's job with the Herrmanns had changed all that. Leitha Everett spent her last years in a palatial Harlem apartment building surrounded by the heady vibrancy of the Harlem Renaissance.

Three blocks uptown lived an enterprising young woman who would become M. H. Everett 's bride. Twenty-four-year-old Julia Evans had traveled alone from Virginia to help support her parents and six siblings. Julia worked in a factory as a dressmaker while living as a boarder on West 143rd Street. Somehow, the magician from Georgia met the factory worker from Virginia.[519] On December 6, 1913, M. H. Everett and Julia Evans were married in New York. Since the new groom was frequently off touring with Madame Herrmann, the couple continued living with Sidney and Mandy in Harlem.

In his Harlem neighborhood, M. H. Everett stood out. Sidney Everett worked as a laborer at the Customs House. On a census page filled with railway porters, elevator operators, cooks, seamstresses, janitors, cart drivers, laundresses, stevedores, and hairdressers, M. H. Everett's occupation reads, "musician." The census taker seemingly misheard, failing to correctly note the unlikely profession, "magician."[520] The 1915 New York State census lists M. H. Everett's profession as "actor." Although both Everett couples were still young, neither marriage produced children.

Over the next few years, M. H. Everett toured with Adelaide Herrmann in vaudeville, assisting in her Cagliostro act. Adelaide resurrected the old trick The Artist's Dream, renaming it The Haunted Studio—A Pantomimic Illusionary Fantasy. In the illusion, Adelaide's male character played an artist whose painting of a young woman came to life. M. H. Everett received billing in the role of Andre, a servant.[521]

With Everett at her side, Madame Herrmann experienced a series of devastating personal losses. The eldest of the four Scarsez sisters, Frances Kretschmann, died in London in 1906, followed four years later by the second-eldest sister, Janet Pallme. In 1911, Everett accompanied Adelaide and Adele to England for a final visit with Adele's ailing mother, Mathilde Scarsez Owles, who died the following year.[522] In just six years, Adelaide had lost all three of her sisters.[523] In 1915 Madame Herrmann's eldest niece and namesake, Adelaide Kretschmann Madell, died in New York at age forty-three, leaving behind five young daughters. A few months later, her niece Adele Dewey was widowed after seven years of marriage when her forty-nine-year-old husband, Charles Wellesley Smith, succumbed to cirrhosis of the liver. In 1916, Léon Herrmann's widow, Marie, died in Paris at age fifty-four. Adelaide responded to all this bad news by touring harder than ever.

In 1916, Everett was recognized by two journalists. The *Atlanta Constitution* mentioned him as Boomsky from Americus, although not his name.[524] A journalist in Norfolk stumbled upon Boomsky's story. While interviewing Madame Herrmann backstage, Adelaide called out, "Milton! Get that suitcase out of my dressing room and take it to the hotel."[525]

She asked the reporter, "Do you remember him?"

"Is it Boomsky?" asked the newsman.

Sensing an interesting angle, the reporter shifted his focus from Madame to her assistant. The resulting article in the *Virginian-Pilot and the Norfolk Landmark* was titled, "Remember 'Boomsky' Faithful Retainer?— After Twenty-Six Years He Is Still One of the Herrmann Company."

The article recounted Adelaide's story of picking up thirteen-year-old Milton Hudson Everett in Americus, Georgia. His betrayals long forgotten, Madame Herrmann heaped praise upon her assistant. "His long career with us began the first night in the next town by Professor Herrmann dubbing him 'Boomsky' and that is the name he has been known by to millions of people this wide world over. He's been the real Biblical good and faithful servant all these years."[526] The article continued, "'Can you realize it,' asked Mme. Herrmann, with a sigh, 'Professor Herrmann has been dead twenty years and Boomsky and I still go on with the work he left us to keep him in the memories of the world of people who knew him.'"

A notorious incident has been attributed to M. H. Everett, but likely it was perpetrated by a different magician, also named Everett. In 1917, Everett the Magician attempted a solo show at the Lyric Theater in Hoboken, New Jersey, a 1,800-seat movie house that featured live acts between the feature films. Everett produced two white rats. He held the squirming creatures just over the head of a woman in the audience. She was visibly frightened. Instead of backing off, Everett pretended to throw the rats at the woman. The terrified woman shrieked then fainted dead away. As other patrons carried her, unconscious, to the rest room, "the house was thrown into something of a panic, necessitating the calling of policemen to prevent a riot."[527]

If this magician was M. H., it marked both his comeback and farewell performance. There is no evidence that he performed as a solo magician after this debacle. As Boomsky, he grew up on the edge of the spotlight, not in its full glare. That was where he was comfortable.

William E. Robinson's Tragic End

While Adelaide and Milton Hudson Everett had been endlessly plying the Orpheum circuit, the Herrmanns' former assistants, Will and Dot Robinson, had been performing in England for over a decade. Will Robinson continued to draw large crowds in his role as the Chinese conjuror Chung Ling Soo. Dot still played his assistant, Suee Seen, despite much heartache. Although now legally married, Will and Dot were no longer a couple.[528] Will had always been a ladies' man, chalking up numerous affairs. In 1907, a liaison with an Englishwoman half his age had resulted in a pregnancy. Will stayed with the woman, Lou Blatchford, and they now had three children. He had become a contented family man while Dot was a lonely expat who had nothing but the show. She had to spend her entire public life pretending to be Chinese, standing next to a man who wanted her assistant skills but no longer wanted her.

Chung Ling Soo's big finale was the bullet catch. Unlike Herrmann, who had performed the dangerous trick only a dozen or so times in his entire career, Chung Ling Soo performed it as a regular feature in his show. The master magician was confident in his method, which was as diabolically clever as it was convincing. The audience actually saw the real bullets being loaded into the two rifles. This was very different from Herrmann's method, in which the marked bullets were switched for hollow amalgam fakes, ensuring that the real bullets never went near the guns. Robinson's method was edgier and even more convincing. Instead of using gimmicked bullets, Robinson rigged the guns. Unknown to the audience, the rifles had two barrels. The barrel holding the bullet was not connected to the charge. The other barrel contained a blank. When the rifle erupted with the smoke and flash of a real shot, the actual bullet remained in the gun.

On March 23, 1918, Chung Ling Soo performed at the Wood Green Empire theater in London. He began the bullet catch finale, called in the program, "Condemned to Death by the Boxers." After the gunshots, there was a suspenseful moment of stillness. The audience expected Soo to step forward triumphantly. Instead, the magician stumbled and fell. Horrified, the audience was additionally stunned when the great Chinese conjuror Chung Ling Soo exclaimed in clear English, "Oh my God! Something's happened! Bring down the curtain!"

Fifty-six-year-old Robinson was rushed to a hospital, where he died a few hours later. The death of Chung Ling Soo, reported in front-page headlines throughout England, contained a double shocker. Many fans reacted with disbelief when they learned that the exotic Chinese superstar was actually the American showman William Ellsworth Robinson. Over the many years that he had meticulously maintained his false Chinese persona, both onstage and off, the public had been thoroughly fooled.

The inquest revealed that repeated performances had worn away a small channel in one of the gimmicked guns, allowing gunpowder to trickle into the barrel containing a real bullet, which had ignited and fired the projectile. The determination of the inquest hearings was Death by Misadventure.[529] Rumors persisted in the magic world, however, that Robinson's death had been the result of a deliberate sabotage by a disgruntled assistant.[530]

Adelaide and M. H. were shocked to learn of Will Robinson's death while performing the bullet catch in England. They worried about Dot, with good reason. Will had left Dot just one-third of his estate. His mistress, Lou Blatchford, now owned the show and most everything else. The inquest was highly publicized, and Dot endured the humiliation of the world knowing of her husband's mistress and their children. When Dot later sailed to New York, she didn't tell anyone of her return. If Dot secretly contacted Adelaide, Madame kept it to herself.[531]

Olive Path "Dot" Robinson would die lonely and cancer-ridden in 1934. Her official age was sixty-one, the showgirl's lie now eternally etched on her headstone, as Dot was actually closer to seventy. She was buried in the Robinson family plot at Woodlawn Cemetery in the Bronx, not far from the Herrmann plot.

HERRMANN'S WAND: HOUDINI DROPS IN

In April 1918, Harry Houdini visited Adelaide Herrmann at her Manhattan atelier. M. H. Everett answered the door and led the magician upstairs. The midtown artist loft served as Adelaide's permanent New York home base, though not her residence. The workshop and rehearsal space housed her equipment and possessions, including the treasured heirlooms of Alexander Herrmann. Whenever Madame was between engagements, which was becoming more frequent, her animals and equipment would be moved temporarily to her atelier. Everett traveled down every day from Harlem to tend to Adelaide's dogs, cats, and birds. Madame frequently stopped by to see her pets, which were not allowed in her suite at the New Strand Hotel.

M. H. gestured Houdini into Madame's space, and several dogs ran to greet them. Adelaide, a tiny dog tucked under her arm, welcomed her visitor warmly. M. H. corralled the other dogs and receded to the corner to better observe the great Houdini, a compact, muscular man vibrating with energy. Houdini sighed as he looked all around at the shelves of worn packing cases and stored illusions, all displaying in large letters, "HERRMANN." This was the closest Houdini would ever get to his idol, Alexander Herrmann. Houdini breathed in deeply, as if the musty air smelled like perfume.

It was twenty-two years since that summer in Nova Scotia when the penniless Harry and Bess Houdini had failed to connect with the high-flying Herrmanns. Now, in 1918, Houdini had long since replaced Herrmann as the most famous magician in the world. Adelaide had watched Houdini's ascension from a front-row seat. In 1903 and 1904, respectively, Harry Houdini and Adelaide Herrmann had joined the newly formed Society of American Magicians (SAM). As colleagues and compeers, Houdini and Madame had gradually developed a cordial professional relationship. In 1917, Houdini had been elected as president of the SAM. On the day of his visit to Adelaide's loft, Houdini was acting in his official capacity.

Houdini had two goals that day. First, he hoped to convince Madame to change her mind about performing for an upcoming fundraiser he was organizing at the gigantic New York Hippodrome. She had already declined via a letter. "My Dear Mr. Houdini—My Assistant and I have gone over the matter of my proposed appearance at the Benefit, and we feel that I could not do myself justice on account of the water tank. It would be too risky to attempt the illusion over the footlights. So we will have to forego the pleasure of appearing."[532]

Now, Houdini admitted to Adelaide that he was confused. By "water tank," did Madame refer to the elliptical pool for aquatic acts that could rise up from below onto the enormous Hippodrome stage? Or was she describing Houdini's own Chinese Water Torture Cell? He did not wait for Madame to answer. Either way, it would not be a problem, Houdini assured her. Madame would have the stage to herself. During her act, there would be no water tank of any sort on the stage. All of Madame's needs would be accommodated and her expenses covered. Satisfied, Adelaide Herrmann agreed to appear at the upcoming benefit.

Houdini's second agenda item was more delicate. He began by extolling Alexander Herrmann's legendary generosity, noting how, with the bullet catch, the great magician had put his very life on the line to raise money for worthy causes. Inspired by the great Herrmann, he, Houdini, sought to emulate the Professor's munificence through his role as president of the Society of American Magicians. Why, just the previous November, Houdini's first Hippodrome benefit had raised nearly $10,000 for the survivors of the *Antilles*, the US Navy troop ship that had been sunk by a German U-boat.[533]

Madame Herrmann didn't need reminding. She had attended the *Antilles* benefit. How could she forget the sight of Houdini's other hero, Harry Kellar, being paraded around the Hippodrome stage on a sedan chair while adoring magicians pelted him with yellow chrysanthemums?[534] But Houdini always did ramble on, especially when talking about his favorite subject—himself.

Houdini's upcoming SAM benefit would establish a hospital fund for ailing magicians and showmen. To further honor her late husband, Houdini planned to present a trick he had never performed before—the bullet catch. He had already informed the press. From across the room, M. H. caught Adelaide's eye. Both were stunned. Just a few weeks prior, William E. Robinson had lain mortally wounded in a pool of blood before shocked theatergoers after performing the bullet catch—on Houdini's birthday of all days. They remained deeply shaken. Had Houdini lost his mind?

Madame's eyes narrowed as her veteran's cynicism kicked in. Houdini had known Robinson well. He would have to be both reckless and insane to attempt the dangerous bullet catch. Houdini was a lot of things—vain, ambitious, overbearing—but he was meticulous about safety, and though he was frequently insufferable, he wasn't insane. Adelaide predicted he would milk the publicity, then find an excuse to cancel.

Houdini finished his monologue with a request on behalf of the Society of American Magicians: Would Madame Herrmann consider donating an artifact of Alexander Herrmann's to auction at the performance? Adelaide thought for a moment, then gestured at a shelf. M. H. fetched for her a narrow wooden box. She opened it and removed a gold-tipped wand. M. H. caught his breath, remembering that Christmas in Portland, Oregon, when he was just fifteen. It had rained all week, and the company had all pitched in to surprise Alexander with this beautiful wand. M. H. recalled the many times that he, as Boomsky, had handed that very wand to Alexander just before the curtain rose.

Madame handed the wand to Houdini. She instructed him to direct the money it raised to where it would do the most good. Houdini thanked her and prepared to leave. But as he packed the wand, he noticed that the box contained two more wands of Alexander Herrmann's. Houdini suggested that perhaps he could auction those as well? Madame resisted at first, but Houdini persisted. Finally, somewhat reluctantly, she allowed Houdini to depart with three of her husband's magic wands.

"The Biggest Show of the Year," hailed the New York newspapers on the morning of April 21, the day of the Hippodrome benefit for the Showman's League and SAM Hospital Fund. Thanks to Houdini's tireless efforts, all 5,300 seats of the world's largest theater were filled. As Madame Herrmann and M. H. Everett prepared her act backstage, they exchanged wry smiles as they heard Houdini announce from the stage, in his booming voice, that the manager of the Hippodrome had forbidden him to perform the bullet catch. Instead, he would be performing the even more dangerous Chinese Water Torture Cell escape.

When Houdini introduced the first of the evening's twenty-three acts, Madame was surprised to see a young female magician named Lady Camile take the stage. Her act, "Magical Horticulture," was simple and pretty. From empty pots grew magical flowers, which Lady Camile tossed to audience members. As Madame waited to perform, nine more magicians, a comedian, and a cellist went before her.

Finally, it was Madame's turn. With Hudson Everett's expert assistance, Adelaide Herrmann manipulated billiard balls, produced doves from thin air, and floated a female assistant in the Aerial Suspension. Houdini would later write of her performance in *M.U.M.*, the SAM's monthly publication, "Mme. Adelaide Herrmann, who has individuality enough to be more than the widow, rather than the successor of the Great Alexander, was cordially received. Her performance was full of 'snap' and go, and she did a lot of fine work in the too short time allotted. We are very proud of our only lady member."[535]

After Adelaide's act came more magicians, singers, comedians, the US Navy Octette, and a fancy lariat roping act. Then it was time for the auction of Alexander Herrmann's wand. To Adelaide's surprise, another item was included along with the wand. A scrapbook of Alexander Herrmann's that had belonged to William Robinson had been donated to the auction by magic dealer Francis Martinka. Madame was not happy. She would have liked her husband's scrapbook for herself. But it was too late to protest. The bidding was brisk,

The New York Hippodrome.

starting at $50 and quickly jumping to $100. Harry Kellar, then in Los Angeles, had entered an absentee bid of $150, certain he would win. Applause greeted the announcement of Kellar's bid, but Herrmann's great rival was quickly outmatched. An unknown man named Gleason won the wand and scrapbook for $250, the equivalent of nearly $5,000 today.

Her part of the show finished, Adelaide and her assistants packed up and left, missing the performances of The Royal Midgets, the 100 Happy Hoboes, and the grand finale—Houdini performing his Chinese Water Torture Cell. This was followed by another, even grander grand finale—the US Army's First Battalion, 71st Infantry, NYC, carrying out military drills and exercises.

When reviews appeared in the New York newspapers, Adelaide, surprisingly, came under fire. She was caught completely off guard by harsh criticism from two groups she was closely affiliated with over the auctioning of Alexander's wand. Members of the Actors' Equity Association and the Belgian Relief Fund were angry that Adelaide had prioritized the Showman's League Hospital Fund over their own groups, especially since Adelaide had no direct connection with the Showman's League of America. Founded by William "Buffalo Bill" Cody to benefit the performers and crews of outdoor spectacles, circuses, and tent shows, the Showmen were viewed by many as rough, hard-drinking types, not necessarily worthy of charity.

Madame's mind flashed to the other two wands that Houdini had taken. She quickly typed a letter on Hotel Strand stationery.

April 25, 1918
My dear Mr. Houdini:

There seems to be quite a little jealousy because I gave a Wand to the Showmen's Hospital Benefit and have not given anything to other societies. I have, therefore, decided to show no partiality and will ask you to kindly bring the two wands that were at the loft and that you have, to the Hippodrome, and I will send the boy Hudson around for them. Just call me up one morning at your earliest convenience to let me know when I can send the boy. Hope you are fully rested after your excitement of last Sunday night. With kind regards, I remain, Yours very truly, Adelaide Herrmann[536]

Normal for the time, Madame used the adjective "boy" to identify her Black assistant of nearly thirty years to her colleague, a term she would never have used in M. H.'s presence.

When M. H. Everett arrived at the Hippodrome to fetch the wands, he knocked on Houdini's dressing room door. Houdini responded with a gruff, "Come in." Madame had warned M. H. that his encounter with Houdini might be tense. Houdini was already planning another charity auction and was not happy about returning the wands to Madame. M. H. resisted the urge to let his eyes rove around the star's dressing room. If Houdini realized that Everett was the same Herrmann assistant whose long-ago prison escapades he had noted in his scrapbook, he didn't show it. Had he comprehended that standing before him was Alexander Herrmann's assistant of five years, Houdini would have savored the opportunity to grill Everett about his days working with Herrmann the Great. But Houdini was in a snit. Scowling and silent, he handed M. H. the wands, and Madame's assistant turned and left.

The Hippodrome show and his encounter with Houdini were the closest M. H. Everett would ever get to the Society of American Magicians. The organization's bylaws stated that membership was open to "anyone of the white race, over twenty-one, with a sincere interest in magic." Everett would be in his late sixties, and long retired from performing, when the SAM would finally admit its first African American member more than three decades later.[537]

M. H. Everett in Harlem

Adelaide Herrmann had managed a full touring schedule before the Great War intervened. Now, in her mid-sixties, Madame Herrmann's performing opportunities dwindled, and in 1919 she was sidelined by two serious operations.[538] When Madame Herrmann returned to vaudeville, M. H. Everett did not accompany her. Instead, Adelaide's nephew John Kretschmann became her touring assistant, using the stage name John Ketcham or John Ketchum. When she launched a new act featuring Alexander's old illusion Noah's Ark, it was John, not M. H., who wrangled her thirty performing animals.[539] For all her efforts, she and the other acts now shared the bill with motion pictures, which were quickly edging out live performers.

M. H. had not wanted to leave Madame's employ. However, with the US entry into the war in Europe, M. H. and his brother Sidney had been required to register for the draft. Working as an entertainer provided no protection from being sent to the Belgian front. Dangerous jobs supplying the war effort were a different story. Trading overseas combat for the risk of getting blown up at home, M. H. and Sidney Everett signed on as dye workers at the Butterworth & Judson Chemical Works in Newark, NJ.[540] The plant produced sulfuric acid, a key component of explosives used by the military. The huge operation employed hundreds of African American workers, who were recruited because they were considered less likely to be spies or saboteurs. They were also considered expendable. The pay was decent, but the work was foul and extremely dangerous. In March 1918, an explosion at the Butterworth & Judson plant killed two workers and leveled four buildings. The shock wave was felt for miles.[541] Less than two months later, two hundred workers were killed at a chemical plant explosion in Pittsburgh.[542]

It is not known how long M. H. Everett worked at Butterworth & Judson, but when the war ended, Madame Herrmann hired him again. These days, whenever she was in New York, Adelaide occupied a suite at the Hotel Arlington on West 25th Street off Fifth Avenue. M. H. and Julia now had their own Harlem apartment at 541 Lenox Avenue.[543] M. H. frequently rode the subway downtown to run errands for Adelaide. When Madame traveled, he now stayed behind in New York, watching over her atelier. His job as Adelaide Herrmann's assistant was listed on the census as "messenger for a private family." Julia supplemented the couple's income by working from home as a dressmaker.[544]

M. H. sometimes saw his old friend Dewey, now known as Adele O. Smith, with whom he had performed the Asiatic Trunk Mystery nearly thirty years earlier. Adele visited her aunt Adelaide on her day off from her job as a clerk at Bamberger's Department Store in Newark. Every Sunday, Adele entered Newark's castle-turreted train station, designed by her late husband, Charles Wellesley Smith, and boarded a Manhattan-bound train that took her all the way to Pennsylvania Station, via the new railway tunnels under the Hudson River.[545] The entire twenty-mile trip took only about an hour. From there it was a ten-block walk to the Arlington Hotel.

The summer of 1926 was nostalgic for Adelaide and for M. H. Everett as well. It was the thirtieth anniversary of Alexander's last glorious summer spent yachting about New York's waterways, along with his triumphant July Fourth show at Sing Sing and their splendid week in Halifax, Nova Scotia. The summer's only major annoyance was a forced move from Adelaide's longtime atelier, which had housed her props, animals, and her husband's mementos for nearly thirty years. She temporarily moved everything to a theatrical warehouse on 46th Street as she looked for a new loft. The warehouse was run-down and dirty, but she didn't plan on staying long.

Adelaide's memories surged back when she attended a lovely July dinner party hosted by Howard Thurston and his daughter Jane. The location itself was poignant; Thurston had purchased the mansion next door to what had been Herrmann Manor in Whitestone. The many magic luminaries in attendance, including Harry and Bess Houdini,

Harry and Mildred Rouclere, John Mulholland, and Max Malini, listened in rapt silence as Madame Herrmann told stories of the old days of Herrmann the Great. It was a beautiful evening. Looking back later, Adelaide would treasure its memory as the end of another era. Six weeks later, disaster struck.

THE WAREHOUSE FIRE

It began with an explosion at 10:50 a.m. on Manhattan's far west side. Glass and wire screens were hurled from the top floor windows and thick smoke poured out. The theatrical warehouse at 609 West 46th Street stored sets and costumes of many well-known performers and also housed over two hundred performing animals, including all thirty of Adelaide Herrmann's Noah's Ark creatures. Adelaide's nephew John Kretschmann was at the warehouse when an illegal distillery exploded. A ceiling collapsed on him. Injured and burned, John found a telephone and called Adelaide, who rushed over.[546] Before she arrived, Thomas Collins ran into the burning warehouse, attempting to rescue his boxing kangaroo. Collins's charred body was found later with that of his beloved performing partner. Vaudevillian Albert Friend, nearly hysterical, was rescued from a shed roof he climbed onto after trying in vain to save his ten performing dogs.

The *Daily News* reported that "Mme. Herrmann arrived just in time to wade into the flooded street and scoop up her white kitten, Magic, after it gave a meow of despair and leaped from the burning fourth floor. Her only other pets rescued were two dogs, Mamie and Nellie." All the other animals in the warehouse perished.

"'We were to have left next week to tour the Orpheum circuit,' said Mme. Herrmann weeping. 'Now all my darlings are dead; I had had them for years. Also I have lost all my husband's medals, decorations and letters from kings and presidents, which were stored there.'"[547] It was an enormous blow, thirty years after her husband's death. Everyone expected Adelaide, then seventy-three, to retire. But against the advice of all her friends, the intrepid Madame set out for one final tour, which she titled, "Magic, Grace, and Music."

It was a terrible autumn for magic. On October 31, seven weeks after the warehouse explosion, Harry Houdini died in Detroit. The escape artist had often demonstrated his toughness by challenging audience members to punch him in the stomach. A few days earlier in Montreal, a visitor to the star's dressing room had surprised Houdini with a series of punches to the abdomen before Houdini had a chance to prepare himself. He was gravely injured by the blows but carried on with his tour, finally succumbing to a burst appendix. Houdini died at the same age as Alexander Herrmann—fifty-two.

M. H. Everett heard about Houdini's death the same way as everyone else, from newsboys on street corners waving papers and shouting the headline. When Madame went back on the road, M. H. stayed behind in New York, living with Julia in Harlem. After the warehouse fire, Adelaide had no need of Everett's services during the months she was out of town. On Madame's return, M. H. would resume working part-time as her messenger and assistant, but his hours and income would be minimal. Julia's income as a dressmaker was also not reliable. At around age forty-seven, Milton Hudson Everett applied for a job with the US Post Office and was hired as a clerk.

Adelaide kept going for another year, but she struggled with fatigue. Her friends observed that she remained traumatized over the loss of her animals. In December 1927, Adelaide Herrmann collapsed while performing in Paterson, New Jersey. Her dear friends, Harry and Mildred Rouclere, took her into their home in Ridgewood to recover. For years, the Roucleres had toured their own full-evening magic show. They were among Adelaide's last remaining friends who had also known Alexander. They now owned a hotel in Ridgewood, New Jersey. As she convalesced, Adelaide declared that Mildred was the best nurse any patient ever had.[548] Harry Rouclere had become an enthusiastic aviator.

On Christmas Day, to Adelaide's delight, Harry dressed up as Santa and flew his open biplane over Ridgewood, tossing candy hanging from little parachutes to the children below.[549]

Adelaide willed herself back onto the stage a few weeks later, but she was weak and unsteady. Finally, even Madame had to admit defeat. In April, the seventy-four-year-old Queen of Magic stood on the stage of the Orpheum Theater in Brooklyn and announced her retirement. She moved permanently into a suite at the Hotel Arlington, at 25th Street and Fifth Avenue in Manhattan. Her old friend and assistant Roland Travers kept a room at the Arlington as well. As she watched the steel-framed Empire State Building rise with incredible speed nine blocks north, Madame began writing her memoir.

END OF AN ERA: LONG LIVE THE QUEEN

On Sunday afternoon, December 6, 1931, Adelaide Herrmann arrived at a party given by M. H. and Julia Everett to celebrate their eighteenth wedding anniversary. Their large apartment at 470 West 146th Street "was beautifully decorated with cut flowers and glimmering candles."[550] Place settings were laid out for forty guests. As friends toasted and congratulated the Everetts, Adelaide noted that there was another anniversary to celebrate. It was forty years since her husband had invited a thirteen-year-old boy to dance for him on a tiny stage in Georgia. The Everetts' Harlem friends listened raptly as M. H. and Madame talked of magical times long gone, remembered by only them. They had been through so much together. Here they were after all these years, at this anniversary party in Harlem. M. H. Everett would cherish the memory of that night for the rest of his life.

The weather that February was vicious. As storm after storm battered New York, Madame Herrmann was feeling miserable. She had always had bad teeth, and they had gotten progressively worse. Now she was in constant pain. Her dentist identified several infected teeth that would have to go, and Madame decided to have them all removed at the same time. The day of her appointment, a nasty winter storm blew in, but she refused to cancel. The extractions were a long, painful ordeal. Adelaide was feeling weak and woozy as she stepped out from the dentist's office directly into heavy sleet and freezing rain. As she made her way home, Adelaide soon became thoroughly wet and chilled. She arrived back at the Arlington feeling disoriented, exhausted, and ill. The next day she woke with a cold that swiftly progressed to pneumonia. Adelaide was hospitalized, but her condition deteriorated.

On Friday, February 19, 1932, Adelaide Herrmann, magic's great queen, slipped into a coma and died at age seventy-eight.

Adelaide's death was a shock to those close to her. Just a few days before becoming ill she had been "the same eager, optimistic soul that she had ever been, always ready with her sunny smile, her gracious manners, never discouraged, never bitter, no matter how severe the reverses nor how shattering the disappointments."[551]

"The funeral services on the 22nd of February were attended by a large and imposing assemblage which included many stars of greater and lesser magnitude, all of whom had known and esteemed Madame Herrmann. Everett, the last of the 'Boomskys' who had served her on the stage, sat in a secluded corner with tears welling in his sorrowful dark eyes." The reporter noted that Everett was the only remaining original member of the Herrmann show.[552] Milton Hudson Everett wiped his eyes and said, "A golden age of vaudeville goes with her. And there are few enough who remember it now."[553]

After Bernard M. L. Ernst read the solemn ritual of the Society of American Magicians, Adelaide's friend Harry Rouclere broke her magic wand over her casket. Adelaide Herrmann was interred at Woodlawn Cemetery in the Bronx, next to her mother, Adele Scarsez, and her husband, Alexander.

Adele Owles Smith gave her aunt's nearly finished memoir manuscript to Adelaide's friend, Stella Grenfell Florence, a poet and author, who lovingly edited and typed the memoir. But when Adele approached publishers, they weren't interested. Alexander Herrmann had been dead nearly forty years. Nobody remembered him, or vaudeville for that matter. Even if they had, it was the Great Depression, and books weren't selling. Adele tried for a while, then gave up and put the manuscript in a drawer, where it would remain for the rest of her life, surfacing in 2010, forty-five years after Adele's death in 1965.

M. H. Everett: Last Boomsky Standing (1932–1956)

When Adelaide Herrmann died, Milton Hudson Everett was fifty-three. With Adelaide's passing in 1932, Everett's forty-year connection to the magic world was severed. He had no more known contact with anyone in Madame's family or the magician community.

M. H. Everett continued working as a clerk at the post office.[554] He had started the job a few years before Madame Herrmann retired, though Adelaide had still employed him as a part-time messenger and assistant on his days off. Julia maintained her home-based dressmaking business. When the stock market crashed in 1929, Everett's post office job protected him from the devastating unemployment and poverty that ensued. By 1930, M. H. and Julia had moved into the spacious apartment on West 146th Street. At fifty-five dollars a month, the Everetts' rent was rather high, but their incomes were more than sufficient.

M. H. and Julia subsequently moved to 80 Edgecombe Avenue, a sturdy, five-story apartment building in Harlem.[555] He had started out as a post office clerk, but as he neared sixty, the elderly Everett was demoted to custodian, sweeping the floors. He worked forty hours a week for fifty-seven cents an hour, which came to one hundred dollars a month. With neighborhood rents averaging thirty dollars a month, Everett's salary was enough to keep them comfortable. He remained at the post office until his retirement around 1940.[556]

Times were quickly changing. People no longer had to leave home to be entertained. Every household in the neighborhood, including the Everetts', owned a radio.[557] But Harlem buzzed with live music. On any given night, M. H. and Julia could walk a few blocks to hear jazz played by emerging artists such as Louis Armstrong, Fats Waller, and Cab Calloway. A mile south of the Everetts' home, the magnificent Harlem Opera House now hosted musical stars like Ethel Waters, Ella Fitzgerald, and Duke Ellington. Perhaps, as the Everetts sat in the theater awaiting the performance, M. H. regaled Julia with stories of performing on that same stage at age fifteen with Alexander Herrmann, when Harlem was still an artsy weekend enclave for chic New Yorkers. That same week, serpentine dancer Loie Fuller had enchanted Alexander and inspired Adelaide to create her own dances. Four years after that, M. H. had stood there again, assisting a visibly ill Frederick Bancroft as he kicked off his tragically brief final season.

At age sixty-two, with another world war looming, M. H. Everett once again registered for the draft, but he was not called to serve.[558] M. H. and Julia eventually moved two doors down to 90 Edgecombe Avenue, their final address.[559] Their beloved Harlem gradually changed, becoming poorer. Crime began to increase. Most of the Everetts' neighbors were also aging Harlemites, and they all watched out for each other.

Nothing more is known of Herrmann's first and greatest Boomsky, whose life began in rural Georgia and ended in Jazz-Age Harlem. As the celebrated assistant of the world's greatest magician, he had elevated and redefined the assistant role. He had been more places, met more influential people, and witnessed more remarkable events than most people ever experience.

On October 20, 1956, Milton Hudson Everett died at the age of seventy-seven. Julia purchased a gravesite in Woodlawn Cemetery in the Bronx, over the hill from Alexander Herrmann, Adelaide Herrmann, Adele Scarsez, and Dot Robinson.[560] Julia Everett remained at 90 Edgcombe Avenue until her death in 1962 at age seventy-five. She was buried at Woodlawn Cemetery next to her husband.

The last surviving member of Alexander Herrmann's company, M. H. Everett's friend, colleague, and contemporary, Adele "Dewey" Owles Smith, died in March 1965 at age eighty-six. She was buried next to her husband, Charles Wellesley Smith, in Evergreen Cemetery in Hillside, New Jersey.

~

Epilogue
The Unknown Boomskys

THERE WERE OTHER BOOMSKYS, whose names are not known. Some stayed with the Herrmann company for weeks or months, perhaps even longer. They were never listed in the program nor mentioned in magic books or publications. In the Herrmann era, few Black magicians surfaced in the press. Of those who did, surely some worked for the Herrmanns during their youth. During the research for this book, the name of each "colored magician" listed below surfaced in the mainstream press just briefly in the form of an advertisement or preview for a performance. In parentheses is the year each was referenced in a newspaper.

Prof. Lepps of Wichita, KS (1887)
P. C. Kebble of Independence, KS (1890)
Prof. Harrison of Tallapoosa, AL (1893)
Prof. W. H. Young of Baltimore, MD (1900)
Zem Williams of Atchinson, KS (1906)
Leroy Myers of Nashville, TN (1907)
Lee Martin of Arkansas (1907)
George Watkins (1907)
There were more.

ᴀCKNOWLEDGMENTS

Aᴅᴇʟᴀɪᴅᴇ Hᴇʀʀᴍᴀɴɴ'ꜱ ᴍᴇᴍᴏɪʀ provided the backbone of this work. Every day I give thanks to Madame for writing it.

I owe my Herrmann obsession to my dear mentor, the late James Hamilton. His Herrmann research files, which James passed on to me, provided many wonderful details and insights for this book, as well as bittersweet reminders of his absence. James's close friends, David Haversat and Dr. Timothy Moore, have cushioned his loss with their constant support and encouragement, as well as carte blanche access to their extensive collections of Herrmann images, many of which appear in this volume.

Since long before I wrote a word, Dale Penn has been Boomsky's greatest advocate and cheerleader. In addition to his beautiful Boomsky images, Dale provided feedback on early drafts and an invaluable page-by-page critique of my manuscript. Hiawatha Johnson Jr. read my manuscript twice and delivered detailed, deeply considered notes over many hours of phone conversations. I remain awed and humbled by the wisdom and generosity of these gentlemen.

Early reader Ann Szypulski helped me find my voice and direction, as did Kim Llewellyn, who also edited early versions of the manuscript. Editor Marianne Ward sorted out my jumbled chapters and organized my words into a story with structure and flow.

Many descendants of Isaac and Blanche Willis provided images, memories, and encouragement, including grandchildren Karen

McLaurin, Glenn Willis, Kathleen Willis, Charles Willis, Agnes Lattie, Isaac Willis III, and great-granddaughter Beverly Cox. Sadly, three Willis granddaughters, Yvonne Glover, Sheila Ryan, and Phyllis Marsman passed away before publication. I am grateful that I was able to meet and spend time with them.

Many members of the magic and magic history community contributed images, information, research, and recollections. David Copperfield offered up his library, which yielded Herrmann treasures to this awestruck researcher. Deep thanks to Mike Caveney, Kenrick "Ice" McDonald, George and Sandy Daily, Michael Claxton, Byron Walker, Diego Domingo, Gary Hunt, Charles Greene III, George Schindler, Kobe Van Herwegen, Dan Smith, William Kalush, John Cox, and Michael Perovich. Jim Steinmeyer's books furnished a wealth of information. Several now-deceased magic historians provided generous guidance in my Herrmann research, including Herb Zarrow, Charles Reynolds, Ray Goulet, Matthew Field, and Dr. Edwin Dawes.

Institutions, collections, databases, and individuals that provided information and images include Conjuring Arts Research Center, Houghton Library at Harvard University, Harry Ransom Center at the University of Texas, James Hamilton Archives, New York Public Library's Billy Rose Theater Collection, The University of Iowa (Redpath Chautauqua Bureau archives), The University of Illinois (*New York Clipper* archives), Johns Hopkins University, Library of Congress Rare Books & Special Collections (Eric P. Frazier), Dalhousie University, Nova Scotia Archives, New Brunswick Archives, State of Georgia Historical Newspaper Archives, Moorland-Spingarn Research Center at Howard University, Colchester Historeum (Joanne Hunt, Ryan McLellan, and Sarah Astatkie), Africville Museum (Juanita Peters), Nova Scotia Black Cultural Center, Linda Graves, Hildene, Library of Congress Chronicling America, Newspapers.com, Ancestry.com., READEX Historical African American Newspapers, New Brunswick researchers Robbie Gilmore and Koral Lavorgna, and Woodlawn Cemetery's Susan Olsen and Robert Kestenbaum.

Personal thanks to Moses Bernard Phillips, W. M. B. Cordis, Bettina Covo, Ann Cecil-Sterman, Andrew Sterman, Alexis Cole, Ron and Mary Macnab, Dr. Lynn Jones, Rodney Chesson, Jes Magdalena, Cathy Rodgers, Larry Bramble, Janet Calia, Tara Colavecchio, Eileen Letzeiser, Pat Millson, Alfred and Gail Hahn, Hank Bungay, Jim Bungay, and Patricia Wright. Those in my artist community of Peekskill, NY, who listened to years of Boomsky talk include Terry Vonhightower, Sol Miranda, Emily Kolker, Mary Stark, Patrick Conlon, Maureen Winzig, Lana Yu, Ron Egatz, Ben Parker, Jeorjia Shea, Liz Peterson, Toni Quest, Sone Tower, Scarlet Antonia, Adam Auslander, Tim Trewella, Stella Vlad, Jane Wilson-Marquis, Corinna Makris, Conor Greene, John Curran, James Brooks, Carol Bash, and David Carbone.

Many in the magic community have encouraged and supported me in this project, including Angela Sanchez, Michael Carbonaro, Arnie Kolodner, Jessica Bonvissuto, Just Alan, Benjamin Barnes, Linda Robbins, Mike Robinson, Kayla Drescher, Julie Eng, Carisa Hendrix, Bill Rauscher, Michele Ainsworth, Tom Ewing, Jen Kramer, Rosemary Reid, Connie Boyd, Eric DeCamps, Rory Rennick, Sara Crasson, Bill Austen, Ken Trombly, Phil Schwartz, Robert Olson, Paul Draper, Miranda Allen, Joe and Lisa Patire, Ran'D Shine, and Mina Barden. I am blessed to have had four great magic mentors: Bob Fitch, Jeff McBride, the late Eugene Burger, and the late James Hamilton.

Thank you to Michele DeFilippo, Ronda Rawlins, Kayla Cook, and the crew at 1106 Design, Orna Ross, Joanna Penn, and the Alliance of Independent Authors. I have not yet met Larry Wilmore, but his enthusiasm for Dale Penn's presentation on Boomsky at the Magic Castle in 2019 was the spark I needed to start writing.

Deepest thanks to my beloved partner Bruce MacNab, whose enthusiasm, support, and love have kept me going during this project. A writer and historian as well, Bruce's research rediscovered the forgotten Isaac Willis. Our co-created newspaper feature on Boomsky (with Moses Bernard Phillips), published in the Halifax *Chronicle Herald* in

2017, provided an early foundation for this book. Bruce's honest feedback on early drafts ("There's a book in there somewhere") showed me both what I had and how far I still had to go.

Finally, my dog Phoebe, curled up next to me now, as she was for every moment of this book's writing, will now accept her thank-you yum-yums.

∿

Cast of Characters

In The Role Of Boomsky

Note: One clarification will help avoid confusion. Alexander Herrmann first coined the name Boomsky in 1891, more than ten years after he began casting Black teens as assistants. Henceforth, all previous assistants were *retroactively* referred to as Boomsky, both by the Herrmanns and by the former assistants themselves.

Alexander Osmann (aka Hausmann)
African Mysteries at Egyptian Hall
Osmann assisted Alexander Herrmann at London's Egyptian Hall from December 1872 until spring 1873. The previous spring, Osmann had presented his African Mysteries at the London Polytechnic.

Edward Johnson (1867–1930)
The Great Black Carl, Carl Dante
Edward Johnson joined Alexander Herrmann circa 1881, at around age fourteen. A superb magician, Black Carl also wrote, produced, managed, and starred in large-scale extravaganzas. A longtime star of Black

minstrelsy, he retired from magic in his forties and became the head carriage man at New York's Metropolitan Opera House.

William Adams
Boomsky and the King

This African American teenager accompanied Alexander Herrmann on his three-year grand tour of South America and Europe from 1883 to 1886. William mortified his employers by mistaking the King of Spain for a waiter and engaging His Royal Highness in casual conversation.

Irving Jones (1873–1932)
Songwriter, Singer, and Comedian

Jones assisted Alexander Herrmann in 1886 at the age of thirteen. He later became a star of Black minstrelsy as a singer/songwriter and comedian. In 1903, Jones broke into mainstream vaudeville with his wife and partner, Sadie. The Joneses occasionally appeared on the same Orpheum bill as Adelaide Herrmann. After retiring they lived in Harlem with their son and grandson.

James A. Willis (1869–?)
Professor Willis, The Black Herrmann

James Willis assisted Alexander Herrmann around 1887. A magician and pianist, he led his own company from 1894 to 1903 before entering Black minstrelsy as a magician and music director. He married and settled in Cleveland, where he worked as a music teacher and greeting card writer.

Arthur B. Williams (1871–?)

Professor Arthur, Herrmann's Right-Hand Man
Williams assisted Alexander Herrmann for three seasons, from 1887 to 1890, touring throughout the US and Mexico before making a very public midshow exit. Williams later became a Pullman porter.

Milton Hudson ("Hutchin") Everett (1879–1956)
Everett the Magician

A former field hand from Americus, Georgia, Everett was thirteen years old when hired by Alexander Herrmann in October 1891. Everett was the first assistant Herrmann named Boomsky. Over the next forty years, Everett assisted Alexander, Léon, and Adelaide Herrmann, Frederick Bancroft, and possibly Harry Kellar. After serving in the US Navy, Everett returned to Adelaide Herrmann, then served a prison term for stealing a diamond ring of hers. In a press interview he gave while in prison, he exposed Madame's magic secrets. After his release, Madame Herrmann rehired Everett, who assisted her for the rest of her life. Everett married Julia Evans and lived in Harlem, where he worked for the US Post Office.

Alonzo Moore (1876–1930)
Alonzo: Prince of Magic, The Black Herrmann

Moore was hired by Alexander Herrmann circa 1892, at around age sixteen, but was subsequently stolen away by Herrmann competitor Edward Maro (Walter Best). Moore assisted Maro from 1894 to 1908 while concurrently pursuing a solo career. Alonzo Moore inherited Maro's act and performed for the Redpath Chautauqua Bureau, in Black minstrelsy, and for Chicago's high society until the mid-1920s.

H. H. Dennis
Assistant/Stage Crew

Dennis assisted Alexander Herrmann in 1893–94. He was the only college-educated assistant to play Boomsky. Dennis also served on Herrmann's backstage crew.

Bernard Baker (1872–?)
Herrmann's Horse Whisperer

A horse trainer, showman, magician, and actor, Baker was hired by Alexander Herrmann in 1894 as his stablemaster. After Alexander Herrmann's death, Baker continued with the Herrmann the Great Company before settling in Philadelphia, where his listed his occupation as "actor."

Isaac William Willis (1879–1933)
The Great Boomsky

Isaac Willis was a messenger at the White House when hired by Léon Herrmann. Willis assisted Léon Herrmann periodically from 1898 to 1908, alternating with stints in Black minstrelsy performing as The Great Boomsky. Willis moved to Canada in 1906. He married Blanche Stoutley and built a house in Truro, Nova Scotia, where the couple raised their eight children. After his last tour in 1911, Willis ran a shoeshine and a restaurant before becoming a Red Cap for the Canadian National Railroad.

J. Edward Clarke
After assisting Léon Herrmann in 1903–04, Clarke toured as a magician with the Redpath Chautauqua Bureau.

THE HERRMANN COMPANY

ALEXANDER HERRMANN (1844–1896)

Herrmann the Great, Professor Herrmann

The French-born magician and comedian is considered by many the greatest magician of all time. Herrmann's young helper, Boomsky, was modeled on Alexander's own childhood role as boy assistant to his older brother, Carl. Alexander Herrmann loved American audiences and made twenty US tours over his career.

ADELAIDE SCARSEZ HERRMANN (1853–1932)

The Queen of Magic

Alexander Herrmann's wife and costar was a dancer and trick bicyclist. She initially played Herrmann's boy assistant before switching to grand illusions and serpentine dances. Upon Alexander's sudden death, Adelaide formed the Herrmann the Great Company with her husband's nephew, Léon Herrmann. In 1899 she broke with Léon and went solo, performing as vaudeville's only female magician for nearly three decades.

CARL (COMPARS) HERRMANN (1816–1887)

Professor Herrmann

Alexander Herrmann's older brother was an acclaimed German-born magician. His younger brother Alexander assisted him from age eight, touring throughout Europe and the US. Carl and Alexander were, respectively, the oldest and youngest of sixteen siblings.

Léon Herrmann (1867–1909)

Herrmann the Third, Herrmann the Great

The nephew of Alexander and Carl, Léon Herrmann was born in Paris and spent his boyhood touring with Carl Herrmann. When Alexander died in 1896, Léon stepped into his uncle's role, costarring with Alexander's widow, Adelaide, in the Herrmann the Great Company. After splitting with Adelaide Herrmann, Léon toured Herrmann's full evening show across American for five years until entering vaudeville in 1904.

Marie Herrmann (1862–1916)

The Other Madame Herrmann

The wife and assistant of Léon Herrmann performed illusions and (for French-speaking audiences) a Second Sight act.

William Ellsworth Robinson (1861–1918)

Chung Ling Soo

A brilliant magician and inventor, Robinson and his partner, Dot, toured with Alexander Herrmann and with his successor, Léon, in the Herrmann the Great Company. The Robinsons also assisted Herrmann's rival, Harry Kellar. Later, Robinson achieved stardom portraying Chinese magician Chung Ling Soo, successfully deceiving audiences for many years before his death while performing the bullet catch in 1918.

Olive "Dot" Robinson (1863–1934)

Suee Seen

Considered the world's greatest illusion assistant, Dot Robinson was a former showgirl of indeterminate age. When William Robinson assumed the identity of Chinese magician Chung Ling Soo, Dot became his assistant, Suee Seen.

EDWARD L. BLOOM (1864–1925)
Theatrical Manager

Alexander Herrmann's brilliant and notorious manager oversaw six seasons of record profits before defecting to Herrmann's competitor, Frederick Bancroft. Bloom managed famous clients for forty years, despite two bankruptcies, several arrests, and lawsuits over alimony, child support, unpaid rent, and alleged theft.

ADELE "DEWEY" OWLES SMITH (1879–1965)
Assistant/Illusionist

The niece of Adelaide Herrmann joined Alexander Herrmann's company at age sixteen. She toured with the Herrmann the Great Company and with Adelaide Herrmann in vaudeville. She was the same age as M. H. Everett, with whom she partnered in the first biracial illusion. She married architect Charles Wellesley Smith in 1908. Widowed nine years later, Adele settled in Newark, NJ, where she worked as a clerk at Bamberger's Department Store.

EDWARD THURNAER (1860–1916)
Theatrical Manager / Producer

Thurnaer managed tours for Harry Kellar, Alexander Herrmann, Léon Herrmann, Adelaide Herrmann, and a variety of theater companies, as well as several professional boxers. A brilliant manager, Thurnaer's issues with alcohol interfered with his duties, resulting in frequent changes of employment.

John Kretschmann, aka Ketcham/Ketchum (1878–1947)
Assistant/Stage Crew

Adelaide Herrmann's nephew toured with Alexander Herrmann and the Herrmann the Great Company. After Adelaide and Léon Herrmann's acrimonious split, John infuriated his aunt by choosing to continue with Léon. After Léon's death, John rejoined Adelaide and assisted her for the rest of her career.

Adele Marneuf Scarsez (1808–1895)
The mother of Adelaide Herrmann was the matriarch of Herrmann Manor. A native of Belgium, she lived with Adelaide and Alexander following her husband's death in 1881.

Roland Travers (1891–1970)
Assistant/Magician

Travers temporarily replaced M. H. Everett as Adelaide Herrmann's assistant in 1900, becoming the only white assistant to wear Boomsky's uniform. He performed his own magic act in Adelaide's Merry Widow Company

and later assisted magician Dell O'Dell, who assumed the title Queen of Magic after Adelaide Herrmann's death.

ᴛʜᴇ Rɪᴠᴀʟs

Hᴀʀʀʏ Kᴇʟʟᴀʀ (1849–1922)

America's number two magician was the archrival of Alexander Herrmann and a constant thorn in Herrmann's side. While engaging in a bitter public feud, the two magicians routinely stole each other's assistants and magic secrets. After Alexander Herrmann's death, Kellar became a close friend of his widow, Adelaide.

Fʀᴇᴅᴇʀɪᴄᴋ Bᴀɴᴄʀᴏꜰᴛ (1866–1897)

Bancroft was a successful businessman and ambitious amateur magician. He befriended Alexander Herrmann and Harry Kellar, learned the masters' secrets, then formed his own professional company and stole Herrmann's manager and most of his crew.

Eᴅᴡᴀʀᴅ Mᴀʀᴏ (Wᴀʟᴛᴇʀ Tʀᴜᴍᴀɴ Bᴇsᴛ) (1868–1908)

Maro performed as a magician and musician for the Redpath Chautauqua Bureau. An admirer of Alexander Herrmann, he hired away Herrmann's assistant, Alonzo Moore, who schooled his new boss on Herrmann's secrets and techniques.

Hᴀʀʀʏ Hᴏᴜᴅɪɴɪ (1874–1926)

Within ten years of Alexander Herrmann's death, Harry Houdini had permanently usurped his idol's title of world's greatest magician. Ever the center of attention, Houdini worked tirelessly to insert himself into any story about magicians, even if it was not about him at all.

ENDNOTES

PROLOGUE, AMERICUS, GEORGIA

1. Sumter County History, http://sumtercountyhistory.com/history/1540_1914.htm.
2. Adelaide Herrmann, *Adelaide Herrmann, Queen of Magic* (Putney, VT: Bramble Books, 2012), 175. The story of Milton Hudson Everett's hiring, including the dialogue, comes directly from Madame Herrmann's memoir.
3. The *Julius Cahn–Gus Hill Theatrical Guide* (1905) includes technical specifics of Glover's Opera House.
4. For an explanation and demonstration of this dance term, see Thomas F. DeFrantz, Duke University, *Buck, Wing, and Jig*. https://www.youtube.com/watch?v=A34OD4eA17o.
5. *Adelaide Herrmann, Queen of Magic*, 175. Madame Herrmann spelled out the quote in vernacular, as was the style of her day: "Dat boy up dar."
6. The correct spelling of Milton Hudson Everett's name appears on multiple official documents. His Georgia accent led to confusion and spelling mistakes in his contemporary press and in accounts of him in magic publications. It didn't help that, at different times in his life, Everett went by both Milton and Hudson, or "Hutchin," and sometimes just his initials, M. H.
7. *Adelaide Herrmann, Queen of Magic*, 175.
8. US Federal Census, 1910.

CHAPTER ONE, MONSIEUR ALEXANDRE, CLEVER AND STEALTHY CHILD

9. *Adelaide Herrmann, Queen of Magic*, 11.
10. James Hamilton, *The Herrmann Chronicles* (Oxford, CT: 1868 Press, 2023), 10-11.

CHAPTER TWO, MAGICIANS IN TRAINING

11. Advertisements in London for Alexander Osmann/Hausmann and his "African Mysteries" appeared between March 1872 and March 1873. He was rumored to have toured Europe and England, but no additional information has surfaced.
12. *The Milwaukee Sentinel*, October 7, 1881.
13. The dates of Edward Johnson's employment with Herrmann are not verified. These are best estimates based on circumstantial evidence.
14. *Adelaide Herrmann, Queen of Magic*, 87.
15. *Adelaide Herrmann, Queen of Magic*, 98–99.
16. *Adelaide Herrmann, Queen of Magic*, 98.
17. *Adelaide Herrmann, Queen of Magic*, 98–99.
18. Madame Herrmann's account is nearly identical to several newspaper reminiscences entitled "Boomsky and the King" that were published in later years. She wrote her memoir using scrapbooks, and she likely referred to these articles.
19. *Adelaide Herrmann, Queen of Magic*, 106.
20. Kayala, the Russian Army outpost named by Adelaide Herrmann as the location of Herrmann's Christmas performance, does not appear on modern maps or in internet searches.
21. *Adelaide Herrmann, Queen of Magic*, 109.
22. *L'Indépendance Belge* (Brussels), February 18, 1886.
23. Herrmann's Black assistant was mentioned in several newspaper articles shortly after the company's return from Europe.
24. US Federal Census, 1880.
25. *Kansas City Star and Kansas City Times*, January 30, 1905. The story of Irving Jones's time with Herrmann is derived from a backstage

interview Jones gave to a newspaper reporter nearly twenty years later.

26. James A. Willis advertised himself as a former assistant to Alexander Herrmann, but exact dates or details of his employment are not known. Willis was performing as "The Black Herrmann" by 1893 (the first of several Black Herrmanns). He is mentioned in news clippings from 1893 to 1903.

27. *The Cleveland Leader,* January 1893.

28. *The Cleveland Gazette,* December 15, 1894. James A. Willis was the first magician to call himself The Black Herrmann.

29. Herrmann Weekly Statements ledger 1887–88, James Hamilton Collection.

30. *Adelaide Herrmann, Queen of Magic,* 173.

31. Adelaide contradicts herself. She called Arthur Williams "the first Boomsky," but she later refers to Milton Hudson Everett as the first Boomsky. She also refers to William as Boomsky, although he preceded both Arthur Williams and Milton Hudson Everett.

32. *The Times Union* (Brooklyn), April 23, 1889.

33. There are asterisks around "board" in the Herrmann Weekly Statements ledger.

34. The Mason-Dixon Line, along the southern border of Pennsylvania, was the informal boundary between Northern and Southern states.

35. This story appears in an unidentified, undated newspaper scrap.

36. Mia Bay, *Traveling Black: A Story of Race and Resistance* (Cambridge, MA: Belknap Press, 2021), 139.

37. Larry Tye, *Rising from the Rails: Pullman Porters and the Making of the Black Middle Class* (New York: Henry Holt & Company, 2005). Not all white passengers addressed porters with the insulting title "George," but many did, also calling them "Boy" or worse derogatory terms. Many white passengers treated the porters abominably. It is said the railroads treated them like property, 95.

38. Tye, *Rising from the Rails.* The expectation of tipping to reward service in compensation for the Pullman company's failure to pay a living wage was a new and much-condemned practice in the US.

39. Tye, *Rising from the Rails*. The Pullman porters formed America's first Black labor union, 159-160.
40. Thurgood Marshall (1908–1993) was the son of a Pullman porter. The first African American to be appointed to the Supreme Court, Marshall served as Associate Justice from 1967 to 1991.
41. Jim Crow was the name of a bumbling, dim-witted Black character portrayed in the 1830s by a white actor who blackened his face with burnt cork. The character, who sang a song called "Jump Jim Crow," formed the basis for blackface minstrel caricatures.
42. Tye, *Rising from the Rails, 53.*
43. Herrmann Weekly Statements 1886–87, James Hamilton Collection.
44. Tye, *Rising from the Rails*. In addition to having to purchase their own uniforms, shoes, and all accessories needed for the job, Pullman porters had to pay for their own meals and often their accommodations. When passengers stole Pullman merchandise—a constant occurrence—porters' pay was docked if they had not seen and reported the theft, 90.
45. From a letter by Hobart Bosworth reprinted in *Adelaide Herrmann, Queen of Magic*, 58.
46 . *The Jersey City News*, March 4, 1889.
47. Herrmann Weekly Statements ledger 1887–88, James Hamilton Collection.
48. Program, Hollis Street Theater, Boston, April 1–6, 1889. James Hamilton Collection.
49. *Adelaide Herrmann, Queen of Magic*, 58.
50. Program, Hollis Street Theater.
51. *Adelaide Herrmann, Queen of Magic*, 38. D'Alivini's real name was William Rushton Nelson. Although he billed himself as "The Jap of Japs," he was an Englishman who was fluent in six languages.
52. *The Buffalo Evening News*, January 8, 1889.
53. Excepting times of plague, cremation didn't become popular in the West until the 1970s.
54 . *The Los Angeles Herald*, September 9, 1888, contained an announcement explaining that Herrmann would play a new theater in

San Francisco because the Bush Street Theater was too small for Cremation.

55. *The Buffalo Evening News*, January 8, 1889. Sensitive to this criticism, Herrmann soon moved Cremation from Part Five to an earlier spot in the program.
56. *The Buffalo Evening News*, January 8, 1889.
57. Program from Hollis Street Theater, Boston, April 1–6, 1889. James Hamilton Collection.
58. *The Baltimore Sun*, January 23, 1889.
59. *The Buffalo Evening News*, January 8, 1889.
60. This illusion technique is known by the name of its inventor's first application of the trick, Pepper's Ghost.
61. In her memoir, Adelaide misremembered the incident as taking place at the Academy of Music in Jersey City, where they played one week later.
62. *The Evening World* (New York), October 30, 1890. "Sheol" is the Hebrew word for "hell," the underworld.
63. *The Evening World* (New York), October 30, 1890.
64. *The Evening World* (New York), October 30, 1890. Mainstream publications of the day often published the offensive term "coon" in quotes, acknowledging that the term was problematic while nonetheless attempting to justify the choice to publish it.
65. New York State Census 1905.
66. Tye, *Rising from the Rails, 33.*
67. *Arizona Daily Star*, December 10, 1890.
68. *Adelaide Herrmann, Queen of Magic,* 174.

CHAPTER THREE, THE BIRTH OF BOOMSKY

69. Madame Herrmann related this story of Milton Hudson Everett's hiring multiple times, in her memoir and in newspaper interviews even twenty-five years later.
70. The little dogs were Adelaide's: Fidget, her "black & tan" Yorkshire terrier, plus two chihuahuas, including Lily, purchased by Alexander while in Mexico. The big dog was a Great Dane named Cora.

71. Adelaide Herrmann's suspicions later proved to be accurate. Robinson was indeed a double agent, trafficking secrets between Kellar and Herrmann while also writing articles for the magazine *Scientific American*, exposing the great magicians' methods.

72. Will and Dot would tour together for twenty years before being married in a civil ceremony in 1906.

73. *The Evening World* (New York), January 24, 1891.

74. *Adelaide Herrmann, Queen of Magic*, 138.

75. Ben and Leitha were young adults when they were emancipated and became parents of the first generation of Southern, free-born African Americans. As all parents, they hoped for better lives for their children. But twelve years after the war, the heady possibilities of Reconstruction were shattered by the violent backlash that followed. Peaceful relations largely prevailed in Americus, but every African American person understood the rules of behavior and interaction and the potentially deadly consequences of breaking them.

76. US Federal Census 1880.

77. In the 1890s the average lifespan of African Americans was thirty-five years.

78. The US Federal Census of 1910 lists Leitha Everett's number of births and surviving children.

79. US Federal Census 1880. Ben and his oldest son, fifteen-year-old Daniel, worked as laborers. Leitha worked as a day laborer. The family's only daughter, thirteen-year-old Polly, was employed as a nurse, tending to ill and invalid members of Americus's white families. In 1880, the five youngest Everett sons ranged from twelve-year-old Lewis down to the two-year-old twins, Cook and Fort. According to the Census, Sidney and Milton were in the middle, aged six and five, respectively. But it seems that the census taker mixed up the children's names and ages. Milton Everett always gave his birth year as 1879, but other documents suggest he was born in 1878, which supports Madame Herrmann's claim that he was thirteen when he joined the company.

80. The Herrmanns played Montgomery on October 23 and 24, 1891.

81. Tye, *Rising from the Rails*. In interviews, former porters talked about the dangers of simply walking on the wrong street in the South.

82. *The Montgomery Advertiser*, October 24, 1891.

83. Dot Robinson, formerly Olive Path, is revered as possibly the greatest magician's assistant of all time. She was secretive about her past. While it has been claimed that her real name was Augusta Pfaff, of Ohio, this has been disproven. Genealogy records show that Augusta Pfaff, formerly thought to be Dot, was married in 1881 and has living descendants. There was another Pfaff daughter, which may have been Dot.

84. Robinson did not invent the floating trick Florine. His superior skills as a craftsman enabled him to customize and improve upon it after seeing another magician demonstrate the concept.

85. Jim Steinmeyer, *The Glorious Deception: The Double Life of William Robinson, aka Chung Ling Soo, the "Marvelous Chinese Conjuror"* (New York: Carroll & Graf, 2005), 82–84.

86. Steinmeyer, *The Glorious Deception*, 74–76.

87. Based on an observation by Herrmann's friend, humorist Bill Nye, in a Utah newspaper in 1890.

88. Herrmann's original Strobeika illusion is currently in the collection of David Copperfield.

89. Michael Claxton, *Don't Fool Yourself: The Magical Life of Dell O'Dell* (Chicago: Squash Publishing, 2014), 164. The winch system under the Aerial Suspension platform was described by Roland Travers, a later assistant to Adelaide Herrmann.

90. Sketches from the late 1870s show Herrmann performing the egg trick with a white assistant, but by 1881 Herrmann consistently employed a Black teen for the trick.

91. "He is a Devil!" *The Washington Post*, October 15, 1886.

92. *The Baltimore Sun*, October 20, 1886.

93. The Herrmanns always presented gifts and bonuses to their staff on Christmas Day.

94. Utah became a state four years later, in 1896.

95. *Adelaide Herrmann, Queen of Magic*, 175.

96. "Magicians at Odds," *The Times* (Philadelphia), February 18, 1892. Herrmann had never traveled to India and did indeed plagiarize Kellar's article. Although Alexander frequently expounded about his trips to the Far East, none of the Herrmanns ever traveled or performed outside of Europe and the Americas.
97. It took thirty years for the Statue of Liberty's dark brown copper to slowly turn green.
98. In the revival of Cremation, Dot Robinson played the devil, replacing the puppet operated by Arthur Williams.
99. *The New York Clipper*, April 30, 1892.
100. *The Gazette* (Montreal), April 19, 1892.
101. *The Gazette* (Montreal), April 19, 1892.
102. The Herrmanns' estate was located in what is now the Borough of Queens, part of New York City. Although the house and other buildings no longer exist, the estate's location at Cryder's Point is easily found on maps, in the shadow of the Throgs Neck Bridge.
103. Naphtha, a petroleum distillate, was a "modern" fuel at the time, burned to create steam to power steam engines.
104. Adele Dewey became Adele Owles's stage name when she joined the Herrmann company, and her name appeared in the program with this spelling.
105. Alexander Herrmann was the youngest of sixteen children, all with the same mother. Adelaide Herrmann's mother bore at least six children. Only the four daughters achieved healthy adulthood. Adelaide's oldest sibling, Joseph Scarsez, died in a "lunacy asylum" at age twenty-nine after years of indigence likely due to alcoholism. Another brother, Isadore, was born in Belgium and emigrated with his family to England in 1848 but died prior to Adelaide's birth in 1853.
106. The Flushing Town Hall opened in 1862 and still operates as a performance venue.
107. *Adelaide Herrmann, Queen of Magic*, 176.
108. References to Alonzo Moore's employment with Herrmann are credible, but his dates with the company are uncertain.

109. The song "Ta-ra-ra Boom-de-ay" has never gone out of popular circulation and is heard to the present day.
110. *The Times-Democrat* (New Orleans), November 14, 1892.
111. *New York Herald*, October 23, 1892. The article describes Boomsky as the valet, guarding Herrmann's inner sanctum.
112. "A Wizard's Wife Behind the Scenes," *Times-Picayune* (New Orleans), November 19, 1892. The article mentions Herrmann's two liveried assistants.
113. *The Grand Rapids Herald*, January 29, 1893.
114 . *The Hartford Courant*, May 6, 1893.
115. The method for the multiplying billiard balls was invented by Bautier de Kolta.
116. *The Scranton Tribune*, November 15, 1899.
117. George Corregan Jr., "'Silent' Mora," *New Tops Magazine* 2, 1962, 498.
118. *The Plaindealer* (Detroit), March 31, 1893.
119. *The New York Times*, April 22, 1893.
120. Herrmann debuted Escape from Sing Sing on May 11, 1893, before a group of invited guests at New York's Grand Opera House.

Chapter Four, Veteran Teenaged Assistant

121. In her memoir, Adelaide states that Loie Fuller merely attended a performance, but reviews confirm that Fuller performed with the Herrmann company that week at the Harlem Opera House.
122. It is difficult for modern audiences to appreciate the profound impact of these dances. Surviving archival film footage of Loie Fuller, shot in full light, does not capture the effect.
123. *The New York Evening World*, September 12, 1893.
124. *The Saint Paul Globe*, October 1, 1893.
125. *Adelaide Herrmann, Queen of Magic*, 142.
126. *The Omaha Bee*, October 5, 1893.
127. *Adelaide Herrmann, Queen of Magic*, 142.
128. *The New York Clipper*, multiple issues, 1893.
129. Boston Museum program, January 15–27, 1894.

130. *The Kansas City Star*, March 14, 1894.
131. *The Kansas City Star*, March 14, 1894.
132. *The Kansas City Star*, March 8, 1894.
133. *The Kansas City Star*, March 1, 1894.
134. Herrmann's visit to Kenilworth Tailors is imagined, but the drop-in visit would have been in character for Alexander Herrmann.
135. *The New York Times*, April 4, 1894.
136. "Vicious Horses," *The Jewell County Review* (Mankato, Kansas), June 12, 1890. The article includes a crude sketch of O. Gleason and a Black assistant.
137. "Beautiful Horses," *Pittsburgh Post-Gazette*, April 19, 1894.
138. The heat wave of 1896 has long been considered one of the greatest natural disasters in US history.
139. Adelaide Herrmann stuck to the story that the marksmen were not complicit. This adds to the lore but is likely false. Their commanding officer would have reassured them that they were not being ordered to fire live ammunition at Herrmann, an innocent civilian.
140. Adelaide Herrmann revealed the details of the bullet catch in her memoir.
141. "Plucky Mme. Herrmann," *The Evening World*, August 9, 1894.
142. "Herrmann Not Ill—Out of Danger," *The Evening World*, August 21, 1894.
143. *Los Angeles Daily Herald*, February 15, 1895.
144. *The Gazette* (Montreal), September 1, 1894.
145. *The Gazette* (Montreal), September 3, 1894. This story is almost certainly a gross exaggeration.
146. *San Francisco Examiner*, January 22, 1895.
147. "And the Pig Fled," *Saint Paul Globe*, March 21, 1895.
148. *The Oakland Tribune*, January 29, 1895.
149. *Adelaide Herrmann, Queen of Magic*, 198.
150. Winona is in Minnesota, Eau Claire and Oshkosh are in Wisconsin.
151. *The Weekly Leader*, Winona, Minnesota, April 27, 1895.
152. *New York Standard Union*, May 4, 1895.
153. *New York Tribune*, April 23, 1895.
154. *The Jersey City News*, May 4, 1895.

155. *New York Evening World*, May 10, 1895.

156. *The New York Times*, May 12, 1895.

157. "The Outrage Against Mrs. Herrmann," *The Jersey City News*, May 11, 1895.

Chapter Five, Herrmann's Penultimate Season

158. *Salt Lake Herald*, November 23, 1895.

159. James Hamilton, research files.

160. *The New York Clipper* (undated clipping). Bloom adjusted for the fact that they played seven performances that week, not the standard eight.

161. *The New York Dramatic Mirror*, October 19, 1895.

162. Léon was fresh in Alexander's mind, having just written his uncle a letter first flattering him then imploring him to send money to support Léon's fledgling career. The letter is in David Copperfield's collection.

163. *Vaudeville Magazine* (undated clipping), James Hamilton Collection.

164. *The San Francisco Call*, November 29, 1895.

165. *The San Francisco Chronicle*, December 1, 1895.

166. The Spray of Life illusion involved a fountain of water behind which "moving pictures" were displayed. The Herrmanns retired the piece soon after its debut and few details about it remain.

167. Hamilton, *The Herrmann Chronicles*, 69.

168. According to Adelaide Herrmann, the horse show ran for multiple days, and Herrmann pulled the two-places-at-once stunt more than once, but newspaper reports on the horse show do not support her claim.

169. A yellow ribbon in this case was likely fourth place.

170. Hamilton, *The Herrmann Chronicles*, 70.

171. *The San Francisco Chronicle*, December 3, 1895.

172. *The Omaha Daily Bee*, January 26, 1896, from the account of journalist Max Meyer, who traveled with the Herrmann company for two months.

173. "Mr. Herrmann as Santa Claus," *The Morning Oregonian*, December 26, 1895.

174. "Mr. Herrmann as Santa Claus," *Morning Oregonian*.

175. *The Houston Daily Post*, January 26, 1896. Despite his recent announcement that he was considering his nephew Léon for the role, Herrmann proposed to school Dixey in magic for three years. Then Herrmann would retire and pay Dixey $50,000 per year for five years to head the show. Dixey was given six months to decide.

176. *The San Francisco Chronicle*, December 19, 1895. It is not known why Herrmann would repeat this risky trick in his standard show. All his other performances of the bullet catch were one-time events, either for charity or when Herrmann needed to raise a large sum of money quickly. In this case, perhaps the presence of master assistant and magician William Robinson reassured him.

177. *The San Francisco Call*, December 29, 1895.

178. *The San Francisco Call*, January 26, 1896.

179. *The Chicago Tribune*, January 16, 1896.

180. *The Chicago Tribune*, January 15, 1896.

181. *The Daily Telegram* (Eau Claire, Wisconsin), February 14, 1896. The *New York Mail* quote (which is unverified) is included in the body of this article.

182. Bancroft may have been the first magician to introduce a bevy of dancing girls into his act.

183. *The Evening Times*, Washington, DC, March 3, 1896. This article mentions Boomsky smashing the hat.

184. *The Morning News*, Washington, DC, March 2, 1896.

185. *Brooklyn Life*, March 14, 1896.

186. *Adelaide Herrmann, Queen of Magic*, 189.

187. *The Daily Telegram*, Eau Claire, Wisconsin, April 26, 1896.

188. *The New York Times*, April 28, 1896.

189. *The New York Herald*, May 19, 1896.

190. Edward Bloom stayed on to manage the Palmer's benefit.

191. *The World*, New York, June 16, 1896.

192. *The Cincinnati Enquirer*, June 21, 1896.

193. *The New York Times*, July 5, 1896.

194. The Hudson River town of Sing Sing changed its name to Ossining in 1901 (five years after Herrmann's visit) to distance itself from the association with Sing Sing Prison.

195. The Sing Sing Prison show was one of Herrmann's most written-about performances. Separate reviews appeared in *The World*, *The Brooklyn Daily Eagle*, *The New York Times*, *Philadelphia Enquirer*, *Brooklyn Times Union*, *The Times Democrat*, *The Buffalo Courier*, and possibly others.

196. *The New York Times*, July 5, 1896. A "black-and-tan terrier" is the same as a Yorkshire terrier.

197. *The Brooklyn Times Union*, July 7, 1896.

198. *The Philadelphia Enquirer*, July 6, 1896.

199. *The Philadelphia Enquirer*, July 6, 1896.

200. *The Brooklyn Times Union*, July 7, 1896.

201. *The Brooklyn Times Union*, July 7, 1896.

202. Bruce MacNab, *The Metamorphosis: The Apprenticeship of Harry Houdini* (Fredericton, NB: Goose Lane Editions, 2012), 257–63.

203. This correspondence has not surfaced and remains shrouded in mystery. That Houdini asked Herrmann for a job is accepted as fact among magic historians.

204. *The New York Dramatic Mirror*, August 22, 1896.

205. As previously noted, John Kretschmann's name was spelled a variety of ways in Herrmann programs.

Chapter Six, The Master's Final Bow

206. *The Sunday Leader*, Wilkes-Barre, PA, November 22, 1896.

207. *The Jersey City News*, September 15, 1896.

208. *The Democrat & Chronicle*, Rochester, September 20, 1896.

209. *The Sunday Leader*, Wilkes-Barre, PA, November 22, 1896.

210. *The Jersey City News*, September 15, 1896.

211. *The Sunday Leader*, Wilkes-Barre, PA, November 22, 1896.

212. *The Record Union*, Sacramento, September 17, 1896.

213. *The Butte Miner*, September 27, 1896.

214. *The Hartford Courant*, October 22, 1896.

215. James Hamilton's research notes that Herrmann signed the note on his life insurance policy on November 26, 1896.

216. "Bancroft . . . has . . . Boomsky," *The Atlanta Constitution*, October 11, 1896.

217. *The Norfolk Virginian*, September 30, 1896.

218. *The Detroit Free Press*, December 12, 1896.

219. *The Houston Post*, October 4, 1896.

220. Numerous magic publications have wrongly stated that Bancroft's real name was Bronson and also that he was a dentist. The source of these two items of misinformation was an inaccurate obituary published in the *New York Dramatic Mirror* and the *New York Clipper* after Bancroft's death in 1897. This obituary was subsequently reprinted in several other papers soon thereafter. The misinformation is easily refuted. Frederick Bancroft appears as a child, with his family, on the 1870 and 1880 US Federal Censuses and also on the 1895 Minnesota State and Territorial Censuses. This inaccurate obituary is the only contemporary reference to Bancroft being a dentist, which is not corroborated elsewhere.

221. *The Washington Evening Star*, December 16, 1895.

222. *The New York Clipper*, multiple issues, 1895–96.

223. *Stanyon's Magic*, multiple issues. Bancroft's act was described in detail.

224. *The Atlanta Constitution*, October 18, 1896.

225. *The Atlanta Constitution*, October 13, 1896.

226. *The Morning News* (Savannah), October 11, 1896.

227. Prior to forming his company, Bancroft had befriended Harry Kellar as well as Alexander Herrmann.

228. Two magicians who were especially vicious in their attacks on Bancroft were H. J. Burlingame and T. Nelson Downs.

229. *The Morning Times* (Washington, DC), December 17, 1895.

230. From an untitled, undated article in Houdini Scrapbook 08, Conjuring Arts Research Center.

231. Houdini Scrapbook 08.

232. Houdini Scrapbook 08.

233. *The Times-Democrat* (New Orleans), October 19, 1896.

234. *The Fort Wayne News*, December 4, 1896.

235. Undated, unidentified news clipping from the scrapbook of H. J. Burlingame, Houdini scrapbook collection, Library of Congress.

236. *Oshkosh Northwestern*, December 29, 1896.

237. Bancroft, in 1896, may have been the earliest magician to use a big cat in his show. Bancroft's appearing lion illusion was later performed by The Great Lafayette with the name The Lion's Bride.

238. *The Oshkosh Northwestern*, December 26, 1896.

239. Undated, unidentified news clipping from the scrapbook of H. J. Burlingame, Houdini scrapbook collection, Library of Congress.

240. When it came to the treatment of performing animals, the Herrmanns' kindness was the exception.

241. *The Sun* (New York), November 7, 1896.

242. *The Scranton Tribune*, December 8, 1896.

243. "Legerdemain in a Reformatory," *The Rochester Democrat*, December 16, 1896.

244. *The Democrat and Chronicle* (Rochester), December 18, 1896.

245. Several sources state that Herrmann's last words were to Will Robinson. Adelaide Herrmann's personal account differs. It is possible that Herrmann made this statement to Robinson in the hours or days before his death. Herrmann knew he was seriously ill. He and Robinson were very close. Herrmann was financially irresponsible but not so with his beloved company. The company manager, Edward Thurnaer, drank excessively. Herrmann would have welcomed the reassurance of his longtime chief assistant that whatever might happen, his company would make it home.

246. James Hamilton, "A Short Biography of Alexander Herrmann & Adelaide Herrmann," undated monograph.

247. *The New York Times*, December 21, 1896.

INTERLUDE, BANCROFT'S COMPANY GETS THE NEWS

248. *The Oshkosh Northwestern*, December 29, 1896.

249. *The Courier* (Waterloo, Iowa), January 9, 1897.

250. *The Detroit Free Press*, August 30, 1896.

251. Burlingame scrapbook, Houdini scrapbook collection, Library of Congress.
252. See, for example, *The Oshkosh Northwestern*, December 29, 1896.
253. *Naugatuck Daily News*, April 15, 1897.
254. It is possible that Hudson Everett worked for another magician during Bancroft's unusually long breaks. In a later interview, Everett stated that he worked for Kellar and other magicians, but this has not been confirmed.
255. *The New York Clipper*, September 1897.
256. *The Morning News* (Wilmington, DE), September 9, 1897.
257. *The Evening Journal* (Wilmington, DE), September 10, 1897
258. *The New York Clipper*, September 18, 1897.
259. *The Evening Journal* (Wilmington, DE), September 11, 1897.
260. To remain in Wilmington an extra week, Bloom canceled Bancroft's upcoming dates in Norfolk, Virginia, and Charlotte and Raleigh, North Carolina.
261. *The Evening Journal* (Wilmington, DE), September 13, 1897.
262. *The Philadelphia Enquirer*, September 13, 1897.
263. *The Morning News* (Wilmington, DE), September 13, 1897.
264. *The Wilmington Daily Republican*, September 15, 1897.
265. *The Morning News* (Wilmington, DE), September 16, 1897.
266. *The News Journal* (Wilmington, DE), September 18, 1897.
267. Frederick Bancroft's publicity and reviews do not mention a private railcar. However, it seems likely that Bancroft traveled with a rented private car. While Pullman Palace cars were a distinguishing feature of success for entertainers, they were ubiquitous among the wealthy.
268. In 1908, Frederick Bancroft's body was exhumed and moved to the Bancroft family plot at Kensico Cemetery in Valhalla, New York.
269. *The New York Times*, October 15, 1897.
270. *The Indianapolis News*, October 16, 1897.

CHAPTER SEVEN, THE HERRMANN THE GREAT COMPANY

271. "Attire for Mourners," *The New York Tribune*, February 27, 1897.
272. Robinson's illusion Florine: Child of the Air (originally Astarte: Maid of the Moon) was renamed simply Maid of the Moon in Léon Herrmann's version.
273. *The Chicago Tribune*, August 30, 1897.
274. *The Chicago Tribune*, August 30, 1897.
275. *The Chicago Dispatch*, August 30, 1897.
276. *The San Francisco Call*, October 31, 1897.
277. *The Sacramento Daily Record-Union*, November 10, 1897.
278. *The Sacramento Daily Record-Union*, November 15, 1897.
279. *The Galveston News*, December 5, 1897.
280. *The Quad City Times*, January 22, 1898.
281. Léon Herrmann posters and program from 1895, preserved at University of Ghent, Belgium, announce Marie Herrmann's performing debut in Léon's full-evening show on February 8, 1895.
282. *Mahatma*, December 1898.
283. *The San Francisco Examiner*, July 11, 1898.
284. *The New York Times*, October 5, 1898.
285. *Junction City Union* (Colorado), October 27, 1898. The Herrmann program, including personnel, was printed in the newspaper (James Hamilton Collection). Another program from Kansas City, Missouri, dated October 30, 1898, also lists "Milton Everett – Assistant Electrician."
286. *The Evening Star* (Washington, DC), January 10, 1899.
287. A letter by Harry Houdini, published in *The New York Dramatic Mirror*, November 12, 1904. Houdini's observations were not quite accurate, as racial prejudice was most definitely present in England, although less pointedly than in America.
288. The marketing for A Night in Japan was built on multiple lies. Adelaide Herrmann may have been the only woman magician in America, but in Europe a magician named Okita (Julia Ferret) had been performing a Japanese-themed act for over twenty years. Julia

Ferret deVere was the partner of prominent magician/magic dealer Charles deVere, with whom all the Herrmanns did business.

289. *The Asheville Citizen Times*, January 17, 1899.
290. *The Evening Times* (Washington, DC), January 10, 1899.
291. *The St. Louis Post Dispatch*, April 3, 1899.
292. *The Scranton Tribune*, December 27, 1898. "Madame Herrmann's dances were received very coldly" due to being overdone. But with this reviewer Madame Herrmann "redeemed herself with A Night in Japan."
293. *The Evening Star* (Washington, DC), December 31, 1898.
294. *Nebraska State Journal*, September 17, 1898.
295. Robinson's first view of Ching Ling Foo was long thought to have occurred in November 1898, when Foo performed at Boyd's Theater in Omaha, based on the recollections of David P. Abbott, published nearly a decade later. However, this encounter could not have occurred as Abbott states, since the Herrmann company was performing in Iowa at the time.
296. Letter from William E. Robinson to Harry Houdini, quoted in Todd Karr, *The Silence of Chung Ling Soo* (Los Angeles: The Miracle Factory, 2001).
297. *Mahatma* 1-5, December 1898, 189.
298. Willis family lore is that Isaac Willis was spotted by Herrmann the Great when the magician performed at the White House, but it is not accurate. None of the Herrmann magicians ever performed at the White House.
299. Isaac Willis's salary is unknown, but the Herrmanns paid their African American employees far more than traditional jobs that were open to Blacks, although far less than their white employees.
300. "Directory of the Inhabited Alleys of Washington, DC," 1912. Jackson Hall Alley no longer exists. The Willis home was located at the approximate spot where Washington's Newseum sits today. Many of the city's Black residents, as well as recent white immigrants, lived in ramshackle housing built in the city's alleys. In the early twentieth century, many of these alleys were labeled hotbeds of crime and disease. The larger alleys were eventually

turned into named streets, while housing was eliminated in the smaller alleys.

301. John Willis was born in 1855. Isabel Willis was born in 1865.
302. *The Evening Times* (Washington, DC), January 10, 1899.
303. Naval service public record, where Milton Everett's rank is listed as "mess attendant." In later tellings, Everett referred to his position in the Navy as "cabin boy."
304. *The Boston Globe*, May 21, 1899.

Chapter Eight, Rival Herrmanns, Rival Boomskys

305. *The New York Times*, July 16, 1899.
306. *Adelaide Herrmann, Queen of Magic*, 209–10.
307. *The Democrat and Chronicle* (Rochester), April 9, 1901.
308. *The Boston Globe*, May 23, 1899. The show "closed with the trunk mystery in which a pretty young woman and a colored assistant change places under seemingly impossible conditions."
309. *The Buffalo Review*, August 29, 1899.
310. *The Times-Democrat* (New Orleans), January 21, 1900.
311. *The Chicago Tribune*, January 29, 1900.
312. Inroads were slowly being made by other women. Emma Reno, a magician trained by her husband, became successful on the Chautauqua circuit.
313. *The Times Picayune* (New Orleans), December 28, 1897.
314. Over the years Adelaide Herrmann named several pets Magic.
315. "Strange Pet of a Woman," *The Wheeling Daily Intelligencer*, August 8, 1899.
316. *The New York Times*, September 3, 1899.
317. *The Washington Times*, December 17, 1899.
318. *The New York Times*, September 1, 1900.
319. Everett's motive for stealing Adelaide's ring has never been revealed. Gambling debts are a strong possibility.
320. "An Experience That Destroyed the Queen of Magic's Faith in Omens," ___ *Tribune*, December 1901. (The newspaper clipping is torn and the full name of the newspaper is missing.)

321. *The Omaha World Herald*, September 8, 1900.
322. "How Herrmann Did His Great Acts of Magic," *The Detroit Journal*, December 15, 1900.
323. "How Herrmann Did His Great Acts of Magic," *The Detroit Journal*, December 15, 1900. This article was reprinted in other US newspapers.
324. Notebook of Harry Houdini, Library of Congress.
325. Milton Hudson Everett quoted in *The Detroit Journal*, March 19, 1902.
326. *The Buffalo Courier*, April 6, 1902.
327. *The Sphinx*, March 1902.
328. *Topeka State Journal*, October 13, 1899.
329. Jesse L. Lasky, *I Blow My Own Horn* (Garden City: Doubleday, 1957), 59.
330. *The Morning News* (Savannah), September 14, 1899.
331. *The Morning News* (Savannah), September 14, 1899.
332. *The Kansas City Journal*, September 12, 1897.
333. *The Topeka State Journal*, October 13, 1899.
334. *The Sioux City Journal*, October 20, 1899.
335. *The Courier-Journal* (Louisville, KY), December 5, 1899.
336. *The St. Joseph-Gazette Herald* (MO), October 14, 1899.
337. *The South Bend Tribune* (IN), November 25, 1899.
338. *The Courier-Journal* (Louisville, KY), December 5, 1899.
339. *The Star-Gazette* (Elmira, NY), January 5, 1900.
340. Léon Herrmann tour program, the David Copperfield collection.
341. *The Star-Gazette* (Elmira, NY), January 11, 1900.
342. *The Raleigh Times*, February 7, 1900.
343. *The Times Democrat* (New Orleans), September 14, 1900.
344. *The Daily Picayune* (New Orleans), September 13, 1900.
345. *The Montgomery Advertiser*, September 2, 1900.
346. *The Morning Post* (Raleigh), August 18, 1900.
347. Tye, *Rising from the Rails*.
348. *The Indianapolis News*, September 29, 1900.
349. *The Indianapolis Journal*, September 29, 1900.
350. *The Des Moines Register*, October 6, 1900.

351. *The El Paso Herald*, November 7, 1900.

352. *The El Paso Herald*, November 7, 1900.

353. *The San Francisco Chronicle*, November 26, 1900.

354. Lasky, *I Blow My Own Horn*, 59. Jesse Lasky describes the Herrmanns' dog as a "frizzled poodle," but reviewers mention the Chihuahua, and in a company photo, Blanche Lasky holds a Chihuahua.

355. *The Star-Gazette* (Elmira, NY), March 20, 1901. In this telling, the canine is "a tiny Mexican dog."

356. *The Gazette* (Montreal), April 30, 1901.

357. *The New York Tribune*, May 28, 1901.

358. *The Indianapolis Freeman*, August 10, 1901.

359. *Victoria Daily Times* (BC), October 16, 1901.

360. *Victoria Daily Times* (BC), October 17, 1901.

361. *Victoria Daily Times* (BC), October 17, 1901.

362. *The Province* (Vancouver, BC), October 18, 1901.

363. *Vancouver Daily World*, October 18, 1901

364. *The Akron Beacon Journal*, March 15, 1902.

365. *Newark Daily Advertiser*, February 1902, as related in *The Linking Ring*, the monthly magazine of the International Brotherhood of Magicians, November 1960.

366. *The Boston Globe*, April 8, 1902.

367. *The Boston Globe*, April 8, 1902.

368. *The Boston Post*, April 9, 1902.

369. *The Boston Globe*, April 10, 1902.

370. *The Boston Globe*, April 13, 1902.

371. Adelaide's blind rage provoked statements she would later have deeply regretted. In her memoir, she spoke of both Léon Herrmann and Hudson Everett in glowing terms.

372. *The San Francisco Examiner*, November 23, 1902.

373. *The San Francisco Examiner*, November 23, 1902.

374. *The Raleigh Times*, February 7, 1900.

375. A supporting act joined Léon Herrmann, the Musical Goolmans, who, according to the *Indianapolis Journal*, "rendered a performance on instruments more novel in appearance than melodious in tone."

The season's "new" illusions were Princess Mohameda—Léon and Marie's version of the Trilby levitation—and The Voyage Instantaneous, a revised version of Ya-Ko-Yo, Instant Chinese Immigration.

376. *The Sioux City Journal*, Iowa, December 26, 1902.

377. *The Richmond Item* (Indiana), April 13, 1903.

378. Lasky, *I Blow My Own Horn*, 60.

379. An eyewitness account reported in *The Sphinx*, September 1928.

380. *Los Angeles Express*, October 22, 1902.

381. Lasky, *I Blow My Own Horn*, 52–53.

382. Lasky, *I Blow My Own Horn*, Jesse L. Lasky, 59.

383. Lasky, *I Blow My Own Horn*, 59–60.

Chapter Nine, Isaac Willis, The Great Boomsky

384. Yuval Taylor and Jake Austen, *Darkest America: Black Minstrelsy from Slavery to Hip-Hop* (New York: W. W. Norton, 2012).

385. Taylor and Austen, *Darkest America*. Modern readers are surprised to learn that African Americans attended white minstrel shows, yet many did, 35-36.

386. There are no known instances of theater balconies collapsing.

387. *The Belleville Telescope* (Kansas), April 6, 1894.

388. *The Buffalo Courier*, October 20, 1896.

389. Black Carl married at least two women in his travels. Two wives showed up at his bedside after he suffered a stroke.

390. *The Brooklyn Daily Eagle*, January 17, 1899.

391. *The Fort Worth Telegram*, September 27, 1905.

392. *The Evening Capital* (Annapolis), February 23, 1907.

393. *The Evening Capital*, February 23, 1907.

394. *The Voice Republican*, July 18, 1912.

395. *The Evening Capital*, February 23, 1907.

396. *The Indianapolis Freeman*, September 9, 1899.

397. *The Napa Journal*, March 7, 1903.

398. *The Indianapolis Freeman*, June 20, 1903.

399. *The Indianapolis Freeman*, July 11, 1903. "Clarinet" was consistently spelled "clarionet" in news articles and programs.

400. *The New York Clipper*, May 1903.

401. *The Evening Messenger* (Marshall, Texas), August 31, 1903.

402. Napoleon Johnson, *The Indianapolis Freeman*, August 15, 1903.

403. In ads and reviews, Cooper's ventriloquist figures were referred to as his wooden-headed family.

404. George Schindler, in conversation with the author in 2021. By 1909, John W. Cooper was one of the few Black performers working in mainstream vaudeville. After retiring to Brooklyn, Cooper taught ventriloquism to a young beginner named Shari Lewis. With Schindler's assistance, Cooper's daughter preserved her father's legacy. Cooper was posthumously admitted into the Ventriloquism Hall of Fame.

405. Kraton was such a sensation that he organized his own hooping troupe. In early 1912 he traveled to England to perform. He died later that year, at age thirty, in an English tuberculosis sanitorium.

406. *The Sphinx*, vol. 3, 4.

407. Quote attributed to Black Carl by Jim Magus, "A History of Blacks in Magic," *The Linking Ring*, November 1983.

408. *The Fort Worth Star*, August 21, 1903.

409. Johnson, *Freeman*, September 19, 1903.

410. *The Commercial Dispatch* (Columbia, Mississippi), November 24, 1903.

411. *Montgomery Advertiser* (Alabama), December 5, 1903.

412. *Fort Worth Star*, August 21, 1903.

413. *Durham Sun* (NC), October 6, 1903.

414. *Gaffney Ledger* (SC), October 23, 1903.

415. Johnson, *Freeman*, October 24, 1903.

416. *The Daily Sentinel* (Grand Junction, CO), April 29, 1904.

417. Johnson, *Freeman*, December 19, 1903.

418. Johnson, *Freeman*, October 8, 1904.

419. *Arkansas City Daily News*, January 1, 1904.

420. *The Missoulian* (Montana), June 22, 1904.

421. *Great Falls Tribune*, June 13, 1904.

422. *The Evening-Times-Republican* (Marshallton, Iowa), July 27, 1904.

423. *The Kansas City Star*, July 31, 1904.

424. *Jonesboro Weekly Sun* (Arkansas), September 1, 1904.

425. Johnson, *Freeman*, October 15, 1904.

426. Johnson, *Freeman*, October 22, 1904.

427. Johnson, *Freeman*, November 19, 1904.

428. Johnson, *Freeman*, December 10, 1904.

429. Johnson, *Freeman*, December 17, 1904.

430. Isaac Willis possibly leased or borrowed the Noah's Ark illusion from Léon Herrmann. Isaac had assisted Léon in Noah's Ark the season prior going out on his own.

431. Johnson, *Freeman*, January 7, 1905.

432. Johnson, *Freeman*, January 14, 1905.

433. *The Nashville American*, March 10, 1905.

434. Johnson, *Freeman*, May 27, 1905.

435. Johnson, *Freeman*, May 27, 1905.

436. Johnson, *Freeman*, May 27, 1905.

437. Johnson, *Freeman*, July 1, 1905.

438. *The Post* (Sydney, NS), July 12, 1905, quoting the *Quebec Chronicle*.

439. Johnson, *Freeman*, July 1, 1905.

440. Johnson, *Freeman*, July 8, 1905.

441. *The Casket* (Antigonish, NS), July 13, 1905.

442. *Hants Journal* (Windsor, NS), July 27, 1905.

443. *The Post* (Sydney, NS), July 12, 1905.

444. *News & Sentinel* (Amherst, NS), July 8, 1905.

445. Nova Scotia, which shares no land border with the US, was not a major destination for African Americans escaping slavery via the Underground Railroad, most of whom arrived in Ontario and Quebec.

446. Africville no longer exists. As Halifax grew, the city taxed the residents of Africville yet failed to expand basic services—paved roads, water, sewers, garbage collection—to the neighborhood, while simultaneously squeezing the community between polluting factories and expanded rail lines. As the neighborhood deteriorated, the city declared Africville a slum. In a widely condemned move,

in the 1960s the City of Halifax seized the land and bulldozed all of Africville's homes. The residents were given $500 each, not nearly enough to purchase another home. Many were moved to public housing. In 2010, the government issued an official apology for the razing of Africville.

447. *The Acadian Recorder* (Halifax, NS), June 26, 1905.

448. Johnson, *Freeman*, October 28, 1905.

449. 1901 Canada Census.

450. *The Herald* (Halifax, NS), November 10, 1903.

451. *The Evening Mail* (Halifax, NS), May 16, 1904.

452. *The Evening Mail* (Halifax, NS), March 27, 1905.

453. Isaac Willis was with Richards and Pringle's Famous Georgia Minstrels from July 1903 to October or November 1905. The tour worked straight through with just one week off for Christmas.

454. *The Indianapolis Freeman*, November 4, 1905.

455. Léon Herrmann's program listed personnel, including Boomsky. But unlike the rest of the cast and crew, whose names were printed, Boomsky was played by "himself."

456. J. E. Clarke toured as a magician with the Maryland Jubilee Company, a Black vocal quartet, in 1905. His exact dates assisting Herrmann are not known.

457. No evidence has surfaced connecting William Keeling Smith (later Eugene Hellman) with Herrmann. Circumstantially, he was the right age (fourteen) to play Boomsky just as Léon Herrmann replaced Isaac Willis. "Hellman," his stage name, is suspiciously similar to "Herrmann."

458. *The Times Democrat* (New Orleans), August 31, 1903.

459. *The Austin-American Statesman*, September 11, 1903.

460. Lasky, *I Blow My Own Horn*, 61.

461. Theodore Roosevelt attended Léon Herrmann's show at the Columbia Theater in Washington, DC, during the first week of March 1904.

462. *The Sioux City Journal*, December 9, 1904.

463. *The Sphinx*, March 1904.

464. Lasky, *I Blow My Own Horn*, 63.

465. *The Democrat and Chronicle* (Rochester, NY), September 27, 1904.

466. *The Tribune* (Scranton), October 9, 1905.

467. Mme. Sa-Hera and her husband performed in American vaudeville from 1907 to 1910.

468. *The Indianapolis News*, January 10, 1906.

469. Léon Herrmann, *The New York Clipper*, July 1906.

470. *The News and Sentinel* (Amherst, NS), July 8, 1906.

471. *The Transcript* (Moncton, NB), July 14, 1906.

472. *The New York Clipper*, July 1906.

473. *The Herald* (Halifax, NS), July 24, 1906.

474. *The Evening Mail* (Halifax, NS), August 31, 1906.

475. *The Evening Mail* (Halifax, NS), November 26, 1906.

476. *The Evening Mail* (Halifax, NS), May 10, 1907.

477. *The Chicago Tribune*, December 15, 1907.

478. "'I Nevaire Play Ze Pokaire,' Says Herrmann," *The Omaha Daily News*, February 5, 1905. In this interview, Léon revealed his plans to train his nephew, Lucién, as his assistant and eventual successor.

479. Charles Greene III, *Ionia: Magician Princess, Secrets Unlocked* (self-published, 2022), 125. Clementine deVere was the daughter of inventor and magic dealer Charles deVere and Julia Ferret, the magician Okita.

480. Benjamin Rucker spelled "Herman" using just one "r" and one "n." Other Black Herrmanns used two of either or both, copying Alexander Herrmann.

481. *The Broad Ax* (Salt Lake City), November 15, 1913.

482. Obituaries of Black Carl ran in the *Detroit Free Press* and the *New York Age*, among others.

483. *The Chicago Tribune*, December 28, 1910.

484. *The Lincoln Sentinel*, July 18, 1912.

485. In the 1910 US Federal Census, Alonzo Moore is listed as a "servant" in the household of Allie Best. Perhaps he was a servant, or this was a prudent way to disguise a closer relationship.

486. *The Indianapolis Freeman*, February 26, 1916.

487. *The Indianapolis Freeman*, March 11, 1916.

488. From an undated, unidentified newspaper obituary of Alonzo Moore.

489. Anecdotal reports suggest that Alonzo Moore occasionally used the name Alonzo White, but that name has not been found on any promotional materials, advertisements, or newspaper reviews related to magic.

490. *The Evening Mail* (Halifax, NS), October 8, 1907.

491. *The Evening Mail* (Halifax, NS), January 20, 1908.

492. *The Evening Mail* (Halifax, NS), January 24, 1908.

493. *The Evening Mail* (Halifax, NS), April 24, 1908.

494. Canada Census 1911.

495. *Ancestors in the Attic*, season 4, episode 7, "Slavery Roots," written and directed by Jamie Kastner, aired January 28, 2010, on History Television. The episode examines the search for Edward Stoutley's true story by his descendants from his later Ontario marriage. Stoutley was light-skinned, and his Ontario descendants were raised to believe that they were white. The documentarians speculated that Edward Stoutley had a traumatic brain injury, which led his Nova Scotia descendants to view him with more compassion and forgiveness. At the time, information on Stoutley's arrest record and alcohol abuse had not yet come to light.

496. *The New York Age*, November 16, 1911. Isaac Willis stopped in Boston and visited magic collector and historian David Price, but Price did not mention Isaac Willis in his book *Magic: A Pictorial History of Conjurers in the Theater.*

497. The new owners of the Crescent Theater were speculating on 135th Street becoming a main commercial thoroughfare to rival 125th Street to the south and 145th Street to the north. The gamble did not pay off. The Crescent Theater closed a few years later.

498. Rotharlo from Nova Scotia quoted in Stanley Hall's "Notes and News from Canada," *The Linking Ring*, vol. 9, 10.

499. Rhadolph Marcelliee, "The Black Magician, *The Success Book, Volume 2*, by Jay Marshall and Frances Marshall.

500. *Truro Daily News*, August 10, 1932.

501. *The New York Times*, March 4, 1933.

502. *The Billboard*, March 11, 1933.
503. Undated newsletter of the Canadian National Railroad, Willis family.

CHAPTER TEN, M. H. EVERETT AND ADELAIDE HERRMANN

504. *The Courier* (Harrisburg, PA), November 23, 1906.
505. *The Kansas City Star and Kansas City Times*, January 30, 1905.
506. Henry Ridgely Evans, *The Sphinx*, March 1903.
507. Everett is listed on a program from Denver's Tabor Opera House, October 1905.
508. On October 24, 1905, Adelaide Herrmann and Company played at the Vancouver Opera House. Richards & Pringle's Famous Georgia Minstrels played there the next night, October 25. Hudson Everett and Isaac Willis performed on the same stage on consecutive nights. That was likely Isaac Willis's last performance with the Famous Georgia Minstrels.
509. After her tour folded, Adelaide Herrmann booked a few weeks of run-outs from New York for her company in November and December 1905 and early January 1906. They played small cities in New Jersey, Pennsylvania, and Ohio. The show was well-received, but houses were modest. Theater managers noted in the *New York Clipper* that many women and children attended.
510. Jim Steinmeyer, *The Last Greatest Magician in the World: Howard Thurston Versus Houdini & The Battles of the American Wizards* (New York: Penguin, 2012), 96.
511. US Federal Census 1900. Roland Travers McKitrick (1881–1970) performed on the vaudeville circuit and eventually settled in New York, where he died at age eighty-eight after being struck by a car.
512. Harry Houdini, *Conjuror's Monthly*, 1908.
513. Herrmann 1887–88 Tour Expense Ledger. This expense ledger contains one page at the back documenting the single week of Adelaide's 1908 Cuba tour.
514. The magazine *Variety* provided regular updates.

515. A favorite triple-stranded pearl necklace, which Madame wore for years, appears in no photos after 1908.

516. Ship manifest. Adelaide's nephew John Kretschmann was scheduled to sail on the same ship but did not board. It's likely that he stayed behind with Adelaide as she pursued legal action against manager Harry Clark.

517. In census reports and other documents, Everett, like many entertainers, usually shaved at least two years from his true age.

518. US Federal Census 1910. All members of the Everett family are marked as literate.

519. Julia Evans's landlady may have been related to Sidney Everett's wife, Mandy.

520. US Federal Census 1910. The Everetts lived at 125 West 131st Street in New York.

521. Adelaide Herrmann's stage plot, properties list, and lighting instructions for The Haunted Studio. James Hamilton Collection.

522. Steamship manifest, Ancestry.com.

523. Adelaide Herrmann's older sisters were Frances Scarsez Kretschmann (1841–1906), Janet Scarsez Pallme (1842–1910), and Mathilde Scarsez Owles (1851–1912).

524. *The Atlanta Constitution*, May 3, 1916.

525. *Virginian-Pilot and The Norfolk Landmark*, April 7, 1916.

526. *Virginian-Pilot and The Norfolk Landmark*, April 7, 1916.

527. *The New York Clipper*, December 19, 1917. It cannot be verified that this Everett the Magician was Milton Hudson Everett. There were several magicians named Everett, and nowhere in the article is Everett described as "colored."

528. William Robinson and Dot Robinson were not legally married during their time with the Herrmanns since Will was already married to another woman. Eventually that marriage was annulled, and Will and Dot were married in 1906. One year later, Will left Dot for Lou Blatchford.

529. Steinmeyer, *The Glorious Deception*, 398–405.

530. William Kalush and Larry Sloman, *The Secret Life of Houdini: The Making of America's First Superhero* (New York: Atria Books, 2006), 337.

531. Dot Robinson returned from England late in 1918 and lived in the Bronx.

532. Adelaide Herrmann in a letter to Harry Houdini dated April 8, 1918. Harry Ransom Center, University of Texas.

533. The *Antilles*, a passenger vessel, had been commandeered by the US Navy and was transporting troops when it was sunk by a German U-boat on October 17, 1917, resulting in the loss of sixty-seven lives. These were the first American casualties of World War I.

534 Kenneth Silverman, *Houdini!!!* (New York: HarperCollins, 1996), 225–6.

535 *M.U.M.*, April 1918.

536 Adelaide Herrmann, letter to Harry Houdini dated April 25, 1918. Harry Ransom Center, University of Texas.

537 Inquiry and research have failed to identify the name and date of admission of the SAM's first Black member.

538 Adelaide's two surgeries in 1919 are mentioned in multiple sources, but the specifics were never made public.

539 Herrmann's durable Noah's Ark illusion had survived previous tours by Alexander Herrmann (1892–93), Léon Herrmann (1901–02), and possibly Isaac Willis/The Great Boomsky (1905).

540 World War I draft registration card of Milton Hudson Everett.

541 *The New York Times*, March 25, 1918.

542 *The Drumright Weekly Derrick* (Oklahoma), May 18, 1918.

543 The Everetts' apartment building at 541 Lenox Avenue still stands.

544 US Federal Census 1920.

545 The station that Charles Wellesley Smith designed was torn down and replaced by Newark's current Penn Station, which opened in 1935.

546 Adelaide Herrmann's residence at the Arlington Hotel at Fifth Avenue and 26th Street was about one and a half miles from the warehouse.

547 *The Daily News* (New York), September 8, 1926.

548 *The Ridgewood Herald*, February 26, 1932.

549 Herb Zarrow, in conversation with the author in the summer of 2001.

550 *Inter-State Tattler* (New York), December 17, 1931.

551 Tribute by Stella Grenfell Florence in *Adelaide Herrmann, Queen of Magic*, 245.

552 *The Sphinx*, March 20, 1932.

553 M. H. Everett quoted in James Hamilton, "Adelaide Herrmann, Queen of Magic," *Genii*, August 2000.

554 US Federal Census 1930.

555 80 Edgecombe Avenue still stands.

556 US Federal Census 1940. Milton Hudson Everett was still working at the post office when the 1940 US Census was taken. In 1941, when he registered for the draft, he was listed as unemployed. Ancestry.com.

557 US Federal Census 1930.

558 WWII draft card, Milton Hudson Everett.

559 90 Edgecombe Avenue still stands.

560 Benjamin Rucker (Black Herman) is also buried at Woodlawn Cemetery. The grave of Herrmann historian James Hamilton, whose research formed much of the basis of this book, adjoins the Herrmann plot at Woodlawn Cemetery.

RECOMMENDED READING

Bay, Mia. *Traveling Black: A Story of Race and Resistance*. Cambridge, MA: The Belknap Press of Harvard University Press, 2021.

Burlingame, Hardin J. *Herrmann the Great: The Famous Magician's Wonderful Tricks*. Chicago: Laird & Lee, 1905.

Caveney, Mike, and William P. Miesel. *Kellar's Wonders*. Pasadena, CA: Mike Caveney's Magic Words, 2003.

Christopher, Milbourne, and Maurine Brooks Christopher. *The Illustrated History of Magic*. New York: Carroll & Graf Pub., 2006.

Copperfield, David, Richard Wiseman, David Britland, and Homer Liwag. *David Copperfield's History of Magic*. New York: Simon & Schuster, 2021.

Current, Richard Nelson, and Marcia Ewing Current. *Loie Fuller: Goddess of Light*. Boston: Northeastern University Press, 1997.

DuBois, W. E. B. *Souls of Black Folks*. New York: Dover, 1994.

Dyson, Michael Eric. *Entertaining Race: Performing Blackness in America*. New York: St. Martin's Press, 2021.

Foster, Cecil. *They Call Me George: The Untold Story of Black Train Porters and the Birth of Modern Canada*. Windsor, ON: Biblioasis, 2019.

Hamilton, James. *The Herrmann Chronicles*. Oxford, CT: 1878 Press, 2023.

Herrmann, Adelaide, and Margaret Steele. *Adelaide Herrmann, Queen of Magic: Memoirs, Published Writings, Collected Ephemera*. Putney, VT: Bramble Books, 2012.

Kalush, William, and Larry Sloman. *The Secret Life of Houdini: The Making of America's First Superhero*. Atria Books, 2006.

Karr, Todd, and Chung Ling Soo. *The Silence of Chung Ling Soo*. Los Angeles: Miracle Factory, 2001.

Lasky, Jesse L., and Don Weldon. *I Blow My Own Horn*. Garden City: Doubleday, 1957.

MacNab, Bruce. *The Metamorphosis: The Apprenticeship of Harry Houdini*. Fredericton, NB: Goose Lane Editions, 2012.

Magus, Jim. *Magical Heroes: The Lives and Legends of Great African American Magicians*. Marietta, GA: Magus Enterprises, 1995.

Pallme, Hermann. *Entertaining by Magic*. New York: M. Witmark & Sons, 1906.

Porteous, Samuel D. *Ching Ling Foo: America's First Chinese Superstar*. Hong Kong: Drowsy Emperor Press, 2020.

Price, David. *Magic: A Pictorial History of Conjurers in the Theater*. New York: Cornwall Books, 1985.

Silverman, Kenneth. *Houdini!!!: The Career of Ehrich Weiss: American Self-Liberator, Europe's Eclipsing Sensation, World's Handcuff King & Prison Breaker—Nothing on Earth Can Hold Houdini a Prisoner!* New York: Harper Perennial, 1997.

Snyder, Robert W. *The Voice of the City: Vaudeville and Popular Culture in New York*. New York: Ivan R. Dee, 1898.

Steinmeyer, Jim. *The Glorious Deception: The Double Life of William Robinson, aka Chung Ling Soo the "Marvelous Chinese Conjurer."* New York: Carroll & Graf, 2006.

Steinmeyer, Jim. *The Last Greatest Magician in the World: Howard Thurston Versus Houdini & The Battles of the American Wizards*. New York: Jeremy P. Tarcher/Penguin, 2012.

Taylor, Yuval, and Jake Austen. *Darkest America: Black Minstrelsy from Slavery to Hip-Hop*. New York: W. W. Norton, 2012.

Tye, Larry. *Rising from the Rails: Pullman Porters and the Making of the Black Middle Class*. New York: Henry Holt and Company, 2005.

Washington, Eric K. *Boss of the Grips: The Life of James H. Williams and the Red Caps of Grand Central Terminal*. New York: Liveright Publishing Corporation, a division of W. W. Norton & Company, 2019.

Wise, Tim J. *White Like Me: Reflections on Race from a Privileged Son; the Remix*. Berkeley, CA: Soft Skull Press, 2011.

ILLUSTRATION CREDITS

ILLUSTRATIONS WERE PROVIDED BY THE FOLLOWING PRIVATE AND INSTITUTIONAL COLLECTIONS:

Alamy, 13.

Ancestry.com, 206.

Mike Caveney, 16, 160, 170, 229, 311.

Michael Claxton, 218, 259.

Library of Congress, 2, 36, 77, 82, 184, 324.

Library of Congress Special Collections, 222.

David Copperfield, 50, 204.

Digital Library of Georgia Historic Newspapers, 3.

George and Sandy Daily, xx, 209.

Linda Graves, 303.

James Hamilton Legacy Collection, 20, 21, 44, 104, 174, 189, 199, 210, 306, 314.

David Haversat, 8, 12, 22, 107, 115, 116, 245, 250, 253, 291.

Harvard University, Houghton Library, 71.

Howard University, Moorland-Spingarn Research Center, Harry Bowman Black Vaudeville Collection, 191.

University of Iowa, Redpath Chautauqua Bureau Archives, 261, 262.

Dr. Timothy Moore, 15, 84, 187, 226.

Newspapers.com, 48, 109, 193, 288, 308.

New York Public Library, 192.

Nova Scotia Archives, 275, 277, 301.

Dale Penn, 73, 225.

Michael Perovich, 235.

Family of Isaac Willis, 201, 297, 298, 299, 300.

About the Author

MARGARET STEELE turned to writing after thirty years in parallel performing careers: as a magician and as a Juilliard-trained oboist. She is the editor of *Adelaide Herrmann, Queen of Magic: Memoirs, Published Writings, and Collected Ephemera* (Bramble Books, 2012). Margaret has presented her groundbreaking research on women in magic for the New-York Historical Society, HISTORY, and NPR. *The Great Boomsky* is her first book as author.

∽

Coming Soon! *Adelaide Herrmann, Queen of Magic: Memoirs, Published Writings, and Collected Ephemera, Second Edition.* Currently out of print, Madame Herrmann's thrilling memoir was discovered and published seventy years after her death. Expanded by 20 percent with new material, the new edition is a companion volume to *The Great Boomsky* and completes the story of the Herrmann dynasty of magicians. Learn more at www.floatingladypublishing.com.

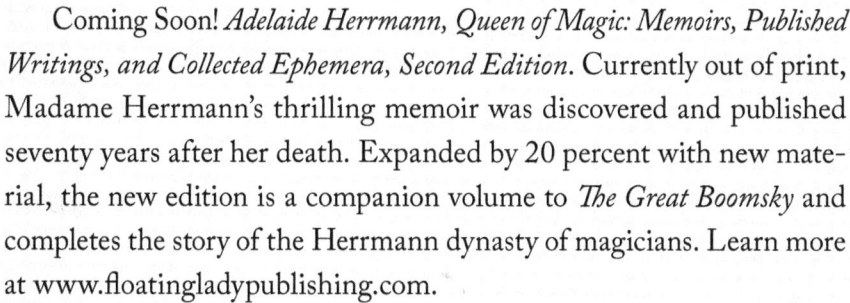

INDEX

X-Y-Z

www.ingramcontent.com/pod-product-compliance
Lightning Source LLC
Chambersburg PA
CBHW051256120626
46547CB00015B/1970